M000164002

Hearthside

Prayers & Meditations
for Every Day of the Year

Daily Guidance

COMPILED BY MARTIN H. MANSER

CUMBERLAND HOUSE
NASHVILLE, TENNESSEE

Library of Congress Cataloging-in-Publication Data

Daily guidance : prayers and meditations for every day of the year / compiled by Martin H. Manser.
    p. cm. — (The hearthside devotional library)
    ISBN 1-58182-235-9 (pbk. : alk. paper)
    1. Devotional calendars. I. Manser, Martin H. II. Series.
BV4810.D253 2001
242'.2—dc21   2001037265

Daily
Guidance

CONTENTS

PREFACE

These readings from the Bible have been compiled with the aim of providing a source of daily encouragement and guidance for Christians. The extracts have been specially chosen to give inspiration—and at times challenge—to believers. The readings are accompanied by extracts from hymns, which can be used to make a personal response to God and his word.

The Bible portions and hymns in this book could perhaps best be complemented by following a plan of reading through the whole Bible. In this way a personal devotional time with God becomes a daily opportunity to "seek [the Lord's] face" (Psalm 27:8) as God speaks to us about out lives "face to face, as a man speaks with his friend" (Exodus 33:11).

Where to find help when you're feeling...

Afraid	Sept 16, Oct 12, Nov 25
Anxious/worried	Mar 16, Sept 17
Bitter/critical	Apr 10, Oct 4
Depressed/discouraged	Jan 2, Feb 20
You have failed	Mar 11, Nov 4
In need of guidance	Jan 4, Jun 21, Oct 31, Dec 4
Ill or in pain	Sept 14, Sept 15
Lonely	Sept 19, Nov 13
In need of peace	Jan 8, Nov 1
Saddened through bereavement	Oct 24, Nov 3
Tempted	Apr 6, Jul 10, Jul 31
Thankful	Jan 13, Mar 13, Apr 9, Apr 15
Tired	Jan 6, Nov 27
Weak	Mar 9, Dec 5
In need of wisdom	Oct 16

Daily Guidance

The perfect guidance of God

I will instruct thee and teach thee in the way which thou shalt go: I will guide thee with mine eye.

Psalm 32:8, KJV

If you spend yourselves in behalf of the hungry and satisfy the needs of the oppressed, then your light will rise in the darkness, and your night will become like the noonday. The LORD will guide you always; he will satisfy your needs in a sun-scorched land and will strengthen your frame. You will be like a well-watered garden, like a spring whose waters never fail.

Isaiah 58:10–11

Jesus said to him, "I am the way, and the truth, and the life. No one comes to the Father except through me."

John 14:6, NRSV

> All the way my Saviour leads me:
>   What have I to ask beside?
> Can I doubt His tender mercy
>   Who through life has been my Guide?
> Heavenly peace, divinest comfort,
>   Here by faith in Him to dwell!
> For I know whate'er befall me,
>   Jesus doeth all things well.
>
> All the way my Saviour leads me;
>   O the fulness of His love!
> Perfect rest to me is promised
>   In my Father's house above.
> When my spirit, clothed immortal,
>   Wings its flight to realms of day,
> This, my song through endless ages,
>   Jesus led me all the way.

Frances Jane Van Alstyne, 1820–1915

The Good Shepherd

The LORD is my shepherd; I shall not want. He maketh me to lie down in green pastures: he leadeth me beside the still waters. He restoreth my soul: he leadeth me in the paths of righteousness for his name's sake. Yea, though I walk through the valley of the shadow of death, I will fear no evil: for thou art with me; thy rod and thy staff they comfort me. Thou preparest a table before me in the presence of mine enemies: thou anointest my head with oil; my cup runneth over. Surely goodness and mercy shall follow me all the days of my life: and I will dwell in the house of the LORD for ever.

Psalm 23:1–6, KJV

I am the good shepherd; the good shepherd lays down His life for the sheep. . . . I am the good shepherd, and I know My own and My own know Me, even as the Father knows Me and I know the Father; and I lay down My life for the sheep. . . .
   My sheep hear My voice, and I know them, and they follow Me.

John 10:11,14–15,27, NASB

Green pastures are before me
   Which yet I have not seen;
Bright skies will soon be o'er me,
   Where the dark clouds have been:
My hope I cannot measure,
   My path to life is free;
My Saviour has my treasure,
   And He will walk with me.

Anna Laetitia Waring, 1820–1910

Knowing Jesus

All things have been delivered to Me by My Father, and no one knows the Son except the Father. Nor does anyone know the Father except the Son, and the one to whom the Son wills to reveal Him.

Matthew 11:27, NKJV

And this is eternal life, that they may know You, the only true God, and Jesus Christ whom You have sent.

John 17:3, NKJV

I keep asking that the God of our Lord Jesus Christ, the glorious Father, may give you the Spirit of wisdom and revelation, so that you may know him better.

Ephesians 1:17

I want to know Christ and the power of his resurrection and the sharing of his sufferings by becoming like him in his death, if somehow I may attain the resurrection from the dead.

Philippians 3:10–11, NRSV

More about Jesus would I know,
More of His grace to others show,
More of His saving fulness see,
More of His love—who died for me.

More, more about Jesus,
More, more about Jesus;
More of His saving fulness see,
More of His love who died for me.

Eliza Edmunds Hewitt, 1851–1920

JANUARY 4

Bearing fruit

Blessed is the man that walketh not in the counsel of the ungodly, nor standeth in the way of sinners, nor sitteth in the seat of the scornful. But his delight is in the law of the LORD; and in his law doth he meditate day and night. And he shall be like a tree planted by the rivers of water, that bringeth forth his fruit in his season; his leaf also shall not wither; and whatsoever he doeth shall prosper.

Psalm 1:1–3, KJV

The fruit of the righteous is a tree of life, and he who wins souls is wise.

Proverbs 11:30, NKJV

I am the vine, you are the branches. He who abides in Me, and I in him, bears much fruit; for without Me you can do nothing. If anyone does not abide in Me, he is cast out as a branch and is withered; and they gather them and throw them into the fire, and they are burned. If you abide in Me, and My words abide in you, you will ask what you desire, and it shall be done for you. By this My Father is glorified, that you bear much fruit; so you will be My disciples.

John 15:5–8, NKJV

Forth in Thy Name, O Lord, I go,
　My daily labour to pursue,
Thee only Thee, resolved to know
　In all I think, or speak, or do.

The task Thy wisdom hath assigned
　O let me cheerfully fulfil,
In all my works Thy presence find,
　And prove Thy good and perfect will.

Charles Wesley, 1707–88

God, the Creator

In the beginning God created the heaven and the earth.

Genesis 1:1, KJV

And God said, Let us make man in our image, after our likeness: and let them have dominion over the fish of the sea, and over the fowl of the air, and over the cattle, and over all the earth, and over every creeping thing that creepeth upon the earth. So God created man in his own image, in the image of God created he him; male and female created he them.

Genesis 1:26–27, KJV

In the beginning was the Word, and the Word was with God, and the Word was God. The same was in the beginning with God. All things were made by him; and without him was not any thing made that was made.

John 1:1–3, KJV

Praise to the Lord, the Almighty,
   the King of creation;
O my soul, praise Him, for He is
   thy health and salvation;
  All ye who hear,
   Brothers and sisters, draw near,
Praise Him in glad adoration.

Praise to the Lord, Who doth prosper
   thy work and defend thee;
Surely His goodness and mercy
   here daily attend thee:
  Ponder anew
  What the Almighty can do,
If with His love He befriend thee.

Joachim Neander, 1650–80
translated by Catherine Winkworth, 1829–78,
and others

Depending upon God

Why do you say, O Jacob, and complain, O Israel, "My way is hidden from the LORD; my cause is disregarded by my God"? Do you not know? Have you not heard? The LORD is the everlasting God, the Creator of the ends of the earth. He will not grow tired or weary, and his understanding no one can fathom. He gives strength to the weary and increases the power of the weak. Even youths grow tired and weary, and young men stumble and fall; but those who hope in the LORD will renew their strength. They will soar on wings like eagles; they will run and not grow weary, they will walk and not be faint.

Isaiah 40:27–31

Happy the man whose hopes rely
On Israel's God! He made the sky,
　And earth, and sea, with all their train:
His truth for ever stands secure;
He saves the oppressed, He feeds the poor,
　And none shall find His promise vain.

I'll praise Him while he lends me breath;
And when my voice is lost in death,
　Praise shall employ my nobler powers:
My days of praise shall ne'er be past,
While life, and thought, and being last,
　Or immortality endures.

Isaac Watts, 1674–1748

The blood of Christ

In Him we have redemption through His blood, the forgiveness of sins, according to the riches of His grace.

Ephesians 1:7, NKJV

Therefore, my friends, since we have confidence to enter the sanctuary by the blood of Jesus, by the new and living way that he opened for us through the curtain (that is, through his flesh), and since we have a great priest over the house of God, let us approach with a true heart in full assurance of faith, with our hearts sprinkled clean from an evil conscience and our bodies washed with pure water.

Hebrews 10:19–22, NRSV

"Man of Sorrows!" what a name
For the Son of God, Who came
Ruined sinners to reclaim!
    Hallelujah! what a Saviour!

Bearing shame and scoffing rude,
In my place condemned He stood;
Sealed my pardon with His blood:
    Hallelujah what a Saviour!

Philipp Paul Bliss, 1838–76

God's perfect peace

Oh how great is thy goodness, which thou hast laid up for them that fear thee; which thou hast wrought for them that trust in thee before the sons of men!

Psalm 31:19, KJV

"Behold, God is my salvation, I will trust and not be afraid; for the LORD GOD is my strength and song, and He has become my salvation." Therefore you will joyously draw water from the springs of salvation.

Isaiah 12:2–3, NASB

Those of steadfast mind you keep in peace—in peace because they trust in you. Trust in the LORD forever, for in the LORD GOD you have an everlasting rock.

Isaiah 26:3–4, NRSV

Like a river glorious
  Is God's perfect peace,
Over all victorious
  In its bright increase;
Perfect, yet it floweth
  Fuller every day;
Perfect, yet it groweth
  Deeper all the way.

Stayed upon Jehovah
  Hearts are fully blest,
Finding, as He promised,
  Perfect peace and rest.

Frances Ridley Havergal, 1836–79

Submitting to our Father

Endure hardship as discipline; God is treating you as sons. For what son is not disciplined by his father? If you are not disciplined (and everyone undergoes discipline), then you are illegitimate children and not true sons. Moreover, we have all had human fathers who disciplined us and we respected them for it. How much more should we submit to the Father of our spirits and live! Our fathers disciplined us for a little while as they thought best; but God disciplines us for our good, that we may share in his holiness. No discipline seems pleasant at the time, but painful. Later on, however, it produces a harvest of righteousness and peace for those who have been trained by it.

Hebrews 12:7–11

Submit yourselves therefore to God. Resist the devil, and he will flee from you.

James 4:7, KJV

Search me, O God, and know my heart: try me, and know my thoughts: And see if there be any wicked way in me, and lead me in the way everlasting.

Psalm 139:23–24, KJV

Have Thine own way, Lord, have Thine own way;
Thou art the potter, I am the clay.
Mould me and make me after thy will,
While I am waiting yielded and still.

Adelaide Addison Pollard, 1862–1934

The Christian's priority

Blessed are the gentle, for they shall inherit the earth.

Blessed are those who hunger and thirst for righteousness, for they shall be satisfied.

Blessed are the merciful, for they shall receive mercy.

Blessed are the pure in heart, for they shall see God.

Matthew 5:5–8, NASB

But seek ye first the kingdom of God, and his righteousness; and all these things shall be added unto you.

Matthew 6:33, KJV

Seek ye first, not earthly pleasure,
Fading joy and failing treasure;
But the love that knows no measure
　Seek ye first.

Seek this first: be pure and holy,
Like the Master, meek and lowly,
Yielded to His service wholly:
　Seek this first.

Georgianna Mary Taylor, 1848–1915

God's holy word

O how love I thy law! it is my meditation all the day. Thou through thy commandments hast made me wiser than mine enemies: for they are ever with me. I have more understanding than all my teachers: for thy testimonies are my meditation. I understand more than the ancients, because I keep thy precepts. . . . Thy word is a lamp unto my feet, and a light unto my path.

Psalm 119:97–100,105, KJV

From childhood you have known the sacred writings that are able to instruct you for salvation through faith in Christ Jesus. All scripture is inspired by God and is useful for teaching, for reproof, for correction, and for training in righteousness, so that everyone who belongs to God may be proficient, equipped for every good work.

2 Timothy 3:15–17, NRSV

Lord, Thy Word abideth,
And our footsteps guideth;
Who its truth believeth
Light and joy receiveth.

O that we, discerning
Its most holy learning,
Lord, may love and fear Thee,
Evermore be near Thee!

Henry Williams Baker, 1821–77

Worshiping Jesus

While He was in Bethany at the home of Simon the leper, and reclining at the table, there came a woman with an alabaster vial of very costly perfume of pure nard; and she broke the vial and poured it over His head. But some were indignantly remarking to one another, "Why has this perfume been wasted? For this perfume might have been sold for over three hundred denarii, and the money given to the poor." And they were scolding her. But Jesus said, "Let her alone; why do you bother her? She has done a good deed to Me. For you always have the poor with you, and whenever you wish you can do good to them; but you do not always have Me. She has done what she could; she has anointed My body beforehand for the burial. Truly I say to you, wherever the gospel is preached in the whole world, what this woman has done will also be spoken of in memory of her."

Mark 14:3–9, NASB

How sweet the Name of Jesus sounds
  In a believer's ear!
It soothes his sorrows, heals his wounds,
  And drives away his fear.

Jesus! my Shepherd, Brother, Friend,
  My Prophet, Priest and King,
My Lord, my Life, my Way, my End,
  Accept the praise I bring.

John Newton, 1725–1807

A life of praise

But you are a chosen generation, a royal priesthood, a holy nation, His own special people, that you may proclaim the praises of Him who called you out of darkness into His marvelous light; who once were not a people but are now the people of God, who had not obtained mercy but now have obtained mercy.

1 Peter 2:9–10, NKJV

Through Jesus, therefore, let us continually offer to God a sacrifice of praise—the fruit of lips that confess his name. And do not forget to do good and to share with others, for with such sacrifices God is pleased.

Hebrews 13:15–16

Fill Thou my life, O Lord my God,
  In every part with praise,
That my whole being may proclaim
  Thy being and Thy ways.

Horatius Bonar, 1808–89

Christ, our rock

I waited patiently for the LORD; and he inclined unto me, and heard my cry. He brought me up also out of an horrible pit, out of the miry clay, and set my feet upon a rock, and established my goings. And he hath put a new song in my mouth, even praise unto our God: many shall see it, and fear, and shall trust in the LORD. Blessed is that man that maketh the LORD his trust, and respecteth not the proud, nor such as turn aside to lies.

Psalm 40:1–4, KJV

But now the righteousness of God apart from the law is revealed, being witnessed by the Law and the Prophets, even the righteousness of God, through faith in Jesus Christ, to all and on all who believe. For there is no difference; for all have sinned and fall short of the glory of God, being justified freely by His grace through the redemption that is in Christ Jesus, whom God set forth as a propitiation by His blood, through faith.

Romans 3:21–25, NKJV

My hope is built on nothing less
Than Jesus' blood and righteousness;
I dare not trust the sweetest frame,
But wholly lean on Jesus' Name.

On Christ, the solid Rock, I stand;
All other ground is sinking sand.

Edward Mote, 1797–1874

"Come to me"

Faith comes from hearing the message, and the message is heard through the word of Christ.

Romans 10:17

Why do you spend your money for that which is not bread, and your labor for that which does not satisfy? Listen carefully to me, and eat what is good, and delight yourselves in rich food. Incline your ear, and come to me; listen, so that you may live. I will make with you an everlasting covenant, my steadfast, sure love for David.

Isaiah 55:2–3, NRSV

Come to Me, all you who labor and are heavy laden, and I will give you rest. Take My yoke upon you and learn from Me, for I am gentle and lowly in heart, and you will find rest for your souls. For My yoke is easy and My burden is light.

Matthew 11:28–30, NKJV

I heard the voice of Jesus say,
  "Come unto Me and rest;
Lay down, thou weary one, lay down
  Thy head upon My breast!"
I came to Jesus as I was,
  Weary, and worn, and sad;
I found in Him a resting-place,
  And He has made me glad.

Horatius Bonar, 1808–89

God, the compassionate one

He will not always chide: neither will he keep his anger for ever. He hath not dealt with us after our sins; nor rewarded us according to our iniquities. For as the heaven is high above the earth, so great is his mercy toward them that fear him. As far as the east is from the west, so far hath he removed our transgressions from us. Like as a father pitieth his children, so the LORD pitieth them that fear him. For he knoweth our frame; he remembereth that we are dust.

Psalm 103:9–14, KJV

Who is a God like unto thee, that pardoneth iniquity, and passeth by the transgression of the remnant of his heritage? he retaineth not his anger for ever, because he delighteth in mercy. He will turn again, he will have compassion upon us; he will subdue our iniquities; and thou wilt cast all their sins into the depths of the sea.

Micah 7:18–19, KJV

Great God of wonders! all Thy ways
   Are matchless, godlike, and divine;
But the fair glories of Thy grace,
   More godlike and unrivalled shine:

Who is a pardoning God like Thee?
Or who has grace so rich and free?

Samuel Davies, 1723–61

Christ is risen!

I declare to you, brothers, that flesh and blood cannot inherit the kingdom of God, nor does the perishable inherit the imperishable. Listen, I tell you a mystery: We will not all sleep, but we will all be changed—in a flash, in the twinkling of an eye, at the last trumpet. For the trumpet will sound, the dead will be raised imperishable, and we will be changed. For the perishable must clothe itself with the imperishable, and the mortal with immortality. When the perishable has been clothed with the imperishable, and the mortal with immortality, then the saying that is written will come true: "Death has been swallowed up in victory."

"Where, O death, is your victory? Where, O death, is your sting?"

The sting of death is sin, and the power of sin is the law. But thanks be to God! He gives us the victory through our Lord Jesus Christ.

Therefore, my dear brothers, stand firm. Let nothing move you. Always give yourselves fully to the work of the Lord, because you know that your labor in the Lord is not in vain.

1 Corinthians 15:50–58

Christ is risen! Hallelujah!
  Risen our victorious Head!
Sing His praises! Hallelujah!
  Christ is risen from the dead.
Gratefully our hearts adore Him
  As His light once more appears,
Bowing down in joy before Him,
  Rising up from grief and tears.

Christ is risen! Hallelujah!
  Risen our victorious Head!
Sing His praises! Hallelujah!
  Christ is risen from the dead.

John Samuel Bewley Monsell, 1811–75

Amazing grace!

From his fullness we have all received, grace upon grace. The law indeed was given through Moses; grace and truth came through Jesus Christ.

John 1:16–17, NRSV

And you He made alive, who were dead in trespasses and sins, in which you once walked according to the course of this world, according to the prince of the power of the air, the spirit who now works in the sons of disobedience, among whom also we all once conducted ourselves in the lusts of our flesh, fulfilling the desires of the flesh and of the mind, and were by nature children of wrath, just as the others. But God, who is rich in mercy, because of His great love with which He loved us, even when we were dead in trespasses, made us alive together with Christ (by grace you have been saved), and raised us up together, and made us sit together in the heavenly places in Christ Jesus, that in the ages to come He might show the exceeding riches of His grace in His kindness toward us in Christ Jesus. For by grace you have been saved through faith, and that not of yourselves; it is the gift of God, not of works, lest anyone should boast.

Ephesians 2:1–9, NKJV

Amazing grace! how sweet the sound
   That saved a wretch like me;
I once was lost, but now am found;
   Was blind, but now I see.

'Twas grace that taught my heart to fear,
   And grace my fears relieved;
How precious did that grace appear,
   The hour I first believed!

John Newton, 1725–1807

The law of the Lord

The law of the LORD is perfect, converting the soul: the testimony of the LORD is sure, making wise the simple. The statutes of the LORD are right, rejoicing the heart: the commandment of the LORD is pure, enlightening the eyes. The fear of the LORD is clean, enduring for ever: the judgments of the LORD are true and righteous altogether. More to be desired are they than gold, yea, than much fine gold: sweeter also than honey and the honeycomb. Moreover by them is thy servant warned: and in keeping of them there is great reward. . . . Let the words of my mouth, and the meditation of my heart, be acceptable in thy sight, O LORD, my strength, and my redeemer.

Psalm 19:7–11,14, KJV

Jesus, I can trust Thee,
  Trust Thy written Word,
Though Thy voice of pity
  I have never heard:
When Thy Spirit teacheth,
  To my taste how sweet!
Only may I hearken,
  Sitting at Thy feet.

Mary Jane Walker, 1816–78

The coming of the Spirit

When the Counselor comes, whom I will send to you from the Father, the Spirit of truth who goes out from the Father, he will testify about me. And you also must testify, for you have been with me from the beginning.

John 15:26–27

So Jesus said to them again, "Peace be with you; as the Father has sent Me, I also send you." And when He had said this, He breathed on them and said to them, "Receive the Holy Spirit. If you forgive the sins of any, their sins have been forgiven them; if you retain the sins of any, they have been retained."

John 20:21–23, NASB

But you shall receive power when the Holy Spirit has come upon you; and you shall be witnesses to Me in Jerusalem, and in all Judea and Samaria, and to the end of the earth.

Acts 1:8, NKJV

Breathe on me, Breath of God,
  Fill me with life anew;
That I may love what Thou dost love
  And do what Thou wouldst do.

Breathe on me, Breath of God,
  Till I am wholly Thine;
Until this earthly part of me
  Glows with Thy fire divine.

Edwin Hatch, 1835–89

True obedience

Then the Pharisees went out and laid plans to trap him in his words. They sent their disciples to him along with the Herodians. "Teacher," they said, "we know you are a man of integrity and that you teach the way of God in accordance with the truth. You aren't swayed by men, because you pay no attention to who they are. Tell us then, what is your opinion? Is it right to pay taxes to Caesar or not?"

But Jesus, knowing their evil intent, said, "You hypocrites, why are you trying to trap me? Show me the coin used for paying the tax." They brought him a denarius, and he asked them, "Whose portrait is this? And whose inscription?"

"Caesar's," they replied.

Then he said to them, "Give to Caesar what is Caesar's, and to God what is God's."

Matthew 22:15–21

Let every person be subject to the governing authorities; for there is no authority except from God, and those authorities that exist have been instituted by God.

Romans 13:1, NRSV

So let our lips and lives express
The holy gospel we profess;
So let our works and virtues shine,
To prove the doctrine all divine.

Isaac Watts, 1674–1748

The strength of Christ in us

And lest I should be exalted above measure through the abundance of the revelations, there was given to me a thorn in the flesh, the messenger of Satan to buffet me, lest I should be exalted above measure. For this thing I besought the Lord thrice, that it might depart from me. And he said unto me, My grace is sufficient for thee: for my strength is made perfect in weakness. Most gladly therefore will I rather glory in my infirmities, that the power of Christ may rest upon me. Therefore I take pleasure in infirmities, in reproaches, in necessities, in persecutions, in distresses for Christ's sake: for when I am weak, then am I strong.

2 Corinthians 12:7–10, KJV

Not that I speak in regard to need, for I have learned in whatever state I am, to be content: I know how to be abased, and I know how to abound. Everywhere and in all things I have learned both to be full and to be hungry, both to abound and to suffer need. I can do all things through Christ who strengthens me.

Philippians 4:11–13, NKJV

Jesus, my strength, my hope,
  On Thee I cast my care,
With humble confidence look up,
  And know Thou hear'st my prayer.
Give me on Thee to wait,
  Till I can all things do,
On Thee, almighty to create,
  Almighty to renew.

Charles Wesley, 1707–88

Our life in Christ

For you have died and your life is hidden with Christ in God.

Colossians 3:3, NASB

For the Lord to whom they could turn is the Spirit, and wherever the Spirit of the Lord is, men's souls are set free.

But all of us who are Christians have no veils on our faces, but reflect like mirrors the glory of the Lord. We are transformed in ever-increasing splendor into his own image, and this is the work of the Lord who is the Spirit.

2 Corinthians 3:17–18, PHILLIPS

Beloved, we are God's children now; what we will be has not yet been revealed. What we do know is this: when he is revealed, we will be like him, for we will see him as he is. And all who have this hope in him purify themselves, just as he is pure.

1 John 3:2–3, NRSV

Our life is hid with Christ,
  With Christ in God above;
Upward our hearts would go to Him,
  Whom, seeing not, we love.

When He who is our life
  In glory shall appear,
We too shall be revealed with Him,
  And His bright raiment wear.

In Him we then shall be
  Transformed and glorified,
For we shall see Him as He is,
  And in His light abide.

Horatius Bonar, 1808–89

Listening to the Lord

As Jesus and his disciples were on their way, he came to a village where a woman named Martha opened her home to him. She had a sister called Mary, who sat at the Lord's feet listening to what he said. But Martha was distracted by all the preparations that had to be made. She came to him and asked, "Lord, don't you care that my sister has left me to do the work by myself? Tell her to help me!"

"Martha, Martha," the Lord answered, "you are worried and upset about many things, but only one thing is needed. Mary has chosen what is better, and it will not be taken away from her."

Luke 10:38–42

Therefore do not worry about tomorrow, for tomorrow will worry about its own things. Sufficient for the day is its own trouble.

Matthew 6:34, NKJV

O that I could for ever sit
With Mary at the Master's feet!
  Be this my happy choice:
My only care, delight, and bliss,
My joy, my heaven on earth, be this—
  To hear the Bridegroom's voice!

Charles Wesley, 1707–88

Following Jesus

As Jesus passed along the Sea of Galilee, he saw Simon and his brother Andrew casting a net into the sea—for they were fishermen. And Jesus said to them, "Follow me and I will make you fish for people." And immediately they left their nets and followed him. As he went a little farther, he saw James son of Zebedee and his brother John, who were in their boat mending the nets. Immediately he called them; and they left their father Zebedee in the boat with the hired men, and followed him.

Mark 1:16–20, NRSV

As they were walking along the road, a man said to him, "I will follow you wherever you go."

Jesus replied, "Foxes have holes and birds of the air have nests, but the Son of Man has no place to lay his head."

He said to another man, "Follow me."

But the man replied, "Lord, first let me go and bury my father."

Jesus said to him, "Let the dead bury their own dead, but you go and proclaim the kingdom of God."

Still another said, "I will follow you, Lord; but first let me go back and say good-by to my family."

Jesus replied, "No one who puts his hand to the plow and looks back is fit for service in the kingdom of God."

Luke 9:57–62

Jesus calls us! O'er the tumult
    Of our life's wild restless sea,
Day by day His sweet voice soundeth,
    Saying, "Christian, follow Me":

Jesus calls us! By Thy mercies,
    Saviour, make us hear Thy call,
Give our hearts to Thy obedience,
    Serve and love Thee best of all.

Cecil Frances Alexander, 1818–95

Our help on life's journey

Now as Samuel was offering up the burnt offering, the Philistines drew near to battle against Israel. But the LORD thundered with a loud thunder upon the Philistines that day, and so confused them that they were overcome before Israel. And the men of Israel went out of Mizpah and pursued the Philistines, and drove them back as far as below Beth Car. Then Samuel took a stone and set it up between Mizpah and Shen, and called its name Ebenezer, saying, "Thus far the LORD has helped us."

1 Samuel 7:10–12, NKJV

But thou art holy, O thou that inhabitest the praises of Israel. Our fathers trusted in thee: they trusted, and thou didst deliver them. They cried unto thee, and were delivered: they trusted in thee, and were not confounded.

Psalm 22:3–5, KJV

Here I raise my Ebenezer,
   Hither by Thy help I'm come,
And I hope by Thy good pleasure
   Safely to arrive at home.
Jesus sought me when a stranger,
   Wandering from the fold of God;
He, to rescue me from danger,
   Interposed His precious blood.

Robert Robinson, 1735–90

Christ's second coming

And then shall appear the sign of the Son of man in heaven: and then shall all the tribes of the earth mourn, and they shall see the Son of man coming in the clouds of heaven with power and great glory.

Matthew 24:30, KJV

For the Lord Himself will descend from heaven with a shout, with the voice of the archangel and with the trumpet of God, and the dead in Christ will rise first. Then we who are alive and remain will be caught up together with them in the clouds to meet the Lord in the air, and so we shall always be with the Lord. Therefore comfort one another with these words.

1 Thessalonians 4:16–18, NASB

Behold, He is coming with clouds, and every eye will see Him, even they who pierced Him. And all the tribes of the earth will mourn because of Him. Even so, Amen.

Revelation 1:7, NKJV

Lo! He comes with clouds descending,
  Once for favoured sinners slain;
Thousand thousand saints attending
  Swell the triumph of His train:
    Hallelujah!
  God appears on earth to reign.

Every eye shall now behold Him
  Robed in dreadful majesty;
Those who set at nought and sold Him,
  Pierced and nailed Him to the tree,
    Deeply wailing,
Shall the true Messiah see.

John Cennick, 1718–55
and
Charles Wesley, 1707–88

The Light of the World

Then Jesus spoke to them again, saying, "I am the light of the world. He who follows Me shall not walk in darkness, but have the light of life."

John 8:12, NKJV

In him was life, and that life was the light of men. The light shines in the darkness, but the darkness has not understood it.

There came a man who was sent from God; his name was John. He came as a witness to testify concerning that light, so that through him all men might believe. He himself was not the light; he came only as a witness to the light. The true light that gives light to every man was coming into the world.

John 1:4–9

This is the judgment, that the Light has come into the world, and men loved the darkness rather than the Light, for their deeds were evil. For everyone who does evil hates the Light, and does not come to the Light for fear that his deeds will be exposed. But he who practices the truth comes to the Light, so that his deeds may be manifested as having been wrought in God.

John 3:19–21, NASB

I heard the voice of Jesus say,
   "I am this dark world's Light;
Look unto Me, thy morn shall rise,
   And all thy day be bright."
I looked to Jesus, and I found
   In Him my Star, my Sun;
And in that light of life I'll walk
   Till travelling days are done.

Horatius Bonar, 1808–89

The precious blood of Christ

But if we walk in the Light as He Himself is in the Light, we have fellowship with one another, and the blood of Jesus His Son cleanses us from all sin.

1 John 1:7, NASB

And whosoever of you will be the chiefest, shall be servant of all. For even the Son of man came not to be ministered unto, but to minister, and to give his life a ransom for many.

Mark 10:44–45, KJV

You know that you were ransomed from the futile ways inherited from your ancestors, not with perishable things like silver or gold, but with the precious blood of Christ, like that of a lamb without defect or blemish. He was destined before the foundation of the world, but was revealed at the end of the ages for your sake. Through him you have come to trust in God, who raised him from the dead and gave him glory, so that your faith and hope are set on God.

1 Peter 1:18–21, NRSV

Just as I am without one plea
But that Thy blood was shed for me,
And that Thou bidd'st me come to Thee,
　O Lamb of God, I come.

Just as I am, Thou wilt receive,
Wilt welcome, pardon, cleanse, relieve;
Because Thy promise I believe,
　O Lamb of God, I come.

Just as I am, of that free love
The breadth, length, depth, and height to prove,
Here for a season, then above,
　O Lamb of God, I come.

Charlotte Elliott, 1789–1871

JANUARY 30

The children of God

For all who are being led by the Spirit of God, these are sons of God. For you have not received a spirit of slavery leading to fear again, but you have received a spirit of adoption as sons by which we cry out, "Abba! Father!" The Spirit Himself testifies with our spirit that we are children of God, and if children, heirs also, heirs of God and fellow heirs with Christ, if indeed we suffer with Him so that we may also be glorified with Him.

Romans 8:14–17, NASB

Consider the incredible love that the Father has shown us in allowing us to be called "children of God"—and that is not just what we are called, but what we are. This explains why the world will no more recognise us than it recognised Christ.

1 John 3:1, PHILLIPS

Behold, what wondrous grace
  The Father hath bestowed
On sinners of a mortal race
  To call them sons of God.

Nor doth it yet appear
  How great we must be made;
But when we see our Saviour here,
  We shall be like our Head.

Isaac Watts, 1674–1748

Spiritual power

"Not by might nor by power, but by My Spirit," says the LORD of hosts.

Zechariah 4:6, NKJV

A woman was there who had been subject to bleeding for twelve years. She had suffered a great deal under the care of many doctors and had spent all she had, yet instead of getting better she grew worse. When she heard about Jesus, she came up behind him in the crowd and touched his cloak, because she thought, "If I just touch his clothes, I will be healed." Immediately her bleeding stopped and she felt in her body that she was freed from her suffering.

At once Jesus realized that power had gone out from him.

Mark 5:25–30

But we have this treasure in earthen vessels, that the excellency of the power may be of God, and not of us.

2 Corinthians 4:7, KJV

Holy Spirit, power divine,
Fill and nerve this will of mine;
By Thee may I strongly live,
Bravely bear, and nobly strive.

Samuel Longfellow, 1819–92

God gave us his Son

For God so loved the world, that he gave his only begotten Son, that whosoever believeth in him should not perish, but have everlasting life.

John 3:16, KJV

You see, at just the right time, when we were still powerless, Christ died for the ungodly. Very rarely will anyone die for a righteous man, though for a good man someone might possibly dare to die. But God demonstrates his own love for us in this: While we were still sinners, Christ died for us.

Romans 5:6–8

For I delivered to you as of first importance what I also received, that Christ died for our sins according to the Scriptures, and that He was buried, and that He was raised on the third day according to the Scriptures, and that He appeared to Cephas, then to the twelve.

1 Corinthians 15:3–5, NASB

To God be the glory! great things He hath done!
So loved He the world that He gave us His Son;
Who yielded His life an atonement for sin,
And opened the life-gate that all may go in.

Praise the Lord! praise the Lord! Let the earth hear His voice!
Praise the Lord, praise the Lord! Let the people rejoice!
O come to the Father through Jesus the Son:
And give Him the glory! great things He hath done!

Frances Jane Van Alstyne, 1820–1915

The name of Jesus

Let the same mind be in you that was in Christ Jesus, who, though he was in the form of God, did not regard equality with God as something to be exploited, but emptied himself, taking the form of a slave, being born in human likeness. And being found in human form, he humbled himself and became obedient to the point of death—even death on a cross. Therefore God also highly exalted him and gave him the name that is above every name, so that at the name of Jesus every knee should bend, in heaven and on earth and under the earth, and every tongue should confess that Jesus Christ is Lord, to the glory of God the Father.

Philippians 2:5–11, NRSV

Jesus! the Name high over all,
 In hell, or earth, or sky;
Angels and men before it fall,
 And devils fear and fly.

O that the world might taste and see
 The riches of His grace;
The arms of love that compass me
 Would all mankind embrace.

Charles Wesley, 1707–88

The peace of Christ

Remember that at that time you were separate from Christ, excluded from citizenship in Israel and foreigners to the covenants of the promise, without hope and without God in the world. But now in Christ Jesus you who once were far away have been brought near through the blood of Christ.

For he himself is our peace, who has made the two one and has destroyed the barrier, the dividing wall of hostility, by abolishing in his flesh the law with its commandments and regulations. His purpose was to create in himself one new man out of the two, thus making peace, and in this one body to reconcile both of them to God through the cross, by which he put to death their hostility. He came and preached peace to you who were far away and peace to those who were near. For through him we both have access to the Father by one Spirit.

Ephesians 2:12–18

Having made peace through the blood of His cross.

Colossians 1:20, NKJV

Peace, perfect peace, in this dark world of sin?
The blood of Jesus whispers peace within.

Peace, perfect peace, by thronging duties pressed?
To do the will of Jesus, this is rest.

Peace, perfect peace, our future all unknown?
Jesus we know, and He is on the throne.

Edward Henry Bickersteth, 1825–1906

Come to my heart, Lord Jesus

He was in the world, and the world was made through Him, and the world did not know Him. He came to His own, and those who were His own did not receive Him. But as many as received Him, to them He gave the right to become children of God, even to those who believe in His name, who were born, not of blood nor of the will of the flesh nor of the will of man, but of God.

John 1:10–13, NASB

Blessed be the God and Father of our Lord Jesus Christ, who has blessed us in Christ with every spiritual blessing in the heavenly places, just as he chose us in Christ before the foundation of the world to be holy and blameless before him in love. He destined us for adoption as his children through Jesus Christ, according to the good pleasure of his will.

Ephesians 1:3–5, NRSV

Thou didst leave Thy throne
And Thy kingly crown,
　When Thou camest to earth for me;
But in Bethlehem's home
Was there found no room
　For Thy holy nativity:
O come to my heart, Lord Jesus!
There is room in my heart for Thee.

Emily Elizabeth Steele Elliott, 1836–97

Christ, the living water

Come, all you who are thirsty, come to the waters; and you who have no money, come, buy and eat! Come, buy wine and milk without money and without cost.

Isaiah 55:1

On the last day, that great day of the feast, Jesus stood and cried out, saying, "If anyone thirsts, let him come to Me and drink. He who believes in Me, as the Scripture has said, out of his heart will flow rivers of living water." But this He spoke concerning the Spirit, whom those believing in Him would receive; for the Holy Spirit was not yet given, because Jesus was not yet glorified.

John 7:37–39, NKJV

I heard the voice of Jesus say,
  "Behold, I freely give
The living water—thirsty one,
  Stoop down, and drink, and live!"

I came to Jesus, and I drank
  Of that life-giving stream;
My thirst was quenched, my soul revived,
  And now I live in Him.

Horatius Bonar, 1808–89

Preaching the gospel

For this reason I remind you to rekindle the gift of God that is within you through the laying on of my hands; for God did not give us a spirit of cowardice, but rather a spirit of power and of love and of self-discipline.

Do not be ashamed, then, of the testimony about our Lord or of me his prisoner, but join with me in suffering for the gospel, relying on the power of God, who saved us and called us with a holy calling, not according to our works but according to his own purpose and grace. This grace was given to us in Christ Jesus before the ages began, but it has now been revealed through the appearing of our Savior Christ Jesus, who abolished death and brought life and immortality to light through the gospel.

2 Timothy 1:6–10, NRSV

For I take no special pride in the fact that I preach the gospel. I feel compelled to do so; I should be utterly miserable if I failed to preach it.

1 Corinthians 9:16, PHILLIPS

O Thou who camest from above
　The pure celestial fire to impart,
Kindle a flame of sacred love
　On the mean altar of my heart!

Jesus, confirm my heart's desire
　To work and speak and think for Thee;
Still let me guard the holy fire,
　And still stir up Thy gift in me.

Charles Wesley, 1707–88

Who is on the Lord's side?

Now, therefore, fear the LORD and serve Him in sincerity and truth; and put away the gods which your fathers served beyond the River and in Egypt, and serve the LORD. . . . Choose for yourselves today whom you will serve: whether the gods which your fathers served which were beyond the River, or the gods of the Amorites in whose land you are living; but as for me and my house, we will serve the LORD.

Joshua 24:14–15, NASB

And Elijah came to all the people, and said, "How long will you falter between two opinions? If the LORD is God, follow Him; but if Baal, follow him." But the people answered him not a word.

1 Kings 18:21, NKJV

My sheep listen to my voice; I know them, and they follow me. I give them eternal life, and they shall never perish; no one can snatch them out of my hand. My Father, who has given them to me, is greater than all; no one can snatch them out of my Father's hand. I and the Father are one.

John 10:27–30

Who is on the Lord's side?
  Who will serve the King?
Who will be His helpers
  Other lives to bring?
Who will leave the world's side?
  Who will face the foe?
Who is on the Lord's side?
  Who for Him will go?
By Thy call of mercy,
  By Thy grace divine,
We are on the Lord's side;
  Saviour, we are Thine.

Frances Ridley Havergal, 1836–79

Eternal security

Who will bring any charge against God's elect? It is God who justifies. Who is to condemn? It is Christ Jesus, who died, yes, who was raised, who is at the right hand of God, who indeed intercedes for us. Who will separate us from the love of Christ? Will hardship, or distress, or persecution, or famine, or nakedness, or peril, or sword? As it is written, "For your sake we are being killed all day long; we are accounted as sheep to be slaughtered." No, in all these things we are more than conquerors through him who loved us. For I am convinced that neither death, nor life, nor angels, nor rulers, nor things present, nor things to come, nor powers, nor height, nor depth, nor anything else in all creation, will be able to separate us from the love of God in Christ Jesus our Lord.

Romans 8:33–39, NRSV

The soul that on Jesus has leaned for repose
He will not, He will not, desert to its foes;
That soul, though all hell should endeavour to shake,
He'll never, no never, no never forsake.

"K" in Rippon's *Selection,* 1787

True joy in God

The righteous shall be glad in the LORD, and shall trust in him; and all the upright in heart shall glory.

Psalm 64:10, KJV

They shall see the glory of the LORD, the excellency of our God. . . . A highway shall be there, and a road, and it shall be called the Highway of Holiness. The unclean shall not pass over it. . . . And the ransomed of the LORD shall return, and come to Zion with singing, with everlasting joy on their heads. They shall obtain joy and gladness, and sorrow and sighing shall flee away.

Isaiah 35:2,8,10, NKJV

Come, we that love the Lord,
  And let our joys be known;
Join in a song with sweet accord,
  And thus surround the throne.

Isaac Watts, 1674–1748

Seeing the glory of God

I pray also for those who will believe in me through their message, that all of them may be one, Father, just as you are in me and I am in you. May they also be in us so that the world may believe that you have sent me. I have given them the glory that you gave me, that they may be one as we are one: I in them and you in me. May they be brought to complete unity to let the world know that you sent me and have loved them even as you have loved me.

Father, I want those you have given me to be with me where I am, and to see my glory, the glory you have given me because you loved me before the creation of the world.

John 17:20–24

More of Thyself, O show me hour by hour,
  More of Thy glory, O my God and Lord;
More of Thyself, in all Thy grace and power;
  More of Thy love and truth, incarnate Word!

Horatius Bonar, 1808–89

The word of God

The grass withereth, the flower fadeth: because the spirit of the LORD bloweth upon it: surely the people is grass. The grass withereth, the flower fadeth: but the word of our God shall stand for ever.

Isaiah 40:7–8, KJV

Thy word is true from the beginning: and every one of thy righteous judgments endureth for ever.

Psalm 119:160, KJV

For the word of God is living and powerful, and sharper than any two-edged sword, piercing even to the division of soul and spirit, and of joints and marrow, and is a discerner of the thoughts and intents of the heart. And there is no creature hidden from His sight, but all things are naked and open to the eyes of Him to whom we must give account.

Hebrews 4:12–13, NKJV

How firm a foundation, ye saints of the Lord.
Is laid for your faith in His excellent word;
What more can He say than to you He hath said.
You who unto Jesus for refuge have fled?

"K" in Rippon's *Selection,* 1787

Thy way, O Lord

Give ear to my words, O LORD, consider my meditation. Hearken unto the voice of my cry, my King, and my God: for unto thee will I pray. My voice shalt thou hear in the morning, O LORD; in the morning will I direct my prayer unto thee, and will look up. For thou art not a God that hath pleasure in wickedness: neither shall evil dwell with thee. The foolish shall not stand in thy sight: thou hatest all workers of iniquity. Thou shalt destroy them that speak leasing: the LORD will abhor the bloody and deceitful man. But as for me, I will come into thy house in the multitude of thy mercy: and in thy fear will I worship toward thy holy temple. Lead me, O LORD, in thy righteousness because of mine enemies; make thy way straight before my face.

Psalm 5:1–8, KJV

Thy way, not mine, O Lord,
  However dark it be!
Lead me by Thine own hand,
  Choose out the path for me.

Smooth let it be, or rough,
  It will be still the best;
Winding, or straight, it leads
  Right onward to Thy rest.

Horatius Bonar, 1808–89

True worship

And Ezra opened the book in the sight of all the people, for he was standing above all the people; and when he opened it, all the people stood up. And Ezra blessed the LORD, the great God. Then all the people answered, "Amen, Amen!" while lifting up their hands. And they bowed their heads and worshiped the LORD with their faces to the ground.

Nehemiah 8:5–6, NKJV

After these things I looked, and behold, a great multitude which no one could count, from every nation and all tribes and peoples and tongues, standing before the throne and before the Lamb, clothed in white robes, and palm branches were in their hands; and they cry out with a loud voice, saying,

"Salvation to our God who sits on the throne, and to the Lamb." And all the angels were standing around the throne and around the elders and the four living creatures; and they fell on their faces before the throne and worshiped God, saying,

"Amen, blessing and glory and wisdom and thanksgiving and honor and power and might, be to our God forever and ever. Amen."

Revelation 7:9–12, NASB

Stand up, and bless the Lord,
  Ye people of His choice:
Stand up, and bless the Lord your God
  With heart and soul and voice.

Though high above all praise,
  Above all blessing high,
Who would not fear His holy Name,
  And laud and magnify?

James Montgomery, 1771–1854

A new responsive heart

For I will take you from among the nations, gather you out of all countries. . . . Then I will sprinkle clean water on you, and you shall be clean; I will cleanse you from all your filthiness and from all your idols. I will give you a new heart and put a new spirit within you; I will take the heart of stone out of your flesh and give you a heart of flesh. I will put My Spirit within you and cause you to walk in My statutes, and you will keep My judgments and do them. Then you shall dwell in the land that I gave to your fathers; you shall be My people, and I will be your God.

Ezekiel 36:24–28, NKJV

The love of God has been poured out within our hearts through the Holy Spirit who was given to us.

Romans 5:5, NASB

But when the goodness and loving kindness of God our Savior appeared, he saved us, not because of any works of righteousness that we had done, but according to his mercy, through the water of rebirth and renewal by the Holy Spirit. This Spirit he poured out on us richly through Jesus Christ our Savior, so that, having been justified by his grace, we might become heirs according to the hope of eternal life.

Titus 3:4–7, NRSV

O for a heart to praise my God,
   A heart from sin set free;
A heart that always feels Thy blood
   So freely shed for me;

A heart resigned, submissive, meek,
   My great Redeemer's throne,
Where only Christ is heard to speak,
   Where Jesus reigns alone.

Charles Wesley, 1707–88

The path of commitment

My son, forget not my law; but let thine heart keep my commandments: For length of days, and long life, and peace, shall they add to thee. Let not mercy and truth forsake thee: bind them about thy neck; write them upon the table of thine heart: So shalt thou find favour and good understanding in the sight of God and man.

Trust in the LORD with all thine heart; and lean not unto thine own understanding. In all thy ways acknowledge him, and he shall direct thy paths. Be not wise in thine own eyes: fear the LORD, and depart from evil. It shall be health to thy navel, and marrow to thy bones.

Proverbs 3:1–8, KJV

I am trusting Thee, Lord Jesus,
    Trusting only Thee,
Trusting Thee for full salvation,
    Great and free.

I am trusting Thee to guide me:
    Thou alone shalt lead,
Every day and hour supplying
    All my need.

Frances Ridley Havergal, 1836–79

Seeing Jesus

One thing have I desired of the LORD, that will I seek after; that I may dwell in the house of the LORD all the days of my life, to behold the beauty of the LORD, and to enquire in his temple. For in the time of trouble he shall hide me in his pavilion: in the secret of his tabernacle shall he hide me; he shall set me up upon a rock. And now shall mine head be lifted up above mine enemies round about me: therefore will I offer in his tabernacle sacrifices of joy; I will sing, yea, I will sing praises unto the LORD. Hear, O LORD, when I cry with my voice: have mercy also upon me, and answer me. When thou saidst, Seek ye my face; my heart said unto thee, Thy face, LORD, will I seek.

Psalm 27:4–8, KJV

One thing I do, forgetting those things which are behind and reaching forward to those things which are ahead, I press toward the goal for the prize of the upward call of God in Christ Jesus.

Philippians 3:13–14, NKJV

May I run the race before me,
  Strong and brave to face the foe,
Looking only unto Jesus
  As I onward go.

May His beauty rest upon me
  As I seek the lost to win,
And may they forget the channel,
  Seeing only Him.

Katie Barclay Wilkinson, 1859–1928

"Go and make disciples of all nations"

Ask of me, and I shall give thee the heathen for thine inheritance, and the uttermost parts of the earth for thy possession. . . .

Serve the LORD with fear, and rejoice with trembling. Kiss the Son, lest he be angry, and ye perish from the way, when his wrath is kindled but a little. Blessed are all they that put their trust in him.

Psalm 2:8,11–12, KJV

Then the eleven disciples went away into Galilee, into a mountain where Jesus had appointed them. And when they saw him, they worshipped him: but some doubted. And Jesus came and spake unto them, saying, All power is given unto me in heaven and in earth. Go ye therefore, and teach all nations, baptizing them in the name of the Father, and of the Son, and of the Holy Ghost: Teaching them to observe all things whatsoever I have commanded you: and, lo, I am with you alway, even unto the end of the world. Amen.

Matthew 28:16–20, KJV

Facing a task unfinished,
    That drives us to our knees,
A need that, undiminished,
    Rebukes our slothful ease,
We who rejoice to know Thee,
    Renew before Thy throne
The solemn pledge we owe Thee,
    To go and make Thee known.

Frank Houghton, 1894–1972

Enjoying God

It is a good thing to give thanks unto the LORD, and to sing praises unto thy name, O most High: To shew forth thy lovingkindness in the morning, and thy faithfulness every night, Upon an instrument of ten strings, and upon the psaltery; upon the harp with a solemn sound. For thou, LORD, hast made me glad through thy work: I will triumph in the works of thy hands. O LORD, how great are thy works! and thy thoughts are very deep. A brutish man knoweth not; neither doth a fool understand this. When the wicked spring as the grass, and when all the workers of iniquity do flourish; it is that they shall be destroyed for ever: But thou, LORD, art most high for evermore.

Psalm 92:1–8, KJV

Sweet is the work, my God, my King,
To praise Thy Name, give thanks and sing;
To show Thy love by morning light,
And talk of all Thy truth at night.

My heart shall triumph in the Lord,
And bless His works and bless His Word;
Thy works of grace, how bright they shine,
How deep Thy counsels, how divine!

Isaac Watts, 1674–1748

The way of peace

As a prisoner for the Lord, then, I urge you to live a life worthy of the calling you have received. Be completely humble and gentle; be patient, bearing with one another in love. Make every effort to keep the unity of the Spirit through the bond of peace. There is one body and one Spirit—just as you were called to one hope when you were called—one Lord, one faith, one baptism; one God and Father of all, who is over all and through all and in all.

Ephesians 4:1–6

All of you be submissive to one another, and be clothed with humility, for "God resists the proud, but gives grace to the humble." Therefore humble yourselves under the mighty hand of God, that He may exalt you in due time.

1 Peter 5:5–6, NKJV

May the mind of Christ my Saviour
  Live in me from day to day,
By His love and power controlling
  All I do and say.

May the peace of God my Father
  Rule my life in everything,
That I may be calm to comfort
  Sick and sorrowing.

May the love of Jesus fill me
  As the waters fill the sea;
Him exalting, self abasing,
  This is victory.

Katie Barclay Wilkinson, 1859–1928

FEBRUARY 20

Confidence in Christ

There is therefore now no condemnation to them which are in Christ Jesus.

Romans 8:1, KJV

Seeing then that we have a great High Priest who has passed through the heavens, Jesus the Son of God, let us hold fast our confession. For we do not have a High Priest who cannot sympathize with our weaknesses, but was in all points tempted as we are, yet without sin. Let us therefore come boldly to the throne of grace, that we may obtain mercy and find grace to help in time of need.

Hebrews 4:14–16, NKJV

No condemnation now I dread;
  Jesus, and all in Him, is mine!
Alive in Him, my living Head,
  And clothed in righteousness divine,
Bold I approach the eternal throne,
And claim the crown, through Christ my own.

Charles Wesley, 1707–88

Watch and pray

Then Jesus went with them to a place called Gethsemane; and he said to his disciples, "Sit here while I go over there and pray." He took with him Peter and the two sons of Zebedee, and began to be grieved and agitated. Then he said to them, "I am deeply grieved, even to death; remain here, and stay awake with me." And going a little farther, he threw himself on the ground and prayed, "My Father, if it is possible, let this cup pass from me; yet not what I want but what you want." Then he came to the disciples and found them sleeping; and he said to Peter, "So, could you not stay awake with me one hour? Stay awake and pray that you may not come into the time of trial; the spirit indeed is willing, but the flesh is weak."

Matthew 26:36–41, NRSV

And forgive us our sins; for we also forgive every one that is indebted to us. And lead us not into temptation; but deliver us from evil.

Luke 11:4, KJV

Christian, seek not yet repose;
  Cast thy dreams of ease away;
Thou art in the midst of foes:
  Watch and pray.

Watch, as if on that alone
  Hung the issue of the day;
Pray that help may be sent down:
  Watch and pray.

Charlotte Elliott, 1789–1871

His righteousness

For we are the circumcision, who worship God in the Spirit, rejoice in Christ Jesus, and have no confidence in the flesh, though I also might have confidence in the flesh. If anyone else thinks he may have confidence in the flesh, I more so: circumcised the eighth day, of the stock of Israel, of the tribe of Benjamin, a Hebrew of the Hebrews; concerning the law, a Pharisee; concerning zeal, persecuting the church; concerning the righteousness which is in the law, blameless. But what things were gain to me, these I have counted loss for Christ. Yet indeed I also count all things loss for the excellence of the knowledge of Christ Jesus my Lord, for whom I have suffered the loss of all things, and count them as rubbish, that I may gain Christ and be found in Him, not having my own righteousness, which is from the law, but that which is through faith in Christ, the righteousness which is from God by faith.

Philippians 3:3–9, NKJV

Jesus! the Name to sinners dear,
  The Name to sinners given;
It scatters all their guilty fear,
  It turns their hell to heaven.

His only righteousness I show,
  His saving truth proclaim;
'Tis all my business here below
  To cry, "Behold the Lamb!"

Charles Wesley, 1707–88

Growing in holiness

Godliness has value for all things, holding promise for both the present life and the life to come.

This is a trustworthy saying that deserves full acceptance (and for this we labor and strive), that we have put our hope in the living God, who is the Savior of all men, and especially of those who believe.

Command and teach these things. Don't let anyone look down on you because you are young, but set an example for the believers in speech, in life, in love, in faith and in purity. Until I come, devote yourself to the public reading of Scripture, to preaching and to teaching. Do not neglect your gift, which was given you through a prophetic message when the body of elders laid their hands on you.

Be diligent in these matters; give yourself wholly to them, so that everyone may see your progress. Watch your life and doctrine closely. Persevere in them, because if you do, you will save both yourself and your hearers.

1 Timothy 4:8–16

Take time to be holy, speak oft with thy Lord;
Abide in Him always, and feed on His Word,
Make friends of God's children, help those who are weak;
Forgetting in nothing His blessing to seek.

Take time to be holy, the world rushes on;
Spend much time in secret with Jesus alone.
By looking to Jesus like Him thou shalt be;
Thy friends, in thy conduct, His likeness shall see.

William Dunn Longstaff, 1822–94

Responding to God

Seek the LORD while He may be found; call upon Him while He is near. Let the wicked forsake his way and the unrighteous man his thoughts; and let him return to the LORD, and He will have compassion on him, and to our God, for He will abundantly pardon. "For My thoughts are not your thoughts, nor are your ways My ways," declares the LORD. "For as the heavens are higher than the earth, so are My ways higher than your ways and My thoughts than your thoughts."

Isaiah 55:6–9, NASB

For Christ also hath once suffered for sins, the just for the unjust, that he might bring us to God, being put to death in the flesh, but quickened by the Spirit.

1 Peter 3:18, KJV

Out of my bondage, sorrow and night,
  Jesus, I come, Jesus, I come;
Into Thy freedom, gladness and light,
  Jesus, I come to Thee.
Out of my sickness into Thy health,
Out of my want and into Thy wealth,
Out of my sin and into Thyself,
  Jesus, I come to Thee.

William True Sleeper, 1840–1920

Giving ourselves to God

I appeal to you therefore, brothers and sisters, by the mercies of God, to present your bodies as a living sacrifice, holy and acceptable to God, which is your spiritual worship. Do not be conformed to this world, but be transformed by the renewing of your minds, so that you may discern what is the will of God—what is good and acceptable and perfect.

For by the grace given to me I say to everyone among you not to think of yourself more highly than you ought to think, but to think with sober judgment, each according to the measure of faith that God has assigned. For as in one body we have many members, and not all the members have the same function, so we, who are many, are one body in Christ, and individually we are members one of another. We have gifts that differ according to the grace given to us: prophecy, in proportion to faith; ministry, in ministering; the teacher, in teaching; the exhorter, in exhortation; the giver, in generosity; the leader, in diligence; the compassionate, in cheerfulness.

Romans 12:1–8, NRSV

Take my life, and let it be
Consecrated, Lord, to Thee;
Take my moments and my days,
Let them flow in ceaseless praise.

Take my will, and make it Thine;
It shall be no longer mine:
Take my heart, it is Thine own;
It shall be Thy royal throne.

Take my love; my Lord, I pour
At Thy feet its treasure-store:
Take myself, and I will be
Ever, only, all for Thee!

Frances Ridley Havergal, 1836–79

"I know whom I have believed"

And the grace of our Lord was exceedingly abundant, with faith and love which are in Christ Jesus. This is a faithful saying and worthy of all acceptance, that Christ Jesus came into the world to save sinners, of whom I am chief. However, for this reason I obtained mercy, that in me first Jesus Christ might show all longsuffering, as a pattern to those who are going to believe on Him for everlasting life. Now to the King eternal, immortal, invisible, to God who alone is wise, be honor and glory forever and ever. Amen.

1 Timothy 1:14–17, NKJV

And of this gospel I was appointed a herald and an apostle and a teacher. That is why I am suffering as I am. Yet I am not ashamed, because I know whom I have believed, and am convinced that he is able to guard what I have entrusted to him for that day.

What you heard from me, keep as the pattern of sound teaching, with faith and love in Christ Jesus. Guard the good deposit that was entrusted to you—guard it with the help of the Holy Spirit who lives in us.

2 Timothy 1:11–14

I know not why God's wondrous grace
  To me has been made known,
Nor why—unworthy as I am—
  He claimed me for His own.

But "I know whom I have believed, and am
persuaded that He is able to keep that which
I've committed unto Him against that day."

Daniel Webster Whittle, 1840–1901

Praise the Lord

Praise ye the LORD. Praise ye the LORD from the heavens: praise him in the heights. Praise ye him, all his angels: praise ye him, all his hosts. Praise ye him, sun and moon: praise him, all ye stars of light. Praise him, ye heavens of heavens, and ye waters that be above the heavens. Let them praise the name of the LORD: for he commanded, and they were created. He hath also stablished them for ever and ever: he hath made a decree which shall not pass. . . .

He also exalteth the horn of his people, the praise of all his saints; even of the children of Israel, a people near unto him. Praise ye the LORD.

Psalm 148:1–6,14, KJV

Praise the Lord! ye heavens, adore Him;
  Praise Him, angels in the height;
Sun and moon, rejoice before Him;
  Praise Him, all ye stars and light.

Praise the Lord! for He hath spoken;
  Worlds His mighty voice obeyed;
Laws, that never shall be broken,
  For their guidance He hath made.

Anonymous

Walking with God

And Enoch walked with God: and he was not; for God took him.

Genesis 5:24, KJV

Many peoples shall come and say, "Come, let us go up to the mountain of the LORD, to the house of the God of Jacob; that he may teach us his ways and that we may walk in his paths." For out of Zion shall go forth instruction, and the word of the LORD from Jerusalem. He shall judge between the nations, and shall arbitrate for many peoples; they shall beat their swords into plowshares, and their spears into pruning hooks; nation shall not lift up sword against nation, neither shall they learn war any more.

O house of Jacob, come, let us walk in the light of the LORD!

Isaiah 2:3–5, NRSV

If we say that we have fellowship with Him and yet walk in the darkness, we lie and do not practice the truth; but if we walk in the Light as He Himself is in the Light, we have fellowship with one another, and the blood of Jesus His Son cleanses us from all sin.

1 John 1:6–7, NASB

O for a closer walk with God,
   A calm and heavenly frame,
A light to shine upon the road
   That leads me to the Lamb!

So shall my walk be close with God,
   Calm and serene my frame;
So purer light shall mark the road
   That leads me to the Lamb.

William Cowper, 1731–1800

The Savior's love for us

As they led him away, they seized Simon from Cyrene, who was on his way in from the country, and put the cross on him and made him carry it behind Jesus. A large number of people followed him, including women who mourned and wailed for him. Jesus turned and said to them, "Daughters of Jerusalem, do not weep for me; weep for yourselves and for your children."

Luke 23:26–28

Now it was about the sixth hour, and there was darkness over all the earth until the ninth hour. Then the sun was darkened, and the veil of the temple was torn in two. And when Jesus had cried out with a loud voice, He said, "Father, 'into Your hands I commit My spirit.'" Having said this, He breathed His last.

Luke 23:44–46, NKJV

He himself bore our sins in his body on the tree, so that we might die to sins and live for righteousness; by his wounds you have been healed.

1 Peter 2:24

Give me a sight, O Saviour,
  Of Thy wondrous love to me,
Of the love that brought Thee down to earth,
  To die on Calvary.

O make me understand it,
  Help me to take it in,
What it meant to Thee, the Holy One,
  To bear away my sin.

Katharine Agnes May Kelly, 1869–1942

Great is thy faithfulness

Remember my affliction and roaming, the wormwood and the gall. My soul still remembers tnd sinks within me. This I recall to my mind, therefore I have hope.

Through the LORD's mercies we are not consumed, because His compassions fail not. They are new every morning; great is Your faithfulness. "The LORD is my portion," says my soul, "therefore I hope in Him!"

The LORD is good to those who wait for Him, To the soul who seeks Him. It is good that one should hope and wait quietly for the salvation of the LORD. It is good for a man to bear the yoke in his youth.

Lamentations 3:19–27, NKJV

Great is Thy faithfulness, O God my Father,
  There is no shadow of turning with Thee;
Thou changest not, Thy compassions they fail not,
  As Thou hast been Thou for ever wilt be.

Great is Thy faithfulness!
Great is Thy faithfulness!
  Morning by morning new mercies I see;
All I have needed Thy hand hath provided,—
  Great is Thy faithfulness, Lord, unto me!

Summer and winter, and spring-time and harvest,
  Sun, moon and stars in their courses above,
Join with all nature in manifold witness
  To Thy great faithfulness, mercy and love.

Thomas O. Chisholm, 1866–1960

Jesus, the Lamb of God

The next day John saw Jesus coming toward him, and said, "Behold! The Lamb of God who takes away the sin of the world! This is He of whom I said, 'After me comes a Man who is preferred before me, for He was before me.' I did not know Him; but that He should be revealed to Israel, therefore I came baptizing with water." And John bore witness, saying, "I saw the Spirit descending from heaven like a dove, and He remained upon Him. I did not know Him, but He who sent me to baptize with water said to me, 'Upon whom you see the Spirit descending, and remaining on Him, this is He who baptizes with the Holy Spirit.' And I have seen and testified that this is the Son of God."

Again, the next day, John stood with two of his disciples. And looking at Jesus as He walked, he said, "Behold the Lamb of God!" The two disciples heard him speak, and they followed Jesus.

John 1:29–37, NKJV

Jesus! the prisoner's fetters breaks,
   And bruises Satan's head;
Power into strengthless souls it speaks,
   And life into the dead.

Happy, if with my latest breath
   I may but gasp His Name;
Preach Him to all, and cry in death,
   "Behold, behold the Lamb!"

Charles Wesley, 1707–88

God, our refuge and strength

God is our refuge and strength, a very present help in trouble. Therefore will not we fear, though the earth be removed, and though the mountains be carried into the midst of the sea; Though the waters thereof roar and be troubled, though the mountains shake with the swelling thereof. Selah. There is a river, the streams whereof shall make glad the city of God, the holy place of the tabernacles of the most High. God is in the midst of her; she shall not be moved: God shall help her, and that right early. The heathen raged, the kingdoms were moved: he uttered his voice, the earth melted. The LORD of hosts is with us; the God of Jacob is our refuge. Selah.

Psalm 46:1–7, KJV

A safe stronghold our God is still,
  A trusty shield and weapon;
He'll help us clear from all the ill
  That hath us now o'ertaken.
The ancient prince of hell
Hath risen with purpose fell;

Strong mail of craft and power
He weareth in this hour;
  On earth is not his fellow.

Martin Luther, 1483–1546
translated by Thomas Carlyle, 1795–1881

Becoming like Jesus

Let no evil talk come out of your mouths, but only what is useful for building up, as there is need, so that your words may give grace to those who hear. And do not grieve the Holy Spirit of God, with which you were marked with a seal for the day of redemption. Put away from you all bitterness and wrath and anger and wrangling and slander, together with all malice, and be kind to one another, tender-hearted, forgiving one another, as God in Christ has forgiven you. Therefore be imitators of God, as beloved children, and live in love, as Christ loved us and gave himself up for us, a fragrant offering and sacrifice to God.

Ephesians 4:29–5:2, NRSV

More of Thy glory let me see,
    Thou Holy, Wise, and True!
I would Thy living image be,
    In joy and sorrow too.

Fill me with gladness from above,
    Hold me by strength divine!
Lord, let the glow of Thy great love
    Through my whole being shine.

Johann Caspar Lavater, 1741–1801
translated by Elizabeth Lee Smith, 1817–98

Victory through Christ

These things I have spoken unto you, that in me ye might have peace. In the world ye shall have tribulation: but be of good cheer; I have overcome the world.

John 16:33, KJV

Be sober, be vigilant; because your adversary the devil walks about like a roaring lion, seeking whom he may devour. Resist him, steadfast in the faith, knowing that the same sufferings are experienced by your brotherhood in the world. But may the God of all grace, who called us to His eternal glory by Christ Jesus, after you have suffered a while, perfect, establish, strengthen, and settle you. To Him be the glory and the dominion forever and ever. Amen.

1 Peter 5:8–11, NKJV

Yield not to temptation, for yielding is sin;
Each victory will help you some other to win;
Fight manfully onward; dark passions subdue;
Look ever to Jesus, He will carry you through.

Ask the Saviour to help you,
Comfort, strengthen, and keep you;
He is willing to aid you,
He will carry you through.

Horatio Richmond Palmer, 1834–1907

MARCH 6

With Christ in glory

My prayer is not for them [Jesus' disciples] alone. I pray also for those who will believe in me through their message, that all of them may be one, Father, just as you are in me and I am in you. May they also be in us so that the world may believe that you have sent me. I have given them the glory that you gave me, that they may be one as we are one: I in them and you in me. May they be brought to complete unity to let the world know that you sent me and have loved them even as you have loved me.

Father, I want those you have given me to be with me where I am, and to see my glory, the glory you have given me because you loved me before the creation of the world.

Righteous Father, though the world does not know you, I know you, and they know that you have sent me. I have made you known to them, and will continue to make you known in order that the love you have for me may be in them and that I myself may be in them.

John 17:20–26

O Jesus, Thou hast promised,
  To all who follow Thee,
That where Thou art in glory
  There shall Thy servant be;
And, Jesus, I have promised
  To serve Thee to the end:
O give me grace to follow,
  My Master and my Friend.

John Ernest Bode, 1816–74

Faith for life's struggles

And while they were sailing he fell asleep. A windstorm swept down on the lake, and the boat was filling with water, and they were in danger. They went to him and woke him up, shouting, "Master, Master, we are perishing!" And he woke up and rebuked the wind and the raging waves; they ceased, and there was a calm. He said to them, "Where is your faith?" They were afraid and amazed, and said to one another, "Who then is this, that he commands even the winds and the water, and they obey him?"

Luke 8:23–25, NRSV

They returned to Lystra and to Iconium and to Antioch, strengthening the souls of the disciples, encouraging them to continue in the faith, and saying, "Through many tribulations we must enter the kingdom of God."

Acts 14:21–22, NASB

Begone, unbelief;
  My Saviour is near,
And for my relief
  Will surely appear:
By prayer let me wrestle,
  And He will perform;
With Christ in the vessel,
  I smile at the storm.

Why should I complain
  Of want or distress,
Temptation or pain?
  He told me no less;
The heirs of salvation,
  I know from His Word,
Through much tribulation
Must follow their Lord.

John Newton, 1725–1807

The grace of God

The Lord did not set His love on you nor choose you because you were more in number than any other people, for you were the least of all peoples; but because the Lord loves you, and because He would keep the oath which He swore to your fathers, the Lord has brought you out with a mighty hand, and redeemed you from the house of bondage, from the hand of Pharaoh king of Egypt.

Deuteronomy 7:7–8, NKJV

Grace be to you and peace from God the Father, and from our Lord Jesus Christ, who gave himself for our sins, that he might deliver us from this present evil world, according to the will of God and our Father: to whom be glory for ever and ever. Amen.

Galatians 1:3–5, KJV

Come, Thou Fount of every blessing,
  Tune my heart to sing Thy grace;
Streams of mercy, never ceasing,
  Call for songs of loudest praise.
Teach me some melodious measure,
  Sung by flaming tongues above;
O the vast, the boundless treasure
  Of my Lord's unchanging love!

O to grace how great a debtor
  Daily I'm constrained to be!
Let that grace, Lord, like a fetter,
  Bind my wandering heart to Thee.
Prone to wander, Lord, I feel it,
  Prone to leave the God I love;
Take my heart, O take and seal it.
  Seal it from Thy courts above!

Robert Robinson, 1735–90

The boundless love of Christ

For this reason I bow my knees before the Father, from whom every family in heaven and on earth derives its name, that He would grant you, according to the riches of His glory, to be strengthened with power through His Spirit in the inner man, so that Christ may dwell in your hearts through faith; and that you, being rooted and grounded in love, may be able to comprehend with all the saints what is the breadth and length and height and depth, and to know the love of Christ which surpasses knowledge, that you may be filled up to all the fullness of God.

Now to Him who is able to do far more abundantly beyond all that we ask or think, according to the power that works within us, to Him be the glory in the church and in Christ Jesus to all generations forever and ever. Amen.

Ephesians 3:14–21, NASB

It passeth knowledge, that dear love of Thine,
My Saviour, Jesus, yet this soul of mine
Would of Thy love, in all its breadth and length,
Its height and depth, its everlasting strength,
　Know more and more.

Mary Shekleton, 1827–83

Finding the lost sheep

Now the tax collectors and "sinners" were all gathering around to hear him. But the Pharisees and the teachers of the law muttered, "This man welcomes sinners and eats with them."

Then Jesus told them this parable: "Suppose one of you has a hundred sheep and loses one of them. Does he not leave the ninety-nine in the open country and go after the lost sheep until he finds it? And when he finds it, he joyfully puts it on his shoulders and goes home. Then he calls his friends and neighbors together and says, 'Rejoice with me; I have found my lost sheep.' I tell you that in the same way there will be more rejoicing in heaven over one sinner who repents than over ninety-nine righteous persons who do not need to repent."

Luke 15:1–7

I will sing the wondrous story
  Of the Christ who died for me;
How He left His home in glory
  For the cross on Calvary.
I was lost: but Jesus found me,
  Found the sheep that went astray;
Threw His loving arms around me
  Drew me back into His way.

Francis Harold Rawley, 1854–1952

Not worthy to be children

And when he came to himself, he said, How many hired servants of my father's have bread enough and to spare, and I perish with hunger! I will arise and go to my father, and will say unto him, Father, I have sinned against heaven, and before thee, and am no more worthy to be called thy son: make me as one of thy hired servants. And he arose, and came to his father. But when he was yet a great way off, his father saw him, and had compassion, and ran, and fell on his neck, and kissed him. And the son said unto him, Father, I have sinned against heaven, and in thy sight, and am no more worthy to be called thy son. But the father said to his servants, Bring forth the best robe, and put it on him; and put a ring on his hand, and shoes on his feet: and bring hither the fatted calf, and kill it; and let us eat, and be merry: For this my son was dead, and is alive again; he was lost, and is found. And they began to be merry.

Luke 15:17–24, KJV

Not worthy, Lord, to gather up the crumbs
  With trembling hand that from Thy table fall,
A weary heavy-laden sinner comes
  To plead Thy promise and obey Thy call.

I am not worthy to be thought Thy child,
  Nor sit the last and lowest at Thy board;
Too long a wanderer, and too oft beguiled,
  I only ask one reconciling word.

Edward Henry Bickersteth, 1825–1906

The power of God's word

Wherewithal shall a young man cleanse his way? by taking heed thereto according to thy word. With my whole heart have I sought thee: O let me not wander from thy commandments. Thy word have I hid in mine heart, that I might not sin against thee. Blessed art thou, O LORD: teach me thy statutes. With my lips have I declared all the judgments of thy mouth. I have rejoiced in the way of thy testimonies, as much as in all riches. I will meditate in thy precepts, and have respect unto thy ways. I will delight myself in thy statutes: I will not forget thy word.

Psalm 119:9–16, KJV

"I have heard what the prophets have said who prophesy lies in My name, saying, 'I have dreamed, I have dreamed!' How long will this be in the heart of the prophets who prophesy lies? Indeed they are prophets of the deceit of their own heart, who try to make My people forget My name by their dreams which everyone tells his neighbor, as their fathers forgot My name for Baal.

"The prophet who has a dream, let him tell a dream; and he who has My word, let him speak My word faithfully. What is the chaff to the wheat?" says the LORD. "Is not My word like a fire?" says the LORD, "and like a hammer that breaks the rock in pieces?"

Jeremiah 23:25–29, NKJV

Come, O Thou all-victorious Lord,
  Thy power to us make known;
Strike with the hammer of Thy Word,
  And break these hearts of stone.

Give us ourselves and Thee to know,
  In this our gracious day;
Repentance unto life bestow,
  And take our sins away.

Charles Wesley, 1707–88

The greatness of God

Thy mercy, O LORD, is in the heavens; and thy faithfulness reacheth unto the clouds. Thy righteousness is like the great mountains; thy judgments are a great deep: O LORD, thou preservest man and beast. How excellent is thy lovingkindness, O God! therefore the children of men put their trust under the shadow of thy wings. They shall be abundantly satisfied with the fatness of thy house; and thou shalt make them drink of the river of thy pleasures. For with thee is the fountain of life: in thy light shall we see light. O continue thy lovingkindness unto them that know thee; and thy righteousness to the upright in heart. Let not the foot of pride come against me, and let not the hand of the wicked remove me. There are the workers of iniquity fallen: they are cast down, and shall not be able to rise.

Psalm 36:5–12, KJV

Unresting, unhasting, and silent as light,
Nor wanting, nor wasting, Thou rulest in might;
Thy justice like mountains high soaring above,
Thy clouds which are fountains of goodness and love.

To all life Thou givest, to both great and small;
In all life Thou livest, the true life of all;
We blossom and flourish as leaves on the tree,
And wither and perish—but nought changeth Thee.

Immortal, invisible, God only wise,
In light inaccessible hid from our eyes,
Most blessed, most glorious the Ancient of Days,
Almighty, victorious, Thy great Name we praise.

Walter Chalmers Smith, 1824–1908

"Teach us to pray"

One day it happened that Jesus was praying in a certain place, and after he had finished, one of his disciples said,

"Lord, teach us how to pray, as John used to teach his disciples."

"When you pray," returned Jesus, "you should say, 'Father, may your name be honoured—may your kingdom come. Give us the bread we need for each day, and forgive us our failures, for we forgive everyone who fails us; and keep us clear of temptation.'"

Luke 11:1–4, PHILLIPS

Have faith in God. For assuredly, I say to you, whoever says to this mountain, "Be removed and be cast into the sea," and does not doubt in his heart, but believes that those things he says will be done, he will have whatever he says. Therefore I say to you, whatever things you ask when you pray, believe that you receive them, and you will have them.

Mark 11:22–24, NKJV

O Thou by whom we come to God,
  The Life, the Truth, the Way,
The path of prayer Thyself hast trod;
  Lord, teach us how to pray.

Prayer is the soul's sincere desire,
  Uttered or unexpressed;
The motion of a hidden fire
  That trembles in the breast.

James Montgomery, 1771–1854

Born of the Spirit

Now there was a Pharisee named Nicodemus, a leader of the Jews. He came to Jesus by night and said to him, "Rabbi, we know that you are a teacher who has come from God; for no one can do these signs that you do apart from the presence of God." Jesus answered him, "Very truly, I tell you, no one can see the kingdom of God without being born from above." Nicodemus said to him, "How can anyone be born after having grown old? Can one enter a second time into the mother's womb and be born?" Jesus answered, "Very truly, I tell you, no one can enter the kingdom of God without being born of water and Spirit. What is born of the flesh is flesh, and what is born of the Spirit is spirit. Do not be astonished that I said to you, 'You must be born from above.' The wind blows where it chooses, and you hear the sound of it, but you do not know where it comes from or where it goes. So it is with everyone who is born of the Spirit."

John 3:1–8

Blessed assurance, Jesus is mine:
O what a foretaste of glory divine!
Heir of salvation, purchase of God,
Born of His Spirit, washed in His blood.

This is my story, this is my song,
Praising my Saviour all the day long.

Frances Jane Van Alstyne, 1820–1915

Leaving our cares with Jesus

Rejoice in the Lord alway: and again I say, Rejoice. Let your moderation be known unto all men. The Lord is at hand. Be careful for nothing; but in every thing by prayer and supplication with thanksgiving let your requests be made known unto God. And the peace of God, which passeth all understanding, shall keep your hearts and minds through Christ Jesus.

Philippians 4:4–7, KJV

Humble yourselves therefore under the mighty hand of God, that he may exalt you in due time: Casting all your care upon him; for he careth for you.

1 Peter 5:6–7, KJV

Are we weak and heavy-laden,
   Cumbered with a load of care?
Precious Saviour, still our refuge:
   Take it to the Lord in prayer.

Do thy friends despise, forsake thee?
   Take it to the Lord in prayer;
In His arms He'll take and shield thee,
   Thou wilt find a solace there.

Joseph Medlicott Scriven, 1819–86

The greatest is love

This love of which I speak is slow to lose patience—it looks for a way of being constructive. It is not possessive: it is neither anxious to impress nor does it cherish inflated ideas of its own importance.

Love has good manners and does not pursue selfish advantage. It is not touchy. It does not keep account of evil or gloat over the wickedness of other people. On the contrary, it shares the joy of those who live by the truth.

Love knows no limit to its endurance, no end to its trust, no fading of its hope; it can outlast anything. Love never fails.

For if there are prophecies they will be fulfilled and done with, if there are "tongues" the need for them will disappear, if there is knowledge it will be swallowed up in truth. For our knowledge is always incomplete and our prophecy is always incomplete, and when the complete comes, that is the end of the incomplete.

When I was a little child I talked and felt and thought like a little child. Now that I am a man I have finished with childish things.

At present we are men looking at puzzling reflections in a mirror. The time will come when we shall see reality whole and face to face! At present all I know is a little fraction of the truth, but the time will come when I shall know it as fully as God has known me!

In this life we have three lasting qualities—faith, hope and love. But the greatest of them is love.

1 Corinthians 13:4–13, PHILLIPS

God only knows the love of God;
O that it now were shed abroad
  In this poor stony heart!
For love I sigh, for love I pine;
This only portion, Lord, be mine,
  Be mine this better part!

Charles Wesley, 1707–88

"Pass me not"

Then it happened, as He was coming near Jericho, that a certain blind man sat by the road begging. And hearing a multitude passing by, he asked what it meant. So they told him that Jesus of Nazareth was passing by. And he cried out, saying, "Jesus, Son of David, have mercy on me!" Then those who went before warned him that he should be quiet; but he cried out all the more, "Son of David, have mercy on me!" So Jesus stood still and commanded him to be brought to Him. And when he had come near, He asked him, saying, "What do you want Me to do for you?" He said, "Lord, that I may receive my sight." Then Jesus said to him, "Receive your sight; your faith has made you well." And immediately he received his sight, and followed Him, glorifying God. And all the people, when they saw it, gave praise to God.

Luke 18:35–43, NKJV

Pass me not, O gentle Saviour,
  Hear my humble cry;
While on others Thou art calling,
  Do not pass me by.

Saviour! Saviour!
  Hear my humble cry,
And while others Thou art calling,
  Do not pass me by.

Frances Jane Van Alstyne, 1820–1915

Knowing forgiveness

Blessed is he whose transgression is forgiven, whose sin is covered. Blessed is the man unto whom the LORD imputeth not iniquity, and in whose spirit there is no guile. When I kept silence, my bones waxed old through my roaring all the day long. For day and night thy hand was heavy upon me: my moisture is turned into the drought of summer. Selah. I acknowledged my sin unto thee, and mine iniquity have I not hid. I said, I will confess my transgressions unto the LORD; and thou forgavest the iniquity of my sin. Selah.

Psalm 32:1–5, KJV

If we say that we have no sin, we deceive ourselves, and the truth is not in us. If we confess our sins, he is faithful and just to forgive us our sins, and to cleanse us from all unrighteousness.

1 John 1:8–9, KJV

Just as I am, and waiting not
To rid my soul of one dark blot,
To Thee, whose blood can cleanse each spot,
  O Lamb of God, I come.

Just as I am—Thy love unknown
Has broken every barrier down—
Now to be Thine, yea, Thine alone,
  O Lamb of God, I come.

Charlotte Elliott, 1789–1871

"Crucify him!"

But the chief priests and elders persuaded the multitude that they should ask Barabbas, and destroy Jesus. The governor answered and said unto them, Whether of the twain will ye that I release unto you? They said, Barabbas. Pilate saith unto them, What shall I do then with Jesus which is called Christ? They all say unto him, Let him be crucified. And the governor said, Why, what evil hath he done? But they cried out the more, saying, Let him be crucified. When Pilate saw that he could prevail nothing, but that rather a tumult was made, he took water, and washed his hands before the multitude, saying, I am innocent of the blood of this just person: see ye to it. Then answered all the people, and said, His blood be on us, and on our children. Then released he Barabbas unto them: and when he had scourged Jesus, he delivered him to be crucified.

Matthew 27:20–26, KJV

My song is love unknown,
  My Saviour's love to me,
Love to the loveless shown,
  That they might lovely be.
    O who am I,
      That for my sake
      My Lord should take
    Frail flesh, and die?

Sometimes they strew His way,
  And His sweet praises sing;
Resounding all the day
  Hosannas to their King.
    Then "Crucify!"
      Is all their breath,
      And for His death
    They thirst and cry.

Samuel Crossman, 1624–83

Jesus on the cross

Now as they came out, they found a man of Cyrene, Simon by name. Him they compelled to bear His cross. And when they had come to a place called Golgotha, that is to say, Place of a Skull, they gave Him sour wine mingled with gall to drink. But when He had tasted it, He would not drink. Then they crucified Him, and divided His garments, casting lots, that it might be fulfilled which was spoken by the prophet: "They divided My garments among them, and for My clothing they cast lots." Sitting down, they kept watch over Him there. And they put up over His head the accusation written against Him: THIS IS JESUS THE KING OF THE JEWS. Then two robbers were crucified with Him, one on the right and another on the left. And those who passed by blasphemed Him, wagging their heads and saying, "You who destroy the temple and build it in three days, save Yourself! If You are the Son of God, come down from the cross."

Matthew 27:32–40, NKJV

There is a green hill far away,
  Outside a city wall,
Where the dear Lord was crucified
  Who died to save us all.

We may not know, we cannot tell
  What pains He had to bear;
But we believe it was for us
  He hung and suffered there.

O dearly, dearly has He loved,
  And we must love Him too,
And trust in His redeeming blood,
  And try His works to do.

Cecil Frances Alexander, 1818–95

Forgiveness from the cross

Two others also, who were criminals, were being led away to be put to death with Him.

When they came to the place called The Skull, there they crucified Him and the criminals, one on the right and the other on the left. But Jesus was saying, "Father, forgive them; for they do not know what they are doing." And they cast lots, dividing up His garments among themselves. And the people stood by, looking on. And even the rulers were sneering at Him, saying, "He saved others; let Him save Himself if this is the Christ of God, His Chosen One."

Luke 23:32–35, NASB

Is it nothing to you, all you who pass by? Look around and see. Is any suffering like my suffering that was inflicted on me, that the LORD brought on me in the day of his fierce anger?

Lamentations 1:12

All ye that pass by,
To Jesus draw nigh;
To you is it nothing that Jesus should die?
Your ransom and peace,
Your surety He is,
Come, see if there ever was sorrow like His.

He dies to atone
For sins not His own;
Your debt He hath paid, and your work he hath done.
Ye all may receive
The peace He did leave,
Who made intercession, "My Father, forgive!"

Charles Wesley, 1707–88

The Prince of glory dies

Now from the sixth hour until the ninth hour there was darkness over all the land. And about the ninth hour Jesus cried out with a loud voice, saying, "Eli, Eli, lama sabachthani?" that is, "My God, My God, why have You forsaken Me?" Some of those who stood there, when they heard that, said, "This Man is calling for Elijah!" Immediately one of them ran and took a sponge, filled it with sour wine and put it on a reed, and offered it to Him to drink. The rest said, "Let Him alone; let us see if Elijah will come to save Him." And Jesus cried out again with a loud voice, and yielded up His spirit.

Matthew 27:45–50, NKJV

When I survey the wondrous cross,
  On which the Prince of glory died,
My richest gain I count but loss,
  And pour contempt on all my pride.

See, from His head, His hands, His feet,
  Sorrow and love flow mingled down;
Did e'er such love and sorrow meet,
  Or thorns compose so rich a crown?

Were the whole realm of nature mine,
  That were an offering far too small;
Love so amazing, so divine,
  Demands my soul, my life, my all.

Isaac Watts, 1674–1748

"It is finished"

And that is what the soldiers did. Meanwhile, standing near the cross of Jesus were his mother, and his mother's sister, Mary the wife of Clopas, and Mary Magdalene. When Jesus saw his mother and the disciple whom he loved standing beside her, he said to his mother, "Woman, here is your son." Then he said to the disciple, "Here is your mother." And from that hour the disciple took her into his own home.

After this, when Jesus knew that all was now finished, he said (in order to fulfill the scripture), "I am thirsty." A jar full of sour wine was standing there. So they put a sponge full of the wine on a branch of hyssop and held it to his mouth. When Jesus had received the wine, he said, "It is finished." Then he bowed his head and gave up his spirit.

John 19:25–30, NRSV

Lifted up was He to die,
"It is finished!" was His cry;
Now in heaven exalted high:
  Hallelujah! what a Saviour!

When He comes, our glorious King,
All his ransomed home to bring,
Then anew this song we'll sing:
  Hallelujah! what a Saviour!

Philipp Paul Bliss, 1838–76

The piercing of Jesus' side

Then the Jews, because it was the day of preparation, so that the bodies would not remain on the cross on the Sabbath (for that Sabbath was a high day), asked Pilate that their legs might be broken, and that they might be taken away. So the soldiers came, and broke the legs of the first man and of the other who was crucified with Him; but coming to Jesus, when they saw that He was already dead, they did not break His legs. But one of the soldiers pierced His side with a spear, and immediately blood and water came out. And he who has seen has testified, and his testimony is true; and he knows that he is telling the truth, so that you also may believe. For these things came to pass to fulfill the Scripture, "NOT A BONE OF HIM SHALL BE BROKEN." And again another Scripture says, "THEY SHALL LOOK ON HIM WHOM THEY PIERCED."

John 19:31–37, NASB

Rock of Ages, cleft for me,
Let me hide myself in Thee;
Let the water and the blood,
From Thy riven side which flowed,
Be of sin the double cure,
Cleanse me from its guilt and power.

Nothing in my hand I bring,
Simply to Thy cross I cling;
Naked, come to Thee for dress;
Helpless, look to Thee for grace;
Foul, I to the fountain fly;
Wash me, Saviour, or I die.

Augustus Montague Toplady, 1740–78

"He has risen!"

Now upon the first day of the week, very early in the morning, they came unto the sepulchre, bringing the spices which they had prepared, and certain others with them. And they found the stone rolled away from the sepulchre. And they entered in, and found not the body of the Lord Jesus. And it came to pass, as they were much perplexed thereabout, behold, two men stood by them in shining garments: And as they were afraid, and bowed down their faces to the earth, they said unto them, Why seek ye the living among the dead? He is not here, but is risen: remember how he spake unto you when he was yet in Galilee, saying, the Son of man must be delivered into the hands of sinful men, and be crucified, and the third day rise again. And they remembered his words.

Luke 24:1–8, KJV

Low in the grave He lay,
　Jesus, my Saviour!
Waiting the coming day,
　Jesus, my Lord!

Up from the grave He arose,
With a mighty triumph o'er His foes;
He arose a Victor from the dark domain,
And He lives for ever with His saints to reign;
He arose! He arose!
Hallelujah! Christ arose!

Robert Lowry, 1826–99

Meeting the risen Jesus

The angel said to the women, "Do not be afraid, for I know that you are looking for Jesus, who was crucified. He is not here; he has risen, just as he said. Come and see the place where he lay. Then go quickly and tell his disciples: 'He has risen from the dead and is going ahead of you into Galilee. There you will see him.' Now I have told you."

So the women hurried away from the tomb, afraid yet filled with joy, and ran to tell his disciples. Suddenly Jesus met them. "Greetings," he said. They came to him, clasped his feet and worshiped him. Then Jesus said to them, "Do not be afraid. Go and tell my brothers to go to Galilee; there they will see me."

Matthew 28:5–10

Lo! Jesus meets us, risen from the tomb;
Lovingly He greets us, scatters fear and gloom;
Let the Church with gladness hymns of triumph sing,
For her Lord now liveth, death hath lost its sting.

Thine be the glory, risen, conquering Son,
Endless is the victory Thou o'er death hast won.

Edmond Louis Budry, 1854–1932
translated by Richard Birch Hoyle, 1875–1939

Sadness turns to joy

Then the disciples went away again to their own homes.

But Mary stood outside by the tomb weeping, and as she wept she stooped down and looked into the tomb. And she saw two angels in white sitting, one at the head and the other at the feet, where the body of Jesus had lain. Then they said to her, "Woman, why are you weeping?" She said to them, "Because they have taken away my Lord, and I do not know where they have laid Him." Now when she had said this, she turned around and saw Jesus standing there, and did not know that it was Jesus. Jesus said to her, "Woman, why are you weeping? Whom are you seeking?" She, supposing Him to be the gardener, said to Him, "Sir, if You have carried Him away, tell me where You have laid Him, and I will take Him away." Jesus said to her, "Mary!" She turned and said to Him, "Rabboni!" (which is to say, Teacher). Jesus said to her, "Do not cling to Me, for I have not yet ascended to My Father; but go to My brethren and say to them, 'I am ascending to My Father and your Father, and to My God and your God.'" Mary Magdalene came and told the disciples that she had seen the Lord, and that He had spoken these things to her.

John 20:10–18, NKJV

Christ, the Lord, is risen today,
Hallelujah!
Sons of men and angels say:
Raise your joys and triumphs high;
Sing, ye heavens, and earth reply.

Vain the stone, the watch, the seal;
Christ hath burst the gates of hell;
Death in vain forbids Him rise;
Christ hath opened paradise.

Charles Wesley, 1707–88

Victory over death

Now if Christ is proclaimed as raised from the dead, how can some of you say there is no resurrection of the dead? If there is no resurrection of the dead, then Christ has not been raised; and if Christ has not been raised, then our proclamation has been in vain and your faith has been in vain. We are even found to be misrepresenting God, because we testified of God that he raised Christ—whom he did not raise if it is true that the dead are not raised. For if the dead are not raised, then Christ has not been raised. If Christ has not been raised, your faith is futile and you are still in your sins. Then those also who have died in Christ have perished. If for this life only we have hoped in Christ, we are of all people most to be pitied.

But in fact Christ has been raised from the dead, the first fruits of those who have died. For since death came through a human being, the resurrection of the dead has also come through a human being; for as all die in Adam, so all will be made alive in Christ. But each in his own order: Christ the first fruits, then at his coming those who belong to Christ. Then comes the end, when he hands over the kingdom to God the Father, after he has destroyed every ruler and every authority and power. For he must reign until he has put all his enemies under his feet. The last enemy to be destroyed is death.

1 Corinthians 15:12–26, NRSV

Jesus lives! thy terrors now
  Can, O death, no more appal us;
Jesus lives! by this we know
  Thou, O grave, canst not enthral us.
Hallelujah!

Christian Fürchtegott Gellert, 1715–69
translated by Frances Elizabeth Cox, 1812–97

"I know that my redeemer lives"

For I know that my redeemer liveth, and that he shall stand at the latter day upon the earth: And though after my skin worms destroy this body, yet in my flesh shall I see God: whom I shall see for myself, and mine eyes shall behold, and not another; though my reins be consumed within me.

Job 19:25–27, KJV

Thus says the LORD, the King of Israel, and his Redeemer, the LORD of hosts: "I am the First and I am the Last; besides Me there is no God. And who can proclaim as I do? Then let him declare it and set it in order for Me, since I appointed the ancient people. And the things that are coming and shall come, let them show these to them. Do not fear, nor be afraid; have I not told you from that time, and declared it? You are My witnesses. Is there a God besides Me? Indeed there is no other Rock; I know not one."

Isaiah 44:6–8, NKJV

I know that my Redeemer lives:
What joy the blest assurance gives!
He lives, He lives, who once was dead;
He lives, my everlasting Head.

Samuel Medley, 1738–99

Jesus, the bread of life

Jesus said to them, "I am the bread of life; he who comes to Me will not hunger, and he who believes in Me will never thirst. But I said to you that you have seen Me, and yet do not believe. All that the Father gives Me will come to Me, and the one who comes to Me I will certainly not cast out. For I have come down from heaven, not to do My own will, but the will of Him who sent Me. This is the will of Him who sent Me, that of all that He has given Me I lose nothing, but raise it up on the last day. For this is the will of My Father, that everyone who beholds the Son and believes in Him will have eternal life, and I Myself will raise him up on the last day."

John 6:35–40, NASB

Jesus, Thou joy of loving hearts,
  Thou fount of life, Thou light of men,
From the best bliss that earth imparts,
  We turn unfilled to Thee again.

Thy truth unchanged hath ever stood;
  Thou savest those that on Thee call;
To them that seek Thee Thou art good,
  To them that find Thee, all in all.

We taste Thee, O Thou living Bread,
  And long to feast upon Thee still;
We drink of Thee, the fountain-head,
  And thirst our souls from Thee to fill.

Latin, c. 11th century
translated by Ray Palmer, 1808–87

Why Jesus died

Men of Israel, I beg you to listen to my words. Jesus of Nazareth was a man proved to you by God himself through the works of power, the miracles and the signs which God showed through him here amongst you—as you very well know. This man, who was put into your power by the predetermined plan and foreknowledge of God, you nailed up and murdered, and you used for your purpose men without the Law! But God would not allow the bitter pains of death to hold him. He raised him to life again—and indeed there was nothing by which death could hold such a man. When David speaks about him he says,

I beheld the Lord always before my face;
For he is on my right hand, that I should not be moved:
Therefore my heart was glad, and my tongue rejoiced;
Moreover my flesh also shall dwell in hope:
Because thou wilt not leave my soul in Hades,
Neither wilt thou give thy holy one to see corruption.
Thou madest known unto me the ways of life;
Thou shalt make me full of gladness with thy countenance.

Acts 2:22–28, PHILLIPS

Was it the nails, O Saviour,
   That bound Thee to the tree?
Nay, 'twas Thine everlasting love,
   Thy love for me, for me.

O wonder of all wonders,
   That through Thy death for me
My open sins, my secret sins,
   Can all forgiven be!

Then melt my heart, O Saviour,
   Bend me, yes, break me down.
Until I own Thee Conqueror,
   And Lord and Sovereign crown.

Katharine Agnes May Kelly, 1869–1942

APRIL 2

Salvation through Jesus

And it came to pass, on the next day, that their rulers, elders, and scribes, as well as Annas the high priest, Caiaphas, John, and Alexander, and as many as were of the family of the high priest, were gathered together at Jerusalem. And when they had set them in the midst, they asked, "By what power or by what name have you done this?" Then Peter, filled with the Holy Spirit, said to them, "Rulers of the people and elders of Israel: If we this day are judged for a good deed done to a helpless man, by what means he has been made well, let it be known to you all, and to all the people of Israel, that by the name of Jesus Christ of Nazareth, whom you crucified, whom God raised from the dead, by Him this man stands here before you whole. This is the 'stone which was rejected by you builders, which has become the chief cornerstone.' Nor is there salvation in any other, for there is no other name under heaven given among men by which we must be saved."

Acts 4:5–12, NKJV

Jesus, we look to Thee,
  Thy promised presence claim;
Thou in the midst of us shalt be,
  Assembled in Thy Name.

Thy Name salvation is,
  Which here we come to prove;
Thy Name is life, and health, and peace,
  And everlasting love.

Present we know Thou art,
  But O Thyself reveal!
Now, Lord, let every bounding heart
  The mighty comfort feel.

Charles Wesley, 1707–88

The foundation of the church

[Paul's farewell to the Ephesian elders] And now, behold, bound in spirit, I am on my way to Jerusalem, not knowing what will happen to me there, except that the Holy Spirit solemnly testifies to me in every city, saying that bonds and afflictions await me. But I do not consider my life of any account as dear to myself, in order that I may finish my course and the ministry which I received from the Lord Jesus, to testify solemnly of the gospel of the grace of God.

And now, behold, I know that all of you, among whom I went about preaching the kingdom, will no longer see my face. Therefore I testify to you this day, that I am innocent of the blood of all men. For I did not shrink from declaring to you the whole purpose of God. Be on guard for yourselves and for all the flock, among which the Holy Spirit has made you overseers, to shepherd the church of God which He purchased with His own blood. I know that after my departure savage wolves will come in among you, not sparing the flock; and from among your own selves men will arise, speaking perverse things, to draw away the disciples after them. Therefore be on the alert, remembering that night and day for a period of three years I did not cease to admonish each one with tears.

Acts 20:22–31, NASB

The church's one foundation
  Is Jesus Christ her Lord;
She is His new creation
  By water and the Word;
From heaven He came and sought her
  To be His holy bride;
With His own blood He bought her,
  And for her life He died.

Samuel John Stone, 1839–1900

Jesus Christ our Lord

Paul, a servant of Jesus Christ, called to be an apostle, separated unto the gospel of God, (Which he had promised afore by his prophets in the holy scriptures,) concerning his Son Jesus Christ our Lord, which was made of the seed of David according to the flesh; and declared to be the Son of God with power, according to the spirit of holiness, by the resurrection from the dead: By whom we have received grace and apostleship, for obedience to the faith among all nations, for his name: Among whom are ye also the called of Jesus Christ: To all that be in Rome, beloved of God, called to be saints: Grace to you and peace from God our Father, and the Lord Jesus Christ.

Romans 1:1–7, KJV

Crown Him the Son of God,
  Before the worlds began:
And ye, who tread where He hath trod,
  Crown Him the Son of man:
Who every grief hath known
  That wrings the human breast,
And takes and bears them for His own,
  That all in Him may rest.

Crown Him the Lord of life,
  Who triumphed o'er the grave,
And rose victorious in the strife
  For those He came to save:
His glories now we sing
  Who died, and rose on high;
Who died eternal life to bring,
  And lives that death may die.

Matthew Bridges, 1800–1894
and
Godfrey Thring, 1823–1903

Not ashamed of the gospel

For I long to see you, that I may impart to you some spiritual gift, so that you may be established—that is, that I may be encouraged together with you by the mutual faith both of you and me. Now I do not want you to be unaware, brethren, that I often planned to come to you (but was hindered until now), that I might have some fruit among you also, just as among the other Gentiles. I am a debtor both to Greeks and to barbarians, both to wise and to unwise. So, as much as is in me, I am ready to preach the gospel to you who are in Rome also.

For I am not ashamed of the gospel of Christ, for it is the power of God to salvation for everyone who believes, for the Jew first and also for the Greek. For in it the righteousness of God is revealed from faith to faith; as it is written, "The just shall live by faith."

Romans 1:11–17, NKJV

I'm not ashamed to own my Lord,
  Or to defend His cause;
Maintain the honour of His Word,
  The glory of His cross.

Isaac Watts, 1674–1748

Commitment to God

Now if we have died with Christ, we believe that we shall also live with Him, knowing that Christ, having been raised from the dead, is never to die again; death no longer is master over Him. For the death that He died, He died to sin once for all; but the life that He lives, He lives to God. Even so consider yourselves to be dead to sin, but alive to God in Christ Jesus.

Therefore do not let sin reign in your mortal body so that you obey its lusts, and do not go on presenting the members of your body to sin as instruments of unrighteousness; but present yourselves to God as those alive from the dead, and your members as instruments of righteousness to God. For sin shall not be master over you, for you are not under law but under grace.

Romans 6:8–14, NASB

In full and glad surrender
  I give myself to Thee,
Thine utterly and only
  And evermore to be.

O come and reign, Lord Jesus;
  Rule over everything!
And keep me always loyal
  And true to Thee, my King.

Frances Ridley Havergal, 1836–79

God's remedy for sin

So from now on we regard no one from a worldly point of view. Though we once regarded Christ in this way, we do so no longer. Therefore, if anyone is in Christ, he is a new creation; the old has gone, the new has come! All this is from God, who reconciled us to himself through Christ and gave us the ministry of reconciliation: that God was reconciling the world to himself in Christ, not counting men's sins against them. And he has committed to us the message of reconciliation. We are therefore Christ's ambassadors, as though God were making his appeal through us. We implore you on Christ's behalf: Be reconciled to God. God made him who had no sin to be sin for us, so that in him we might become the righteousness of God.

As God's fellow workers we urge you not to receive God's grace in vain. For he says, "In the time of my favor I heard you, and in the day of salvation I helped you." I tell you, now is the time of God's favor, now is the day of salvation.

2 Corinthians 5:16–6:2

Tell me the story slowly,
  That I may take it in—
That wonderful redemption,
  God's remedy for sin.
Tell me the story often,
  For I forget so soon;
The early dew of morning
  Has passed away at noon.

Tell me the old, old story,
Tell me the old, old story,
Tell me the old, old story,
  Of Jesus and His love.

Arabella Catherine Hankey, 1834–1911

The Lamb on the throne

And I beheld, and, lo, in the midst of the throne and of the four beasts, and in the midst of the elders, stood a Lamb as it had been slain, having seven horns and seven eyes, which are the seven Spirits of God sent forth into all the earth. And he came and took the book out of the right hand of him that sat upon the throne. And when he had taken the book, the four beasts and four and twenty elders fell down before the Lamb, having every one of them harps, and golden vials full of odours, which are the prayers of saints. And they sung a new song, saying, Thou art worthy to take the book, and to open the seals thereof: for thou wast slain, and hast redeemed us to God by thy blood out of every kindred, and tongue, and people, and nation; and hast made us unto our God kings and priests: and we shall reign on the earth.

Revelation 5:6–10, KJV

Crown Him with many crowns,
  The Lamb upon His throne;
Hark! how the heavenly anthem drowns
  All music but its own.
Awake, my soul, and sing
  Of Him who died for thee,
And hail Him as thy chosen King
  Through all eternity.

Matthew Bridges, 1800–1894
and
Godfrey Thring, 1823–1903

Worthy is the Lamb

Then I looked, and I heard the voice of many angels surrounding the throne and the living creatures and the elders; they numbered myriads of myriads and thousands of thousands, singing with full voice, "Worthy is the Lamb that was slaughtered to receive power and wealth and wisdom and might and honor and glory and blessing!" Then I heard every creature in heaven and on earth and under the earth and in the sea, and all that is in them, singing, "To the one seated on the throne and to the Lamb be blessing and honor and glory and might forever and ever!" And the four living creatures said, "Amen!" And the elders fell down and worshiped.

Revelation 5:11–14, NRSV

Come, let us join our cheerful songs
  With angels round the throne;
Ten thousand thousand are their tongues,
  But all their joys are one.

"Worthy the Lamb that died," they cry,
  "To be exalted thus!"
"Worthy the Lamb," our lips reply,
  "For He was slain for us!"

The whole creation join in one,
  To bless the sacred Name
Of Him that sits upon the throne,
  And to adore the Lamb.

Isaac Watts, 1674–1748

God is love

Beloved, let us love one another, for love is from God; and everyone who loves is born of God and knows God. The one who does not love does not know God, for God is love. By this the love of God was manifested in us, that God has sent His only begotten Son into the world so that we might live through Him. In this is love, not that we loved God, but that He loved us and sent His Son to be the propitiation for our sins. Beloved, if God so loved us, we also ought to love one another. No one has seen God at any time; if we love one another, God abides in us, and His love is perfected in us. By this we know that we abide in Him and He in us, because He has given us of His Spirit. We have seen and testify that the Father has sent the Son to be the Savior of the world.

Whoever confesses that Jesus is the Son of God, God abides in him, and he in God. We have come to know and have believed the love which God has for us. God is love, and the one who abides in love abides in God, and God abides in him.

1 John 4:7–16, NASB

I am so glad that our Father in heaven
Tells of His love in the book He has given:
Wonderful things in the Bible I see;
This is the dearest, that Jesus loves me.

I am so glad that Jesus loves me,
Jesus loves even me.

Though I forget Him, and wander away,
Still He doth love me wherever I stray;
Back to His dear loving arms do I flee,
When I remember that Jesus loves me.

Philipp Paul Bliss, 1838–76

APRIL 11

The suffering servant

Just as there were many who were appalled at him—his appearance was so disfigured beyond that of any man and his form marred beyond human likeness—so will he sprinkle many nations, and kings will shut their mouths because of him. For what they were not told, they will see, and what they have not heard, they will understand.

Who has believed our message and to whom has the arm of the LORD been revealed? He grew up before him like a tender shoot, and like a root out of dry ground. He had no beauty or majesty to attract us to him, nothing in his appearance that we should desire him. He was despised and rejected by men, a man of sorrows, and familiar with suffering. Like one from whom men hide their faces he was despised, and we esteemed him not.

Isaiah 52:14–53:3

O sacred head! sore wounded,
  With grief and shame bowed down,
How scornfully surrounded
  With thorns, Thine only crown!
How pale art Thou with anguish,
  With sore abuse and scorn!
How does that visage languish
  Which once was bright as morn!

Thy brief and bitter passion
  Were all for sinners' gain
Mine, mine was the transgression,
  But Thine the deadly pain:
Lo! here I fall, my Saviour;
  'Tis I deserve Thy place;
Look on me with Thy favour,
  Vouchsafe to me Thy grace.

Paul Gerhardt, 1607–76
attributed to Bernard of Clairvaux, 1091–1153
translated by James Waddell Alexander, 1804–59

Man of sorrows

Surely our griefs He Himself bore, and our sorrows He carried; yet we ourselves esteemed Him stricken, smitten of God, and afflicted. But He was pierced through for our transgressions, He was crushed for our iniquities; the chastening for our well-being fell upon Him, and by His scourging we are healed. All of us like sheep have gone astray, each of us has turned to his own way; but the LORD has caused the iniquity of us all to fall on Him.

He was oppressed and He was afflicted, yet He did not open His mouth; like a lamb that is led to slaughter, and like a sheep that is silent before its shearers, so He did not open His mouth. By oppression and judgment He was taken away; and as for His generation, who considered that He was cut off out of the land of the living for the transgression of my people, to whom the stroke was due? His grave was assigned with wicked men, yet He was with a rich man in His death, because He had done no violence, nor was there any deceit in His mouth.

Isaiah 53:4–9, KJV

Man of Sorrows! what a name
For the Son of God, who came
Ruined sinners to reclaim!
  Hallelujah! what a Saviour!

Bearing shame and scoffing rude,
In my place condemned He stood;
Sealed my pardon with His blood:
  Hallelujah! what a Saviour!

Philipp Paul Bliss, 1838–76

Crowned with glory

Yet it pleased the LORD to bruise Him; He has put Him to grief. When You make His soul an offering for sin, He shall see His seed, He shall prolong His days, and the pleasure of the LORD shall prosper in His hand. He shall see the labor of His soul, and be satisfied. By His knowledge My righteous Servant shall justify many, for He shall bear their iniquities. Therefore I will divide Him a portion with the great, and He shall divide the spoil with the strong, because He poured out His soul unto death, and He was numbered with the transgressors, and He bore the sin of many, and made intercession for the transgressors.

Isaiah 53:10–12, NKJV

Look, ye saints! the sight is glorious;
  See the Man of Sorrows now,
From the fight returned victorious,
  Every knee to Him shall bow:
Crown Him! Crown Him!
  Crowns become the Victor's brow.

Crown the Saviour! angels, crown Him!
  Rich the trophies Jesus brings;
In the seat of power enthrone Him,
  While the vault of heaven rings:
Crown Him! Crown Him!
  Crown the Saviour King of kings!

Thomas Kelly, 1769–1855

Jesus, our Savior

Long ago God spoke to our ancestors in many and various ways by the prophets, but in these last days he has spoken to us by a Son, whom he appointed heir of all things, through whom he also created the worlds. He is the reflection of God's glory and the exact imprint of God's very being, and he sustains all things by his powerful word. When he had made purification for sins, he sat down at the right hand of the Majesty on high.

Hebrews 1:1–3, NRSV

For Christ did not enter a holy place made with hands, a mere copy of the true one, but into heaven itself, now to appear in the presence of God for us; nor was it that He would offer Himself often, as the high priest enters the holy place year by year with blood that is not his own. Otherwise, He would have needed to suffer often since the foundation of the world; but now once at the consummation of the ages He has been manifested to put away sin by the sacrifice of Himself. And inasmuch as it is appointed for men to die once and after this comes judgment, so Christ also, having been offered once to bear the sins of many, will appear a second time for salvation without reference to sin, to those who eagerly await Him.

Hebrews 9:24–28, NASB

Jesus the Saviour reigns,
  The God of truth and love:
When He had purged our stains,
  He took His seat above:
Lift up your heart, lift up your voice;
Rejoice, again I say, Rejoice.

Rejoice in glorious hope;
  Jesus the Judge shall come,
And take His servants up
  To their eternal home:
We soon shall hear the archangel's voice;
The trump of God shall sound, Rejoice!

Charles Wesley, 1707–88

The praise of God's glory

O LORD our Lord, how excellent is thy name in all the earth! who hast set thy glory above the heavens. Out of the mouth of babes and sucklings hast thou ordained strength because of thine enemies, that thou mightest still the enemy and the avenger. When I consider thy heavens, the work of thy fingers, the moon and the stars, which thou hast ordained; what is man, that thou art mindful of him? and the son of man, that thou visitest him? For thou hast made him a little lower than the angels, and hast crowned him with glory and honour. Thou madest him to have dominion over the works of thy hands: thou hast put all things under his feet: all sheep and oxen, yea, and the beasts of the field; the fowl of the air, and the fish of the sea, and whatsoever passeth through the paths of the seas. O LORD our Lord, how excellent is thy name in all the earth!

Psalm 8:1–9, KJV

All creatures of our God and King,
Lift up your voice and with us sing:
  Hallelujah, Hallelujah!
Thou burning sun with golden beam,
Thou silver moon with softer gleam:

O praise Him, O praise Him,
Hallelujah, Hallelujah, Hallelujah!

Let all things their Creator bless,
And worship Him in humbleness,
  O praise Him, Hallelujah!
Praise, praise the Father, praise the Son,
And praise the Spirit, Three in One.

Francis of Assisi, 1182–1226
translated by William Henry Draper, 1855–1933

Crucified... and risen!

[Abraham], contrary to hope, in hope believed, so that he became the father of many nations, according to what was spoken, "So shall your descendants be." And not being weak in faith, he did not consider his own body, already dead (since he was about a hundred years old), and the deadness of Sarah's womb. He did not waver at the promise of God through unbelief, but was strengthened in faith, giving glory to God, and being fully convinced that what He had promised He was also able to perform. And therefore "it was accounted to him for righteousness." Now it was not written for his sake alone that it was imputed to him, but also for us. It shall be imputed to us who believe in Him who raised up Jesus our Lord from the dead, who was delivered up because of our offenses, and was raised because of our justification.

Romans 4:18–25, NKJV

For under the Law I "died," and I am dead to the Law's demands so that I may live for God. I died on the cross with Christ. And my present life is not that of the old "I," but the living Christ within me. The bodily life I now live, I live believing in the Son of God who loved me and sacrificed himself for me.

Galatians 2:19–20, PHILLIPS

One day when heaven was filled with His praises,
  One day when sin was as black as could be,
Jesus came forth to be born of a virgin
  Dwelt amongst men, my example is He!

Living, He loved me; dying, He saved me;
  Buried, He carried my sins far away!
Rising, He Justified freely for ever;
  One day He's coming—O glorious day!

J. Wilbur Chapman, 1859–1918

In all things God works for good

We know that all things work together for good for those who love God, who are called according to his purpose. For those whom he foreknew he also predestined to be conformed to the image of his Son, in order that he might be the firstborn within a large family. And those whom he predestined he also called; and those whom he called he also justified; and those whom he justified he also glorified.

Romans 8:28–30, NRSV

Now I want you to know, brethren, that my circumstances have turned out for the greater progress of the gospel, so that my imprisonment in the cause of Christ has become well known throughout the whole praetorian guard and to everyone else, and that most of the brethren, trusting in the Lord because of my imprisonment, have far more courage to speak the word of God without fear.

Philippians 1:12–14, NASB

Through the love of God our Saviour
  All will be well;
Free and changeless is His favour,
  All, all is well:
Precious is the blood that healed us;
Perfect is the grace that sealed us;
Strong the hand stretched forth to shield us;
  All must be well.

Though we pass through tribulation,
  All will be well;
Christ hath purchased full salvation,
  All, all is well:
Happy still in God confiding,
Fruitful, if in Christ abiding,
Holy, through the Spirit's guiding;
  All must be well.

Mary Peter, 1813–56

God leads his people on

And the LORD went before them by day in a pillar of cloud to lead the way, and by night in a pillar of fire to give them light, so as to go by day and night. He did not take away the pillar of cloud by day or the pillar of fire by night from before the people.

Exodus 13:21–22, NKJV

Trust in the LORD, and do good; so shalt thou dwell in the land, and verily thou shalt be fed. Delight thyself also in the LORD; and he shall give thee the desires of thine heart. Commit thy way unto the LORD; trust also in him; and he shall bring it to pass. And he shall bring forth thy righteousness as the light, and thy judgment as the noonday. Rest in the LORD, and wait patiently for him: fret not thyself because of him who prospereth in his way, because of the man who bringeth wicked devices to pass.

Psalm 37:3–7, KJV

Guide me, O Thou great Jehovah,
  Pilgrim through this barren land;
I am weak, but Thou art mighty,
  Hold me with Thy powerful hand;
    Bread of heaven,
Feed me now and evermore.

William Williams, 1717–91
translated by Peter Williams, 1721–96

Becoming like Jesus

You were taught, with regard to your former way of life, to put off your old self, which is being corrupted by its deceitful desires; to be made new in the attitude of your minds; and to put on the new self, created to be like God in true righteousness and holiness.

Therefore each of you must put off falsehood and speak truthfully to his neighbor, for we are all members of one body. "In your anger do not sin": Do not let the sun go down while you are still angry, and do not give the devil a foothold. He who has been stealing must steal no longer, but must work, doing something useful with his own hands, that he may have something to share with those in need.

Ephesians 4:22–28

O Jesus Christ, grow Thou in me,
    And all things else recede:
My heart be daily nearer Thee,
    From sin be daily freed.

Johann Caspar Lavater, 1741–1801
translated by Elizabeth Lee Smith, 1817–98

Seeking the lost

And Jesus entered and passed through Jericho. And, behold, there was a man named Zacchaeus, which was the chief among the publicans, and he was rich. And he sought to see Jesus who he was; and could not for the press, because he was little of stature. And he ran before, and climbed up into a sycomore tree to see him: for he was to pass that way. And when Jesus came to the place, he looked up, and saw him, and said unto him, Zacchaeus, make haste, and come down; for to day I must abide at thy house. And he made haste, and came down, and received him joyfully. And when they saw it, they all murmured, saying, That he was gone to be guest with a man that is a sinner. And Zacchaeus stood, and said unto the Lord; Behold, Lord, the half of my goods I give to the poor; and if I have taken any thing from any man by false accusation, I restore him fourfold. And Jesus said unto him, This day is salvation come to this house, forsomuch as he also is a son of Abraham.

Luke 19:1–9, KJV

Come, let us sing of a wonderful love,
  Tender and true;
Out of the heart of the Father above,
  Streaming to me and to you:
    Wonderful love
Dwells in the heart of the Father above.

Jesus, the Saviour, this gospel to tell
  Joyfully came;
Came with the helpless and hopeless to dwell,
  Sharing their sorrow and shame;
    Seeking the lost,
Saving, redeeming at measureless cost.

Robert Walmsley, 1831–1905

APRIL 21

Boasting in Jesus

Thus says the LORD: "Let not the wise man glory in his wisdom, let not the mighty man glory in his might, nor let the rich man glory in his riches; but let him who glories glory in this, that he understands and knows Me, that I am the LORD, exercising lovingkindness, judgment, and righteousness in the earth. For in these I delight," says the LORD.

Jeremiah 9:23–24, NKJV

The base things of the world and the things which are despised God has chosen, and the things which are not, to bring to nothing the things that are, that no flesh should glory in His presence. But of Him you are in Christ Jesus, who became for us wisdom from God—and righteousness and sanctification and redemption—that, as it is written, "He who glories, let him glory in the LORD."

1 Corinthians 1:28–31, NKJV

But God forbid that I should boast except in the cross of our Lord Jesus Christ, by whom the world has been crucified to me, and I to the world. For in Christ Jesus neither circumcision nor uncircumcision avails anything, but a new creation.

Galatians 6:14–15, NKJV

Forbid it, Lord, that I should boast
  Save in the death of Christ my God:
All the vain things that charm me most,
  I sacrifice them to His blood.

Isaac Watts, 1674–1748

114

"Seek this first"

So if you have been raised with Christ, seek the things that are above, where Christ is, seated at the right hand of God. Set your minds on things that are above, not on things that are on earth, for you have died, and your life is hidden with Christ in God. When Christ who is your life is revealed, then you also will be revealed with him in glory.

Put to death, therefore, whatever in you is earthly: fornication, impurity, passion, evil desire, and greed (which is idolatry). On account of these the wrath of God is coming on those who are disobedient. These are the ways you also once followed, when you were living that life. But now you must get rid of all such things—anger, wrath, malice, slander, and abusive language from your mouth. Do not lie to one another, seeing that you have stripped off the old self with its practices and have clothed yourselves with the new self, which is being renewed in knowledge according to the image of its creator. In that renewal there is no longer Greek and Jew, circumcised and uncircumcised, barbarian, Scythian, slave and free; but Christ is all and in all!

As God's chosen ones, holy and beloved, clothe yourselves with compassion, kindness, humility, meekness, and patience. Bear with one another and, if anyone has a complaint against another, forgive each other; just as the Lord has forgiven you, so you also must forgive. Above all, clothe yourselves with love, which binds everything together in perfect harmony.

Colossians 3:1–14, NRSV

Seek Him first; then, when forgiven,
Pardoned, made an heir of heaven,
Let your life to Him be given:
 Seek this first.

Georgianna Mary Taylor, 1848–1915

Jesus is on our side

My little children, I am writing these things to you so that you may not sin. And if anyone sins, we have an Advocate with the Father, Jesus Christ the righteous; and He Himself is the propitiation for our sins; and not for ours only, but also for those of the whole world.

1 John 2:1–2, NASB

But He, because He continues forever, has an unchangeable priesthood. Therefore He is also able to save to the uttermost those who come to God through Him, since He always lives to make intercession for them. For such a High Priest was fitting for us, who is holy, harmless, undefiled, separate from sinners, and has become higher than the heavens.

Hebrews 7:24–26, NKJV

Before the throne of God above
    I have a strong, a perfect plea,
A great High Priest, whose Name is Love,
    Who ever lives and pleads for me.

My name is graven in His hands,
    My name is written on His heart;
I know that, while in heaven He stands,
    No tongue can bid me thence depart.

Charitie Lees De Chenez, 1841–1923

Be filled with the Spirit

Therefore be careful how you walk, not as unwise men but as wise, making the most of your time, because the days are evil. So then do not be foolish, but understand what the will of the Lord is. And do not get drunk with wine, for that is dissipation, but be filled with the Spirit, speaking to one another in psalms and hymns and spiritual songs, singing and making melody with your heart to the Lord; always giving thanks for all things in the name of our Lord Jesus Christ to God, even the Father; and be subject to one another in the fear of Christ.

Ephesians 5:15–21, NASB

I delight to do thy will, O my God: yea, thy law is within my heart.

Psalm 40:8, KJV

Let all those that seek thee rejoice and be glad in thee: let such as love thy salvation say continually, The LORD be magnified.

Psalm 40:16, KJV

O fill me with Thy fulness, Lord;
    Until my very heart o'erflow
In kindling thought and glowing word,
    Thy love to tell, Thy praise to show.

O use me, Lord, use even me,
    Just as Thou wilt, and when, and where,
Until Thy blessed face I see,
    Thy rest, Thy joy, Thy glory share.

Frances Ridley Havergal, 1836–79

King of kings, Lord of lords

I saw heaven standing open and there before me was a white horse, whose rider is called Faithful and True. With justice he judges and makes war. His eyes are like blazing fire, and on his head are many crowns. He has a name written on him that no one knows but he himself. He is dressed in a robe dipped in blood, and his name is the Word of God. The armies of heaven were following him, riding on white horses and dressed in fine linen, white and clean. Out of his mouth comes a sharp sword with which to strike down the nations. "He will rule them with an iron scepter." He treads the winepress of the fury of the wrath of God Almighty. On his robe and on his thigh he has this name written: KING OF KINGS AND LORD OF LORDS.

Revelation 19:11–16

Hark, those bursts of acclamation!
Hark, those loud triumphant chords!
Jesus takes the highest station:
O what joy the sight affords!
Crown Him! Crown Him:
King of kings, and Lord of lords!

Thomas Kelly, 1769–1855

God's holiness and love

In the year that king Uzziah died I saw also the Lord sitting upon a throne, high and lifted up, and his train filled the temple. Above it stood the seraphims: each one had six wings; with twain he covered his face, and with twain he covered his feet, and with twain he did fly. And one cried unto another, and said, Holy, holy, holy, is the LORD of hosts: the whole earth is full of his glory. And the posts of the door moved at the voice of him that cried, and the house was filled with smoke. Then said I, Woe is me! for I am undone; because I am a man of unclean lips, and I dwell in the midst of a people of unclean lips: for mine eyes have seen the King, the LORD of hosts. Then flew one of the seraphims unto me, having a live coal in his hand, which he had taken with the tongs from off the altar: And he laid it upon my mouth, and said, Lo, this hath touched thy lips; and thine iniquity is taken away, and thy sin purged.

Isaiah 6:1–7, KJV

Eternal Light! Eternal Light!
  How pure the soul must be,
When, placed within Thy searching sight,
It shrinks not, but with calm delight
  Can live and look on Thee.

There is a way for man to rise
  To that sublime abode:
An offering and a sacrifice,
A Holy Spirit's energies,
  An Advocate with God.

Thomas Binney, 1798–1874

The preciousness of Christ

Again, the kingdom of heaven is like treasure hidden in a field, which a man found and hid; and for joy over it he goes and sells all that he has and buys that field.

Again, the kingdom of heaven is like a merchant seeking beautiful pearls, who, when he had found one pearl of great price, went and sold all that he had and bought it.

Matthew 13:44–46, NKJV

But Christ came as High Priest of the good things to come, with the greater and more perfect tabernacle not made with hands, that is, not of this creation. Not with the blood of goats and calves, but with His own blood He entered the Most Holy Place once for all, having obtained eternal redemption. For if the blood of bulls and goats and the ashes of a heifer, sprinkling the unclean, sanctifies for the purifying of the flesh, how much more shall the blood of Christ, who through the eternal Spirit offered Himself without spot to God, cleanse your conscience from dead works to serve the living God?

Hebrews 9:11–14, NKJV

I've found the pearl of greatest price,
My heart doth sing for joy;
And sing I must, for Christ is mine,
Christ shall my song employ.

Christ is my Prophet, Priest, and King:
My Prophet full of light,
My great High Priest before the throne,
My King of heavenly might.

John Mason, c. 1646–94

The power of sin

Then the LORD said, "My Spirit shall not strive with man forever, because he also is flesh; nevertheless his days shall be one hundred and twenty years." . . . Then the LORD saw that the wickedness of man was great on the earth, and that every intent of the thoughts of his heart was only evil continually. The LORD was sorry that He had made man on the earth, and He was grieved in His heart.

Genesis 6:3, 5–6, NASB

The heart is devious above all else; it is perverse—who can understand it? I the LORD test the mind and search the heart, to give to all according to their ways, according to the fruit of their doings.

Jeremiah 17:9–10, NRSV

Plenteous grace with Thee is found,
  Grace to cover all my sin;
Let the healing streams abound,
  Make and keep me pure within:

Thou of life the fountain art,
  Freely let me take of Thee;
Spring Thou up within my heart,
  Rise to all eternity.

Charles Wesley, 1707–88

Praise God!

I will bless the LORD at all times: his praise shall continually be in my mouth. My soul shall make her boast in the LORD: the humble shall hear thereof, and be glad. O magnify the LORD with me, and let us exalt his name together. I sought the LORD, and he heard me, and delivered me from all my fears. They looked unto him, and were lightened: and their faces were not ashamed. This poor man cried, and the LORD heard him, and saved him out of all his troubles. The angel of the LORD encampeth round about them that fear him, and delivereth them. O taste and see that the LORD is good: blessed is the man that trusteth in him. O fear the LORD, ye his saints: for there is no want to them that fear him. . . . Many are the afflictions of the righteous: but the LORD delivereth him out of them all.

Psalm 34:1–9,19, KJV

Through all the changing scenes of life,
 In trouble and in joy,
The praises of my God shall still
 My heart and tongue employ.

Fear Him, ye saints, and you will then
 Have nothing else to fear;
Make you His service your delight,
 Your wants shall be His care.

Nahum Tate, 1652–1715
and
Nicholas Brady, 1659–1726

"I am with you"

But now thus saith the LORD that created thee, O Jacob, and he that formed thee, O Israel, Fear not: for I have redeemed thee, I have called thee by thy name; thou art mine. When thou passest through the waters, I will be with thee; and through the rivers, they shall not overflow thee: when thou walkest through the fire, thou shalt not be burned; neither shall the flame kindle upon thee. For I am the LORD thy God, the Holy One of Israel, thy Saviour: I gave Egypt for thy ransom, Ethiopia and Seba for thee. Since thou wast precious in my sight, thou hast been honourable, and I have loved thee: therefore will I give men for thee, and people for thy life. Fear not: for I am with thee: I will bring thy seed from the east, and gather thee from the west; I will say to the north, Give up; and to the south, Keep not back: bring my sons from far, and my daughters from the ends of the earth; even every one that is called by my name: for I have created him for my glory, I have formed him; yea, I have made him.

Isaiah 43:1–7, KJV

Fear not, He is with thee, O be not dismayed;
For He is thy God, and will still give thee aid:
He'll strengthen thee, help thee, and cause thee to stand,
Upheld by His righteous, omnipotent hand.

When through the deep waters He calls thee to go,
The rivers of grief shall not thee overflow;
For He will be with thee in trouble to bless,
And sanctify to thee thy deepest distress.

"K" in Rippon's *Selection,* 1787

The greatness of God

O LORD, thou hast searched me, and known me. Thou knowest my downsitting and mine uprising, thou understandest my thought afar off. Thou compassest my path and my lying down, and art acquainted with all my ways. For there is not a word in my tongue, but, lo, O LORD, thou knowest it altogether. Thou hast beset me behind and before, and laid thine hand upon me. Such knowledge is too wonderful for me; it is high, I cannot attain unto it. Whither shall I go from thy spirit? or whither shall I flee from thy presence? If I ascend up into heaven, thou art there: if I make my bed in hell, behold, thou art there. If I take the wings of the morning, and dwell in the uttermost parts of the sea; even there shall thy hand lead me, and thy right hand shall hold me.

Psalm 139:1–10, KJV

Holy and Infinite! Viewless, Eternal!
  Veiled in the glory none can sustain,
None comprehendeth Thy Being supernal,
  Nor can the heaven of heavens contain.

Glorious in holiness, fearful in praises,
  Who shall not fear Thee and who shall not laud?
Anthems of glory Thy universe raises,
  Holy and infinite! Father and God!

Frances Ridley Havergal, 1836–79

Spiritual praise

For you have not come to the mountain that may be touched and that burned with fire, and to blackness and darkness and tempest, and the sound of a trumpet and the voice of words, so that those who heard it begged that the word should not be spoken to them anymore. (For they could not endure what was commanded: "And if so much as a beast touches the mountain, it shall be stoned or shot with an arrow." And so terrifying was the sight that Moses said, "I am exceedingly afraid and trembling.") But you have come to Mount Zion and to the city of the living God, the heavenly Jerusalem, to an innumerable company of angels, to the general assembly and church of the firstborn who are registered in heaven, to God the Judge of all, to the spirits of just men made perfect, to Jesus the Mediator of the new covenant, and to the blood of sprinkling that speaks better things than that of Abel.

Hebrews 12:18–24, NKJV

Praise Him, praise Him! Jesus, our blessed Redeemer;
  For our sins He suffered and bled and died.
He, our Rock, our hope of eternal salvation,
  Hail Him, hail Him! Jesus the crucified.
Loving Saviour, meekly enduring sorrow,
  Crowned with thorns that cruelly pierced His brow;
Once for us rejected, despised, and forsaken,
  Prince of glory, ever triumphant now.

Frances Jane Van Alstyne, 1820–1915

Worshiping God alone

And God spake all these words, saying, I am the LORD thy God, which have brought thee out of the land of Egypt, out of the house of bondage. Thou shalt have no other gods before me. Thou shalt not make unto thee any graven image, or any likeness of any thing that is in heaven above, or that is in the earth beneath, or that is in the water under the earth: Thou shalt not bow down thyself to them, nor serve them: for I the LORD thy God am a jealous God, visiting the iniquity of the fathers upon the children unto the third and fourth generation of them that hate me; and shewing mercy unto thousands of them that love me, and keep my commandments.

Exodus 20:1–6, KJV

We know that whoever is born of God does not sin; but he who has been born of God keeps himself, and the wicked one does not touch him. We know that we are of God, and the whole world lies under the sway of the wicked one. And we know that the Son of God has come and has given us an understanding, that we may know Him who is true; and we are in Him who is true, in His Son Jesus Christ. This is the true God and eternal life. Little children, keep yourselves from idols.

1 John 5:18–21, NKJV

Jesus calls us from the worship
  Of the vain world's golden store,
From each idol that would keep us,
  Saying, "Christian, love me more!"

In our joys and in our sorrow,
  Days of toil and hours of ease,
Still He calls, in cares and pleasures,
  That we love Him more than these.

Cecil Frances Alexander, 1818–95

Serving Christ

Finally, all of you, live in harmony with one another; be sympathetic, love as brothers, be compassionate and humble. Do not repay evil with evil or insult with insult, but with blessing, because to this you were called so that you may inherit a blessing. For, "Whoever would love life and see good days must keep his tongue from evil and his lips from deceitful speech. He must turn from evil and do good; he must seek peace and pursue it. For the eyes of the Lord are on the righteous and his ears are attentive to their prayer, but the face of the Lord is against those who do evil."

Who is going to harm you if you are eager to do good? But even if you should suffer for what is right, you are blessed. "Do not fear what they fear; do not be frightened." But in your hearts set apart Christ as Lord. Always be prepared to give an answer to everyone who asks you to give the reason for the hope that you have. But do this with gentleness and respect, keeping a clear conscience, so that those who speak maliciously against your good behavior in Christ may be ashamed of their slander. It is better, if it is God's will, to suffer for doing good than for doing evil. For Christ died for sins once for all, the righteous for the unrighteous, to bring you to God.

1 Peter 3:8–18

I want a true regard,
  A single, steady aim,
Unmoved by threatening or reward,
  To Thee and Thy great Name;
A jealous, just concern
  For Thine immortal praise;
A pure desire that all may learn
  And glorify Thy grace.

Charles Wesley, 1707–88

A faith for life

Now faith is the substance of things hoped for, the evidence of things not seen. For by it the elders obtained a good testimony. By faith we understand that the worlds were framed by the word of God, so that the things which are seen were not made of things which are visible.

By faith Abel offered to God a more excellent sacrifice than Cain, through which he obtained witness that he was righteous, God testifying of his gifts; and through it he being dead still speaks. By faith Enoch was taken away so that he did not see death, "and was not found, because God had taken him"; for before he was taken he had this testimony, that he pleased God. But without faith it is impossible to please Him, for he who comes to God must believe that He is, and that He is a rewarder of those who diligently seek Him.

Hebrews 11:1–6, NKJV

When we walk with the Lord,
In the light of His word,
　What a glory He shed on our way!
While we do His good will,
He abides with us still,
　And with all who will trust and obey!

Trust and obey!
For there's no other way
　To be happy in Jesus
But to trust and obey.

John Henry Sammis, 1846–1919

Practical Christian unity

And the congregation of those who believed were of one heart and soul; and not one of them claimed that anything belonging to him was his own, but all things were common property to them. And with great power the apostles were giving testimony to the resurrection of the Lord Jesus, and abundant grace was upon them all. For there was not a needy person among them, for all who were owners of land or houses would sell them and bring the proceeds of the sales and lay them at the apostles' feet, and they would be distributed to each as any had need.

Now Joseph, a Levite of Cyprian birth, who was also called Barnabas by the apostles (which translated means Son of Encouragement), and who owned a tract of land, sold it and brought the money and laid it at the apostles' feet.

Acts 4:32–37, NASB

Blest be the tie that binds
  Our hearts in Christian love;
The fellowship of kindred minds
  Is like to that above.

Before our Father's throne
  We pour our ardent prayers;
Our fears, our hopes, our aims are one,
  Our comforts and our cares.

John Fawcett, 1739–1817

Reverence for God's name

You shall not misuse the name of the LORD your God, for the LORD will not hold anyone guiltless who misuses his name.

Exodus 20:7

Again, you have heard that the people in the old days were told— "Thou shalt not forswear thyself, but shalt perform unto the Lord thine oaths," but I say to you, don't use an oath at all. Don't swear by Heaven for it is God's throne, nor by the earth for it is his footstool, nor by Jerusalem for it is the city of the great King. No, and don't swear by your own head, for you cannot make a single hair white or black! Whatever you have to say let your "yes" be a plain "yes" and your "no" be a plain "no"—anything more than this has a taint of evil.

Matthew 5:33–37, PHILLIPS

Shun evil companions; bad language disdain;
God's Name hold in reverence, nor take it in vain;
Be thoughtful and earnest, kind-hearted and true;
Look ever to Jesus, He will carry you through.

Horatio Richmond Palmer, 1834–1907

Resting in God

For thus says the Lord GOD, the Holy One of Israel: "In returning and rest you shall be saved; in quietness and confidence shall be your strength." But you would not, And you said, "No, for we will flee on horses"—therefore you shall flee! And, "We will ride on swift horses"—therefore those who pursue you shall be swift! One thousand shall flee at the threat of one, at the threat of five you shall flee, till you are left as a pole on top of a mountain and as a banner on a hill.

Therefore the LORD will wait, that He may be gracious to you; and therefore He will be exalted, that He may have mercy on you. For the LORD is a God of justice; blessed are all those who wait for Him.

Isaiah 30:15–18, NKJV

Drop Thy still dews of quietness
　Till all our strivings cease:
Take from our souls the strain and stress,
And let our ordered lives confess
　The beauty of Thy peace.

John Greenleaf Whittier, 1807–92

Generous giving

And he looked up, and saw the rich men casting their gifts into the treasury. And he saw also a certain poor widow casting in thither two mites. And he said, Of a truth I say unto you, that this poor widow hath cast in more than they all: For all these have of their abundance cast in unto the offerings of God: but she of her penury hath cast in all the living that she had.

Luke 21:1–4, KJV

But this I say, He which soweth sparingly shall reap also sparingly; and he which soweth bountifully shall reap also bountifully. Every man according as he purposeth in his heart, so let him give; not grudgingly, or of necessity: for God loveth a cheerful giver. And God is able to make all grace abound toward you; that ye, always having all sufficiency in all things, may abound to every good work: (As it is written, He hath dispersed abroad; he hath given to the poor: his righteousness remaineth for ever. Now he that ministereth seed to the sower both minister bread for your food, and multiply your seed sown, and increase the fruits of your righteousness;) being enriched in every thing to all bountifulness, which causeth through us thanksgiving to God.

2 Corinthians 9:6–11, KJV

Take my silver and my gold,
Not a mite would I withhold;
Take my intellect, and use
Every power as Thou shalt choose.

Frances Ridley Havergal, 1836–79

God's special day

Remember the Sabbath day, to keep it holy. Six days you shall labor and do all your work, but the seventh day is the Sabbath of the LORD your God. In it you shall do no work: you, nor your son, nor your daughter, nor your male servant, nor your female servant, nor your cattle, nor your stranger who is within your gates. For in six days the LORD made the heavens and the earth, the sea, and all that is in them, and rested the seventh day. Therefore the LORD blessed the Sabbath day and hallowed it.

Exodus 20:8–11, NKJV

If you turn away your foot from the Sabbath, from doing your pleasure on My holy day, and call the Sabbath a delight, the holy day of the LORD honorable, and shall honor Him, not doing your own ways, nor finding your own pleasure, nor speaking your own words, then you shall delight yourself in the LORD; and I will cause you to ride on the high hills of the earth, and feed you with the heritage of Jacob your father. The mouth of the LORD has spoken.

Isaiah 58:13–14, NKJV

And [Jesus] said to them, "The Sabbath was made for man, and not man for the Sabbath. Therefore the Son of Man is also Lord of the Sabbath."

Mark 2:27–28, NKJV

O Sabbath rest by Galilee!
  O calm of hills above.
Where Jesus knelt to share with Thee
The silence of eternity,
  Interpreted by love.

John Greenleaf Whittier, 1807–92

Living God's way

Come, ye children, hearken unto me: I will teach you the fear of the LORD. What man is he that desireth life, and loveth many days, that he may see good? Keep thy tongue from evil, and thy lips from speaking guile. Depart from evil, and do good; seek peace, and pursue it.

Psalm 34:11–14, KJV

Blessed is the man who finds wisdom, the man who gains understanding, for she is more profitable than silver and yields better returns than gold. She is more precious than rubies; nothing you desire can compare with her. Long life is in her right hand; in her left hand are riches and honor. Her ways are pleasant ways, and all her paths are peace. She is a tree of life to those who embrace her; those who lay hold of her will be blessed.

Proverbs 3:13–18

And there's another country, I've heard of long ago—
Most dear to them that love her, most great to them that know—
We may not count her armies: we may not see her King—
Her fortress is a faithful heart, her pride is suffering—
And soul by soul and silently her shining bounds increase,
And her ways are ways of gentleness and all her paths are peace.

Cecil Spring Rice, 1859–1918

Children and parents

Honour thy father and thy mother: that thy days may be long upon the land which the LORD thy God giveth thee.

Exodus 20:12, KJV

And [Jesus] went down with them, and came to Nazareth, and was subject unto them: but his mother kept all these sayings in her heart. And Jesus increased in wisdom and stature, and in favour with God and man.

Luke 2:51–52, KJV

Children, obey your parents in the Lord: for this is right. Honour thy father and mother; which is the first commandment with promise; that it may be well with thee, and thou mayest live long on the earth. And, ye fathers, provoke not your children to wrath: but bring them up in the nurture and admonition of the Lord.

Ephesians 6:1–4, KJV

And through all His wondrous childhood
  He would honour and obey,
Love, and watch the lowly maiden
  In whose gentle arms He lay.
Christian children all must be
Mild, obedient, good as He.

Cecil Frances Alexander, 1818–95

MAY 13

Obeying Christ

But why do you call Me "Lord, Lord," and do not do the things which I say? Whoever comes to Me, and hears My sayings and does them, I will show you whom he is like: He is like a man building a house, who dug deep and laid the foundation on the rock. And when the flood arose, the stream beat vehemently against that house, and could not shake it, for it was founded on the rock. But he who heard and did nothing is like a man who built a house on the earth without a foundation, against which the stream beat vehemently; and immediately it fell. And the ruin of that house was great.

Luke 6:46–49, NKJV

According to the grace of God which was given to me, as a wise master builder I have laid the foundation, and another builds on it. But let each one take heed how he builds on it. For no other foundation can anyone lay than that which is laid, which is Jesus Christ.

1 Corinthians 3:10–11, NKJV

When we walk with the Lord,
In the light of His Word,
    What a glory He sheds on our way!
While we do His good will,
He abides with us still,
    And with all who will trust and obey!

Trust and obey!
For there's no other way
    To be happy in Jesus
But to trust and obey.

John Henry Sammis, 1846–1919

Building on Christ

Now if any man builds on the foundation with gold, silver, precious stones, wood, hay, straw, each man's work will become evident; for the day will show it because it is to be revealed with fire, and the fire itself will test the quality of each man's work. If any man's work which he has built on it remains, he will receive a reward. If any man's work is burned up, he will suffer loss; but he himself will be saved, yet so as through fire.

Do you not know that you are a temple of God and that the Spirit of God dwells in you? If any man destroys the temple of God, God will destroy him, for the temple of God is holy, and that is what you are.

Let no man deceive himself. If any man among you thinks that he is wise in this age, he must become foolish, so that he may become wise. For the wisdom of this world is foolishness before God. For it is written, "He is THE ONE WHO CATCHES THE WISE IN THEIR CRAFTINESS"; and again, "THE LORD KNOWS THE REASONINGS of the wise, THAT THEY ARE USELESS." So then let no one boast in men. For all things belong to you, whether Paul or Apollos or Cephas or the world or life or death or things present or things to come; all things belong to you, and you belong to Christ; and Christ belongs to God.

1 Corinthians 3:12–23, NASB

Christ is our Corner-stone,
　On Him alone we build;
With His true saints alone
　The courts of heaven are filled;
On His great love
　Our hopes we place
　Of present grace
And joys above.

Latin, 6th or 7th century
translated by John Chandler, 1806–76

The depth of sin

You shall not commit adultery.

Exodus 20:14

You have heard that it was said to the people in the old days, "Thou shalt not commit adultery." But I say to you that every man who looks at a woman lustfully has already committed adultery with her—in his heart.

Yes, if your right eye leads you astray pluck it out and throw it away; it is better for you to lose one of your members than that your whole body should be thrown on to the rubbish-heap.

Yes, if your right hand leads you astray cut it off and throw it away; it is better for you to lose one of your members than that your whole body should go to the rubbish-heap.

Matthew 5:27–30, PHILLIPS

I want a godly fear,
  A quick-discerning eye
That looks to Thee when sin is near,
  And sees the tempter fly;
A spirit still prepared,
  And armed with jealous care,
For ever standing on its guard
  And watching unto prayer.

Charles Wesley, 1707–88

The way to true wisdom

James, a bond-servant of God and of the Lord Jesus Christ,
To the twelve tribes who are dispersed abroad: Greetings.
Consider it all joy, my brethren, when you encounter various trials, knowing that the testing of your faith produces endurance. And let endurance have its perfect result, so that you may be perfect and complete, lacking in nothing.
But if any of you lacks wisdom, let him ask of God, who gives to all generously and without reproach, and it will be given to him. But he must ask in faith without any doubting, for the one who doubts is like the surf of the sea, driven and tossed by the wind. For that man ought not to expect that he will receive anything from the Lord.

James 1:1–7, NASB

Lead us, O Father, in the paths of peace:
  Without Thy guiding hand we go astray,
And doubts appal, and sorrows still increase;
  Lead us through Christ, the true and living Way.

Lead us, O Father, in the paths of truth:
  Unhelped by Thee, in error's maze we grope,
While passion stains and folly dims our youth,
  And age comes on uncheered by faith or hope.

William Henry Burleigh, 1812–71

The Christian's new life

You shall not steal.

Exodus 20:15

No, what you learned was to fling off the ditty clothes of the old way of living, which were rotted through and through with lust's illusions, and, with yourselves mentally and spiritually re-made, to put on the clean fresh clothes of the new life which was made by God's design for righteousness and the holiness which is no illusion.

Finish, then, with lying and let each man tell his neighbour the truth, for we are all parts of the same body. If you are angry, be sure that it is not a sinful anger. Never go to bed angry—don't give the devil that sort of foothold.

The man who used to be a thief must give up stealing, and do an honest day's work with his own hands, so that he may be able to give to those in need.

Ephesians 4:22–28, PHILLIPS

O Jesus, I have promised
  To serve Thee to the end;
Be Thou for ever near me,
  My Master and my Friend:
I shall not fear the battle
  If Thou art by my side,
Nor wander from the pathway
  If Thou wilt be my Guide.

O let me feel Thee near me:
  The world is ever near;
I see the sights that dazzle,
  The tempting sounds I hear;
My foes are ever near me,
  Around me and within;
But, Jesus, draw Thou nearer,
  And shield my soul from sin.

John Ernest Bode, 1816–74

Light upon our way

And the LORD spake unto Moses, saying, Speak unto Aaron and unto his sons, saying, On this wise ye shall bless the children of Israel, saying unto them, The LORD bless thee, and keep thee: The LORD make his face shine upon thee, and be gracious unto thee: The LORD lift up his countenance upon thee, and give thee peace.

Numbers 6:22–26, KJV

Thy testimonies are wonderful: therefore doth my soul keep them. The entrance of thy words giveth light; it giveth understanding unto the simple. I opened my mouth, and panted: for I longed for thy commandments. Look thou upon me, and be merciful unto me, as thou usest to do unto those that love thy name. Order my steps in thy word: and let not any iniquity have dominion over me. Deliver me from the oppression of man: so will I keep thy precepts. Make thy face to shine upon thy servant; and teach me thy statutes.

Psalm 119:129–35, KJV

Lord, upon our blindness
  Thy pure radiance pour;
For Thy loving kindness
  Make us love Thee more;
And, when clouds are drifting
  Dark across our sky,
Then, the veil uplifting,
  Father, be Thou nigh.

William Walsham How, 1823–97

MAY 19

He will keep us from falling

Paul and Timothy, bondservants of Jesus Christ,

To all the saints in Christ Jesus who are in Philippi, with the bishops and deacons: Grace to you and peace from God our Father and the Lord Jesus Christ.

I thank my God upon every remembrance of you, always in every prayer of mine making request for you all with joy, for your fellowship in the gospel from the first day until now, being confident of this very thing, that He who has begun a good work in you will complete it until the day of Jesus Christ.

Philippians 1:1–6, NKJV

Now to Him who is able to keep you from stumbling, and to present you faultless before the presence of His glory with exceeding joy, to God our Savior, who alone is wise, be glory and majesty, dominion and power, both now and forever. Amen.

Jude 24–25, NKJV

The work which His goodness began,
  The arm of His strength will complete;
His promise is Yea and Amen,
  And never was forfeited yet.
Things future, nor things that are now,
  Not all things below nor above,
Can make Him His purpose forgo,
  Or sever my soul from His love.

Augustus Montague Toplady, 1740–78

Jesus is baptized

Then cometh Jesus from Galilee to Jordan unto John, to be baptized
of him. But John forbad him, saying, I have need to be baptized of
thee, and comest thou to me? And Jesus answering said unto him,
Suffer it to be so now: for thus it becometh us to fulfil all righteousness. Then he suffered him. And Jesus, when he was baptized, went
up straightway out of the water: and, lo, the heavens were opened
unto him, and he saw the Spirit of God descending like a dove, and
lighting upon him: And lo a voice from heaven, saying, This is my
beloved Son, in whom I am well pleased.

Matthew 3:13–17, KJV

Come, gracious Spirit, heavenly Dove,
With light and comfort from above,
Be Thou our guardian, Thou our guide,
O'er every thought and step preside.

Lead us to Christ, the living Way,
Nor let us from His pastures stray;
Lead us to holiness, the road
That we must take to dwell with God.

Simon Browne, 1680–1732

The Counselor will come

Now I am going to him who sent me, yet none of you asks me, "Where are you going?" Because I have said these things, you are filled with grief. But I tell you the truth: It is for your good that I am going away. Unless I go away, the Counselor will not come to you; but if I go, I will send him to you. When he comes, he will convict the world of guilt in regard to sin and righteousness and judgment: in regard to sin, because men do not believe in me; in regard to righteousness, because I am going to the Father, where you can see me no longer; and in regard to judgment, because the prince of this world now stands condemned.

I have much more to say to you, more than you can now bear. But when he, the Spirit of truth, comes, he will guide you into all truth. He will not speak on his own; he will speak only what he hears, and he will tell you what is yet to come. He will bring glory to me by taking from what is mine and making it known to you. All that belongs to the Father is mine. That is why I said the Spirit will take from what is mine and make it known to you.

In a little while you will see me no more, and then after a little while you will see me.

John 16:5–16

Come, Holy Spirit, come,
  Let Thy bright beams arise;
Dispel the sorrow from our minds,
  The darkness from our eyes.

Convince us of our sin,
  Then lead to Jesus' blood;
And to our wondering view reveal
  The secret love of God.

Joseph Hart, 1712–68

The day of Pentecost

When the Day of Pentecost had fully come, they were all with one accord in one place. And suddenly there came a sound from heaven, as of a rushing mighty wind, and it filled the whole house where they were sitting. Then there appeared to them divided tongues, as of fire, and one sat upon each of them. And they were all filled with the Holy Spirit and began to speak with other tongues, as the Spirit gave them utterance.

And there were dwelling in Jerusalem Jews, devout men, from every nation under heaven. And when this sound occurred, the multitude came together, and were confused, because everyone heard them speak in his own language. Then they were all amazed and marveled, saying to one another, "Look, are not all these who speak Galileans? And how is it that we hear, each in our own language in which we were born? Parthians and Medes and Elamites, those dwelling in Mesopotamia, Judea and Cappadocia, Pontus and Asia, Phrygia and Pamphylia, Egypt and the parts of Libya adjoining Cyrene, visitors from Rome, both Jews and proselytes, Cretans and Arabs—we hear them speaking in our own tongues the wonderful works of God." So they were all amazed and perplexed, saying to one another, "Whatever could this mean?" Others mocking said, "They are full of new wine."

Acts 2:1–13, NKJV

O Breath of life, come sweeping through us,
Revive your church with life and power;
O Breath of life, come, cleanse, renew us
And fit your church to meet this hour.

O Wind of God, come bend us, break us
Till humbly we confess our need;
Then, in your tenderness remake us,
Revive, restore—for this we plead.

Elizabeth A. P. Head, 1850–1936

Sealed with the Spirit

In whom [Christ] also we have obtained an inheritance, being predestinated according to the purpose of him who worketh all things after the counsel of his own will: That we should be to the praise of his glory, who first trusted in Christ. In whom ye also trusted, after that ye heard the word of truth, the gospel of your salvation: in whom also after that ye believed, ye were sealed with that holy Spirit of promise, which is the earnest of our inheritance until the redemption of the purchased possession, unto the praise of his glory.

Ephesians 1:11–14, KJV

Now he which stablisheth us with you in Christ, and hath anointed us, is God; who hath also sealed us, and given the earnest of the Spirit in our hearts.

2 Corinthians 1:21–22, KJV

Why should the children of a King
  Go mourning all their days?
Great Comforter, descend, and bring
  Some tokens of Thy grace.

Dost Thou not dwell in all Thy saints,
  And seal the heirs of heaven?
When wilt Thou banish my complaints,
  And show my sins forgiven?

Thou art the earnest of His love,
  The pledge of joys to come,
And Thy soft wings, celestial Dove,
  Will safe convey me home.

Isaac Watts, 1674–1748

Do not put out the Spirit's fire

And do not grieve the Holy Spirit of God, by whom you were sealed for the day of redemption. Let all bitterness, wrath, anger, clamor, and evil speaking be put away from you, with all malice. And be kind to one another, tenderhearted, forgiving one another, just as God in Christ forgave you.

Ephesians 4:30–32, NKJV

Rejoice always, pray without ceasing, in everything give thanks; for this is the will of God in Christ Jesus for you.

Do not quench the Spirit. Do not despise prophecies. Test all things; hold fast what is good. Abstain from every form of evil.

Now may the God of peace Himself sanctify you completely; and may your whole spirit, soul, and body be preserved blameless at the coming of our Lord Jesus Christ. He who calls you is faithful, who also will do it.

1 Thessalonians 5:16–24, NKJV

Come down, O Love divine
Seek Thou this soul of mine,
　And visit it with Thine own ardour glowing;
O Comforter, draw near,
Within my heart appear,
　And kindle it, Thy holy flame bestowing.

O let it freely burn,
Till earthly passions turn
　To dust and ashes, in its heat consuming;
And let Thy glorious light
Shine ever on my sight,
　And clothe me round, the while my path illuming.

Bianco da Siena, c. 1350–1434
translated by Richard Frederick Littledale, 1833–90

The moving of the Spirit

We did not follow cleverly invented stories when we told you about the power and coming of our Lord Jesus Christ, but we were eyewitnesses of his majesty. For he received honor and glory from God the Father when the voice came to him from the Majestic Glory, saying, "This is my Son, whom I love; with him I am well pleased." We ourselves heard this voice that came from heaven when we were with him on the sacred mountain.

And we have the word of the prophets made more certain, and you will do well to pay attention to it, as to a light shining in a dark place, until the day dawns and the morning star rises in your hearts. Above all, you must understand that no prophecy of Scripture came about by the prophet's own interpretation. For prophecy never had its origin in the will of man, but men spoke from God as they were carried along by the Holy Spirit.

2 Peter 1:16–21

Come, Holy Ghost, our hearts inspire,
  Let us Thine influence prove,
Source of the old prophetic fire,
  Fountain of light and love.

Come, Holy Ghost, for moved by Thee
  The prophets wrote and spoke;
Unlock the truth, Thyself the key,
  Unseal the sacred Book.

God, through Himself, we then shall know,
  If Thou within us shine,
And sound, with all Thy saints below,
  The depths of love divine.

Charles Wesley, 1707–88

Longing for God

As the hart panteth after the water brooks, so panteth my soul after thee, O God. My soul thirsteth for God, for the living God: when shall I come and appear before God? My tears have been my meat day and night, while they continually say unto me, Where is thy God? When I remember these things, I pour out my soul in me: for I had gone with the multitude, I went with them to the house of God, with the voice of joy and praise, with a multitude that kept holyday. Why art thou cast down, O my soul? and why art thou disquieted in me? hope thou in God: for I shall yet praise him for the help of his countenance. O my God, my soul is cast down within me: therefore will I remember thee from the land of Jordan, and of the Hermonites, from the hill Mizar.

Psalm 42:1–6, KJV

O Love divine, how sweet Thou art!
When shall I find my willing heart
    All taken up by Thee?
I thirst, I faint, I die to prove
The greatness of redeeming love,
    The love of Christ to me.

Charles Wesley, 1707–88

Following Christ

From that time Jesus began to show to His disciples that He must go to Jerusalem, and suffer many things from the elders and chief priests and scribes, and be killed, and be raised the third day. Then Peter took Him aside and began to rebuke Him, saying, "Far be it from You, Lord; this shall not happen to You!" But He turned and said to Peter, "Get behind Me, Satan! You are an offense to Me, for you are not mindful of the things of God, but the things of men."

Then Jesus said to His disciples, "If anyone desires to come after Me, let him deny himself, and take up his cross, and follow Me. For whoever desires to save his life will lose it, but whoever loses his life for My sake will find it. For what profit is it to a man if he gains the whole world, and loses his own soul? Or what will a man give in exchange for his soul? For the Son of Man will come in the glory of His Father with His angels, and then He will reward each according to his works. Assuredly, I say to you, there are some standing here who shall not taste death till they see the Son of Man coming in His kingdom."

Matthew 16:21–28, NKJV

O Love, that wilt not let me go,
I rest my weary soul in Thee;
I give Thee back the life I owe,
That in Thine ocean depths its flow
May richer, fuller be.

George Matheson, 1842–1906

Worship the Lord in holiness

Give unto the LORD, O ye mighty, give unto the LORD glory and strength. Give unto the LORD the glory due unto his name; worship the LORD in the beauty of holiness. The voice of the LORD is upon the waters: the God of glory thundereth: the LORD is upon many waters. The voice of the LORD is powerful; the voice of the LORD is full of majesty. The voice of the LORD breaketh the cedars; yea, the LORD breaketh the cedars of Lebanon. He maketh them also to skip like a calf; Lebanon and Sirion like a young unicorn. The voice of the LORD divideth the flames of fire. . . .The LORD sitteth upon the flood; yea, the LORD sitteth King for ever. The LORD will give strength unto his people; the LORD will bless his people with peace.

Psalm 29:1–7,10–11, KJV

O worship the Lord in the beauty of holiness;
  Bow down before Him, His glory proclaim;
With gold of obedience and incense of lowliness,
  Kneel and adore Him, the Lord is His Name.

John Samuel Bewley Monsell, 1811–75

Life in the Spirit

Live by the Spirit, I say, and do not gratify the desires of the flesh. For what the flesh desires is opposed to the Spirit, and what the Spirit desires is opposed to the flesh; for these are opposed to each other, to prevent you from doing what you want. But if you are led by the Spirit, you are not subject to the law. Now the works of the flesh are obvious: fornication, impurity, licentiousness, idolatry, sorcery, enmities, strife, jealousy, anger, quarrels, dissensions, factions, envy, drunkenness, carousing, and things like these. I am warning you, as I warned you before: those who do such things will not inherit the kingdom of God.

By contrast, the fruit of the Spirit is love, joy, peace, patience, kindness, generosity, faithfulness, gentleness, and self-control. There is no law against such things. And those who belong to Christ Jesus have crucified the flesh with its passions and desires. If we live by the Spirit, let us also be guided by the Spirit. Let us not become conceited, competing against one another, envying one another.

Galatians 5:16–26, NRSV

Holy Spirit, love divine,
Glow within this heart of mine;
Kindle every high desire;
Perish self in Thy pure fire.

Holy Spirit, joy divine,
Gladden Thou this heart of mine;
In the desert ways I'll sing:
Spring, O Well, for ever spring!

Samuel Longfellow, 1819–92

The cleansing of God

Have mercy upon me, O God, according to thy lovingkindness: according unto the multitude of thy tender mercies blot out my transgressions. Wash me throughly from mine iniquity, and cleanse me from my sin. For I acknowledge my transgressions: and my sin is ever before me. Against thee, thee only, have I sinned, and done this evil in thy sight: that thou mightest be justified when thou speakest, and be clear when thou judgest. Behold, I was shapen in iniquity; and in sin did my mother conceive me. Behold, thou desirest truth in the inward parts: and in the hidden part thou shalt make me to know wisdom. Purge me with hyssop, and I shall be clean: wash me, and I shall be whiter than snow. Make me to hear joy and gladness; that the bones ˙ which thou hast broken may rejoice. Hide thy face from my sins, and blot out all mine iniquities.

Psalm 51:1–9, KJV

Have Thine own ways, Lord, have Thine own way;
Search me and try me, Master, today.
Whiter than snow, Lord, wash me just now,
As in Thy presence humbly I bow.

Adelaide Addison Pollard, 1862–1934

Create in me a pure heart

Create in me a clean heart, O God; and renew a right spirit within me. Cast me not away from thy presence; and take not thy holy spirit from me. Restore unto me the joy of thy salvation; and uphold me with thy free spirit. Then will I teach transgressors thy ways; and sinners shall be converted unto thee. Deliver me from bloodguiltiness, O God, thou God of my salvation: and my tongue shall sing aloud of thy righteousness. O Lord, open thou my lips; and my mouth shall shew forth thy praise. For thou desirest not sacrifice; else would I give it: thou delightest not in burnt offering. The sacrifices of God are a broken spirit: a broken and a contrite heart, O God, thou wilt not despise. Do good in thy good pleasure unto Zion: build thou the walls of Jerusalem. Then shalt thou be pleased with the sacrifices of righteousness, with burnt offering and whole burnt offering: then shall they offer bullocks upon thine altar.

Psalm 51:10–19, KJV

A humble, lowly, contrite heart,
  Believing, true, and clean,
Which neither life nor death can part
  From Him that dwells within;

Thy nature, gracious Lord, impart;
  Come quickly from above;
Write Thy new Name upon my heart,
  Thy new best Name of love.

Charles Wesley, 1707–88

Praise the Lord, O my soul

Bless the LORD, O my soul: and all that is within me, bless his holy name. Bless the LORD, O my soul, and forget not all his benefits: who forgiveth all thine iniquities; who healeth all thy diseases; who redeemeth thy life from destruction; who crowneth thee with lovingkindness and tender mercies; who satisfieth thy mouth with good things; so that thy youth is renewed like the eagle's. The LORD executeth righteousness and judgment for all that are oppressed. He made known his ways unto Moses, his acts unto the children of Israel. The LORD is merciful and gracious, slow to anger, and plenteous in mercy. . . .

Bless the LORD, ye his angels, that excel in strength, that do his commandments, hearkening unto the voice of his word. Bless ye the LORD, all ye his hosts; ye ministers of his, that do his pleasure. Bless the LORD, all his works in all places of his dominion: bless the LORD, O my soul.

Psalm 103:1–8,20–22, KJV

Praise, my soul the King of heaven,
  To His feet they tribute bring;
Ransomed, healed, restored, forgiven,
  Who like thee His praise should sing?
    Praise Him! Praise Him!
  Praise the everlasting King.

Angels, help us to adore Him;
  Ye behold Him face to face;
Sun and moon, bow down before Him,
  Dwellers all in time and space.
    Praise Him! Praise Him!
  Praise with us the God of grace.

Henry Francis Lyte, 1793–1847

God's glorious grace

Peter, an apostle of Jesus Christ, To the pilgrims of the Dispersion in Pontus, Galatia, Cappadocia, Asia, and Bithynia, elect according to the foreknowledge of God the Father, in sanctification of the Spirit, for obedience and sprinkling of the blood of Jesus Christ: Grace to you and peace be multiplied.

Blessed be the God and Father of our Lord Jesus Christ, who according to His abundant mercy has begotten us again to a living hope through the resurrection of Jesus Christ from the dead, to an inheritance incorruptible and undefiled and that does not fade away, reserved in heaven for you, who are kept by the power of God through faith for salvation ready to be revealed in the last time. In this you greatly rejoice, though now for a little while, if need be, you have been grieved by various trials, that the genuineness of your faith, being much more precious than gold that perishes, though it is tested by fire, may be found to praise, honor, and glory at the revelation of Jesus Christ, whom having not seen you love. Though now you do not see Him, yet believing, you rejoice with joy inexpressible and full of glory, receiving the end of your faith—the salvation of your souls.

1 Peter 1:1–9, NKJV

On such love, my soul, still ponder,
 Love so great, so rich and free;
Say, while lost in holy wonder,
 "Why, O Lord, such love to me?"
 Hallelujah!
Grace shall reign eternally.

John Kent, 1766–1843

The body and blood of Christ

While they were eating, Jesus took some bread, and after a blessing, He broke it and gave it to the disciples, and said, "Take, eat; this is My body." And when He had taken a cup and given thanks, He gave it to them, saying, "Drink from it, all of you; for this is My blood of the covenant, which is poured out for many for forgiveness of sins. But I say to you, I will not drink of this fruit of the vine from now on until that day when I drink it new with you in My Father's kingdom."

Matthew 26:26–29, NASB

For I received from the Lord that which I also delivered to you, that the Lord Jesus in the night in which He was betrayed took bread; and when He had given thanks, He broke it and said, "This is My body, which is for you; do this in remembrance of Me." In the same way He took the cup also after supper, saying, "This cup is the new covenant in My blood; do this, as often as you drink it, in remembrance of Me." For as often as you eat this bread and drink the cup, you proclaim the Lord's death until He comes.

Therefore whoever eats the bread or drinks the cup of the Lord in an unworthy manner, shall be guilty of the body and the blood of the Lord. But a man must examine himself, and in so doing he is to eat of the bread and drink of the cup. For he who eats and drinks, eats and drinks judgment to himself if he does not judge the body rightly. For this reason many among you are weak and sick, and a number sleep.

1 Corinthians 11:23–30, NASB

Here would I feed upon the bread of God,
  Here drink with Thee the royal wine of heaven;
Here would I lay aside each earthly load,
  Here take afresh the calm of sin forgiven.

Horatius Bonar, 1808–89

The message of the cross

For the message of the cross is foolishness to those who are perishing, but to us who are being saved it is the power of God. For it is written: "I will destroy the wisdom of the wise, and bring to nothing the understanding of the prudent." Where is the wise? Where is the scribe? Where is the disputer of this age? Has not God made foolish the wisdom of this world? For since, in the wisdom of God, the world through wisdom did not know God, it pleased God through the foolishness of the message preached to save those who believe. For Jews request a sign, and Greeks seek after wisdom; but we preach Christ crucified, to the Jews a stumbling block and to the Greeks foolishness, but to those who are called, both Jews and Greeks, Christ the power of God and the wisdom of God. Because the foolishness of God is wiser than men, and the weakness of God is stronger than men.

For you see your calling, brethren, that not many wise according to the flesh, not many mighty, not many noble, are called. But God has chosen the foolish things of the world to put to shame the wise, and God has chosen the weak things of the world to put to shame the things which are mighty.

1 Corinthians 1:18–27, NKJV

We sing the praise of Him who died,
  Of Him who died upon the cross;
The sinner's hope let men deride,
  For this we count the world but loss.

The cross! it takes our guilt away;
  It holds the fainting spirit up;
It cheers with hope the gloomy day,
  And sweetens every bitter cup.

Thomas Kelly, 1769–1855

JUNE 5

Singing joyfully to God

Make a joyful noise unto the LORD, all ye lands. Serve the LORD with gladness: come before his presence with singing. Know ye that the LORD he is God: it is he that hath made us, and not we ourselves; we are his people, and the sheep of his pasture. Enter into his gates with thanksgiving, and into his courts with praise: be thankful unto him, and bless his name. For the LORD is good; his mercy is everlasting; and his truth endureth to all generations.

Psalm 100:1–5, KJV

The glory of the LORD shall endure for ever: the LORD shall rejoice in his works. He looketh on the earth, and it trembleth: he toucheth the hills, and they smoke. I will sing unto the LORD as long as I live: I will sing praise to my God while I have my being. My meditation of him shall be sweet: I will be glad in the LORD. Let the sinners be consumed out of the earth, and let the wicked be no more. Bless thou the LORD, O my soul. Praise ye the LORD.

Psalm 104:31–35, KJV

All people on earth do dwell,
　Sing to the Lord with cheerful voice;
Him serve with fear, His praise forth tell,
　Come ye before Him and rejoice.

William Kethe, d. 1594

JUNE 6

Looking forward to the day of the Lord

But do not ignore this one fact, beloved, that with the Lord one day is like a thousand years, and a thousand years are like one day. The Lord is not slow about his promise, as some think of slowness, but is patient with you, not wanting any to perish, but all to come to repentance. But the day of the Lord will come like a thief, and then the heavens will pass away with a loud noise, and the elements will be dissolved with fire, and the earth and everything that is done on it will be disclosed.

Since all these things are to be dissolved in this way, what sort of persons ought you to be in leading lives of holiness and godliness, waiting for and hastening the coming of the day of God, because of which the heavens will be set ablaze and dissolved, and the elements will melt with fire? But, in accordance with his promise, we wait for new heavens and a new earth, where righteousness is at home. Therefore, beloved, while you are waiting for these things, strive to be found by him at peace, without spot or blemish.

2 Peter 3:8–14, NRSV

O may we thus be found,
   Obedient to His Word,
Attentive to the trumpet's sound,
   And looking for our Lord!
O may we thus ensure
   A lot among the blest;
And watch a moment to secure
   An everlasting rest!

Charles Wesley, 1707–88

The cost of discipleship

Now when Jesus saw a crowd around Him, He gave orders to depart to the other side of the sea. Then a scribe came and said to Him, "Teacher, I will follow You wherever You go." Jesus said to him, "The foxes have holes and the birds of the air have nests, but the Son of Man has nowhere to lay His head." Another of the disciples said to Him, "Lord, permit me first to go and bury my father." But Jesus said to him, "Follow Me, and allow the dead to bury their own dead."

When He got into the boat, His disciples followed Him. And behold, there arose a great storm on the sea, so that the boat was being covered with the waves; but Jesus Himself was asleep. And they came to Him and woke Him, saying, "Save us, Lord; we are perishing!" He said to them, "Why are you afraid, you men of little faith?" Then He got up and rebuked the winds and the sea, and it became perfectly calm. The men were amazed, and said, "What kind of a man is this, that even the winds and the sea obey Him?"

Matthew 8:18–27, NASB

The foxes found rest,
And the birds their nest,
  In the shade of the cedar tree;
But Thy couch was the sod,
O Thou Son of God,
  In the deserts of Galilee:
O come to my heart, Lord Jesus!
  There is room in my heart for Thee.

Emily Elizabeth Steele Elliott, 1836–97

The armor of God

Finally, my brethren, be strong in the Lord and in the power of His might. Put on the whole armor of God, that you may be able to stand against the wiles of the devil. For we do not wrestle against flesh and blood, but against principalities, against powers, against the rulers of the darkness of this age, against spiritual hosts of wickedness in the heavenly places. Therefore take up the whole armor of God, that you may be able to withstand in the evil day, and having done all, to stand. Stand therefore, having girded your waist with truth, having put on the breastplate of righteousness, and having shod your feet with the preparation of the gospel of peace; above all, taking the shield of faith with which you will be able to quench all the fiery darts of the wicked one. And take the helmet of salvation, and the sword of the Spirit, which is the word of God; praying always with all prayer and supplication in the Spirit, being watchful to this end with all perseverance and supplication for all the saints.

Ephesians 6:10–18, NKJV

Soldiers of Christ, arise,
  And put your armour on;
Strong in the strength which God supplies,
  Through His eternal Son;
Strong in the Lord of hosts,
  And in His mighty power;
Who in the strength of Jesus trusts
  Is more than conqueror.

Charles Wesley, 1707–88

JUNE 9

Fight the good fight

Now godliness with contentment is great gain. For we brought nothing into this world, and it is certain we can carry nothing out. And having food and clothing, with these we shall be content. But those who desire to be rich fall into temptation and a snare, and into many foolish and harmful lusts which drown men in destruction and perdition. For the love of money is a root of all kinds of evil, for which some have strayed from the faith in their greediness, and pierced themselves through with many sorrows.

But you, O man of God, flee these things and pursue righteousness, godliness, faith, love, patience, gentleness. Fight the good fight of faith, lay hold on eternal life, to which you were also called and have confessed the good confession in the presence of many witnesses.

1 Timothy 6:6–12, NKJV

Fight the good fight with all thy might;
Christ is thy strength, and Christ thy right;
Lay hold on life, and it shall be
Thy joy and crown eternally.

John Samuel Bewley Monsell, 1811–75

The battle belongs to the Lord

Then the Spirit of the LORD came upon Jahaziel the son of Zechariah, the son of Benaiah, the son of Jeiel, the son of Mattaniah, a Levite of the sons of Asaph, in the midst of the assembly. And he said, "Listen, all you of Judah and you inhabitants of Jerusalem, and you, King Jehoshaphat! Thus says the LORD to you: 'Do not be afraid nor dismayed because of this great multitude, for the battle is not yours, but God's. Tomorrow go down against them. They will surely come up by the Ascent of Ziz, and you will find them at the end of the brook before the Wilderness of Jeruel. You will not need to fight in this battle. Position yourselves, stand still and see the salvation of the LORD, who is with you, O Judah and Jerusalem!' Do not fear or be dismayed; tomorrow go out against them, for the LORD is with you."

2 Chronicles 20:14–17, NKJV

We go in faith, our own great weakness feeling,
    And needing more each day Thy grace to know;
Yet from our hearts a song of triumph pealing:
    "We rest on Thee, and in Thy Name we go."

We rest on Thee, our Shield and our Defender!
    Thine is the battle; Thine shall be the praise
When passing through the gates of pearly splendour,
    Victors, we rest with Thee through endless days.

Edith Adeline Gilling Cherry, 1872–97

Depending on God's strength

Strengthen ye the weak hands, and confirm the feeble knees. Say to them that are of a fearful heart, Be strong, fear not: behold, your God will come with vengeance, even God with a recompence; he will come and save you. Then the eyes of the blind shall be opened, and the ears of the deaf shall be unstopped. Then shall the lame man leap as an hart, and the tongue of the dumb sing: for in the wilderness shall waters break out, and streams in the desert. And the parched ground shall become a pool, and the thirsty land springs of water: in the habitation of dragons, where each lay, shall be grass with reeds and rushes.

Isaiah 35:3–7, KJV

And the Lord said, Simon, Simon, behold, Satan hath desired to have you, that he may sift you as wheat: But I have prayed for thee, that thy faith fail not: and when thou art converted, strengthen thy brethren. And he said unto him, Lord, I am ready to go with thee, both into prison, and to death. And he said, I tell thee, Peter, the cock shall not crow this day, before that thou shalt thrice deny that thou knowest me.

Luke 22:31–34, KJV

Thou seest our weakness, Lord;
  Our hearts are known to Thee:
O lift Thou up the sinking hand,
  Confirm the feeble knee!

Let us in life, in death,
  Thy steadfast truth declare,
And publish with our latest breath
  Thy love and guardian care.

Paul Gerhardt, 1607–76
translated by John Wesley, 1703–91

Separation of the peoples

Then the king will say to those at his right hand, "Come, you that are blessed by my Father, inherit the kingdom prepared for you from the foundation of the world; for I was hungry and you gave me food, I was thirsty and you gave me something to drink, I was a stranger and you welcomed me, I was naked and you gave me clothing, I was sick and you took care of me, I was in prison and you visited me." Then the righteous will answer him, "Lord, when was it that we saw you hungry and gave you food, or thirsty and gave you something to drink? And when was it that we saw you a stranger and welcomed you, or naked and gave you clothing? And when was it that we saw you sick or in prison and visited you?" And the king will answer them, "Truly I tell you, just as you did it to one of the least of these who are members of my family, you did it to me." Then he will say to those at his left hand, "You that are accursed, depart from me into the eternal fire prepared for the devil and his angels; for I was hungry and you gave me no food, I was thirsty and you gave me nothing to drink, I was a stranger and you did not welcome me, naked and you did not give me clothing, sick and in prison and you did not visit me." Then they also will answer, "Lord, when was it that we saw you hungry or thirsty or a stranger or naked or sick or in prison, and did not take care of you?" Then he will answer them, "Truly I tell you, just as you did not do it to one of the least of these, you did not do it to me." And these will go away into eternal punishment, but the righteous into eternal life.

Matthew 25:34–46, NRSV

At His call the dead awaken,
  Rise to life from earth and sea;
All the powers of nature, shaken
  By His look, prepare to flee;
    Careless sinner,
  What will then become of thee?

But those who have confessed,
  Loved and served the Lord below,
He will say, "Come near, ye blessed,
  See the kingdom I bestow;
    You for ever
  Shall my love and glory know."

                    John Newton, 1725–1807

JUNE 13

How unsearchable are his judgments

When I applied my heart to know wisdom and to see the business that is done on earth, even though one sees no sleep day or night, then I saw all the work of God, that a man cannot find out the work that is done under the sun. For though a man labors to discover it, yet he will not find it; moreover, though a wise man attempts to know it, he will not be able to find it.

Ecclesiasties 8:16–17, NKJV

Oh, the depth of the riches both of the wisdom and knowledge of God! How unsearchable are His judgments and His ways past finding out! "For who has known the mind of the LORD? Or who has become His counselor? Or who has first given to Him and it shall be repaid to him?" For of Him and through Him and to Him are all things, to whom be glory forever. Amen.

Romans 11:33–36, NKJV

Holy and Infinite! limitless, boundless
  All Thy perfections and power and praise!
Ocean of Mystery! awful and soundless
  All Thine unsearchable judgements and ways!

Frances Ridley Havergal, 1836–79

Making the most of the time

Continue earnestly in prayer, being vigilant in it with thanksgiving; meanwhile praying also for us, that God would open to us a door for the word, to speak the mystery of Christ, for which I am also in chains, that I may make it manifest, as I ought to speak. Walk in wisdom toward those who are outside, redeeming the time. Let your speech always be with grace, seasoned with salt, that you may know how you ought to answer each one.

Tychicus, a beloved brother, faithful minister, and fellow servant in the Lord, will tell you all the news about me. I am sending him to you for this very purpose, that he may know your circumstances and comfort your hearts, with Onesimus, a faithful and beloved brother, who is one of you. They will make known to you all things which are happening here.

Colossians 4:2–9, NKJV

I would the precious time redeem,
  And longer live for this alone,
To spend, and to be spent, for them
  Who have not yet my Saviour known;
Fully on these my mission prove,
And only breathe, to breathe Thy love.

Charles Wesley, 1707–88

"I am with you"

Moreover if thy brother shall trespass against thee, go and tell him his fault between thee and him alone: if he shall hear thee, thou hast gained thy brother. But if he will not hear thee, then take with thee one or two more, that in the mouth of two or three witnesses every word may be established. And if he shall neglect to hear them, tell it unto the church: but if he neglect to hear the church, let him be unto thee as an heathen man and a publican. Verily I say unto you, Whatsoever ye shall bind on earth shall be bound in heaven: and whatsoever ye shall loose on earth shall be loosed in heaven. Again I say unto you, That if two of you shall agree on earth as touching any thing that they shall ask, it shall be done for them of my Father which is in heaven. For where two or three are gathered together in my name, there am I in the midst of them.

Matthew 18:15–20, KJV

Jesus, where'er Thy people meet,
There they behold Thy mercy-seat;
Where'er they seek Thee Thou art found,
And every place is hallowed ground.

Here may we prove the power of prayer,
To strengthen faith and sweeten care,
To teach our faint desires to rise,
And bring all heaven before our eyes.

William Cowper, 1731–1800

JUNE 16

Jesus loves to answer prayer

And he said unto them, Which of you shall have a friend, and shall go unto him at midnight, and say unto him, Friend, lend me three loaves; for a friend of mine in his journey is come to me, and I have nothing to set before him? And he from within shall answer and say, Trouble me not: the door is now shut, and my children are with me in bed; I cannot rise and give thee. I say unto you, Though he will not rise and give him, because he is his friend, yet because of his importunity he will rise and give him as many as he needeth. And I say unto you, Ask, and it shall be given you; seek, and ye shall find; knock, and it shall be opened unto you. For every one that asketh receiveth; and he that seeketh findeth; and to him that knocketh it shall be opened. If a son shall ask bread of any of you that is a father, will he give him a stone? or if he ask a fish, will he for a fish give him a serpent? Or if he shall ask an egg, will he offer him a scorpion? If ye then, being evil, know how to give good gifts unto your children: how much more shall your heavenly Father give the Holy Spirit to them that ask him?

Luke 11:5–13, KJV

Come my soul, thy suit prepare,
Jesus loves to answer prayer;
He Himself has bid thee pray,
Therefore will not say thee nay.

Thou art coming to a King,
Large petitions with thee bring;
For His grace and power are such,
None can ever ask too much.

John Newton, 1725–1807

The heavenly worship

Also before the throne there was what looked like a sea of glass, clear as crystal.

In the center, around the throne, were four living creatures, and they were covered with eyes, in front and in back. The first living creature was like a lion, the second was like an ox, the third had a face like a man, the fourth was like a flying eagle. Each of the four living creatures had six wings and was covered with eyes all around, even under his wings. Day and night they never stop saying: "Holy, holy, holy is the Lord God Almighty, who was, and is, and is to come." Whenever the living creatures give glory, honor and thanks to him who sits on the throne and who lives for ever and ever, the twenty-four elders fall down before him who sits on the throne, and worship him who lives for ever and ever. They lay their crowns before the throne and say: "You are worthy, our Lord and God, to receive glory and honor and power, for you created all things, and by your will they were created and have their being."

Revelation 4:6–11

Finish then Thy new creation,
  Pure and spotless may we be;
Let us see Thy great salvation,
  Perfectly restored in Thee;
Changed from glory into glory,
  Till in heaven we take our place,
Till we cast our crowns before Thee,
  Lost in wonder, love and praise.

Charles Wesley, 1707–88

Jesus prays for his disciples

I have manifested Your name to the men whom You gave Me out of the world; they were Yours and You gave them to Me, and they have kept Your word. Now they have come to know that everything You have given Me is from You; for the words which You gave Me I have given to them; and they received them and truly understood that I came forth from You, and they believed that You sent Me. I ask on their behalf; I do not ask on behalf of the world, but of those whom You have given Me; for they are Yours; and all things that are Mine are Yours, and Yours are Mine; and I have been glorified in them. I am no longer in the world; and yet they themselves are in the world, and I come to You. Holy Father, keep them in Your name, the name which You have given Me, that they may be one even as We are. While I was with them, I was keeping them in Your name which You have given Me; and I guarded them and not one of them perished but the son of perdition, so that the Scripture would be fulfilled.

John 17:6–12, NASB

In the hour of trial,
   Jesus, pray for me,
Lest by base denial
   I depart from Thee;
When Thou seest me waver,
   With a look recall,
Nor, for fear or favour,
   Suffer me to fall.

James Montgomery, 1771–1854

Proclaim his salvation!

O sing unto the LORD a new song: sing unto the LORD, all the earth. Sing unto the LORD, bless his name; shew forth his salvation from day to day. Declare his glory among the heathen, his wonders among all people. For the LORD is great, and greatly to be praised: he is to be feared above all gods. For all the gods of the nations are idols: but the LORD made the heavens. Honour and majesty are before him: strength and beauty are in his sanctuary. Give unto the LORD, O ye kindreds of the people, give unto the LORD glory and strength. Give unto the LORD the glory due unto his name: bring an offering, and come into his courts. O worship the LORD in the beauty of holiness: fear before him, all the earth.

Psalm 96:1–9, KJV

Ye blessed souls at rest,
  Who ran this earthly race,
And now, from sin released,
  Behold the Saviour's face,
God's praises sound,
  As in His sight
  With sweet delight
Ye do abound.

Ye saints, who toil below,
  Adore your heavenly King,
And, onward as ye go,
  Some joyful anthem sing;
That what He gives,
  And praise Him still
  Through good and ill,
Who ever lives.

Richard Baxter, 1615–91

Jesus, our friend

As the Father loved Me, I also have loved you; abide in My love. If you keep My commandments, you will abide in My love, just as I have kept My Father's commandments and abide in His love. These things I have spoken to you, that My joy may remain in you, and that your joy may be full. This is My commandment, that you love one another as I have loved you. Greater love has no one than this, than to lay down one's life for his friends. You are My friends if you do whatever I command you. No longer do I call you servants, for a servant does not know what his master is doing; but I have called you friends, for all things that I heard from My Father I have made known to you. You did not choose Me, but I chose you and appointed you that you should go and bear fruit, and that your fruit should remain, that whatever you ask the Father in My name He may give you. These things I command you, that you love one another.

John 15:9–17, NKJV

I've found a Friend, O such a Friend!
  He loved me ere I knew Him;
He drew me with the cords of love,
  And thus He bound me to Him;
And round my heart still closely twine
  Those ties which nought can sever;
For I am His, and He is mine,
  For ever and for ever.

I've found a Friend, O such a Friend!
  He bled, He died to save me;
And not alone the gift of life,
  But His own self He gave me.
Nought that I have mine own I'll call,
  I'll hold it for the Giver;
My heart, my strength, my life, my all
  Are His, and His for ever.

James Grindlay Small, 1817–88

The guidance of God

And the angel of God, which went before the camp of Israel, removed and went behind them; and the pillar of the cloud went from before their face, and stood behind them: And it came between the camp of the Egyptians and the camp of Israel; and it was a cloud and darkness to them, but it gave light by night to these: so that the one came not near the other all the night.

Exodus 14:19–20, KJV

Marvellous things did he in the sight of their fathers, in the land of Egypt, in the field of Zoan. He divided the sea, and caused them to pass through; and he made the waters to stand as an heap. In the daytime also he led them with a cloud, and all the night with a light of fire. He clave the rocks in the wilderness, and gave them drink as out of the great depths. He brought streams also out of the rock, and caused waters to run down like rivers.

Psalm 78:12–16, KJV

Open Thou the crystal fountain
  Whence the healing stream doth flow;
Let the fiery, cloudy pillar
  Lead me all my journey through;
    Strong Deliverer,
  Be Thou still my strength and shield.

William Williams, 1717–91
translated by Peter Williams, 1721–96

God, our help in ages past

Lord, thou hast been our dwelling place in all generations. Before the mountains were brought forth, or ever thou hadst formed the earth and the world, even from everlasting to everlasting, thou art God. . . .

O satisfy us early with thy mercy; that we may rejoice and be glad all our days. Make us glad according to the days wherein thou hast afflicted us, and the years wherein we have seen evil. Let thy work appear unto thy servants, and thy glory unto their children. And let the beauty of the LORD our God be upon us: and establish thou the work of our hands upon us; yea, the work of our hands establish thou it.

Psalm 90:1–2, 14–17, KJV

O God, our help in ages past,
　Our hope for years to come,
Our shelter from the stormy blast,
　And our eternal home;

Beneath the shadow of Thy throne
　Thy saints have dwelt secure;
Sufficient is Thine arm alone,
　And our defence is sure.

Isaac Watts, 1674–1748

Real service

Let us have no imitation Christian love. Let us have a genuine hatred for evil and a real devotion to good. Let us have real warm affection for one another as between brothers, and a willingness to let the other man have the credit. Let us not allow slackness to spoil our work and let us keep the fires of the spirit burning, as we do our work for the Lord. Base your happiness on your hope in Christ. When trials come endure them patiently; steadfastly maintain the habit of prayer. Give freely to fellow-Christians in want, never grudging a meal or a bed to those who need them. And as for those who try to make your life a misery, bless them. Don't curse, bless. Share the happiness of those who are happy, and the sorrow of those who are sad. Live in harmony with each other. Don't become snobbish but take a real interest in ordinary people. Don't become set in your own opinions. Don't pay back a bad turn by a bad turn, to anyone. See that your public behaviour is above criticism. As far as your responsibility goes, live at peace with everyone. Never take vengeance into your own hands, my dear friends: stand back and let God punish if he will. For it is written:

Vengeance belongeth unto me: I will recompense, saith the Lord.
And it is also written:

If thine enemy hunger, feed him;
If he thirst, give him to drink:
For in so doing thou shall heap coals of fire upon his head.
Don't allow yourself to be overpowered by evil. Take the offensive—overpower evil with good!

Romans 12:9–21, PHILLIPS

The Lord is King! I own His power,
His right to rule each day and hour;
I own His claim on heart and will,
And His demands I would fulfil.

Darley Terry, 1848–1934

Following Christ's example

Servants, be submissive to your masters with all fear, not only to the good and gentle, but also to the harsh. For this is commendable, if because of conscience toward God one endures grief, suffering wrongfully. For what credit is it if, when you are beaten for your faults, you take it patiently? But when you do good and suffer, if you take it patiently, this is commendable before God. For to this you were called, because Christ also suffered for us, leaving us an example, that you should follow His steps: "Who committed no sin, nor was deceit found in His mouth"; who, when He was reviled, did not revile in return; when He suffered, He did not threaten, but committed Himself to Him who judges righteously; who Himself bore our sins in His own body on the tree, that we, having died to sins, might live for righteousness—by whose stripes you were healed. For you were like sheep going astray, but have now returned to the Shepherd and Overseer of your souls.

1 Peter 2:18–25, NKJV

O let me see Thy footmarks,
　And in them plant mine own:
My hope to follow duly
　Is in Thy strength alone.
O guide me, call me, draw me,
　Uphold me to the end;
And then in heaven receive me,
　My Saviour and my Friend.

John Ernest Bode, 1816–74

JUNE 25

Loving the Lord Jesus

When they had finished breakfast, Jesus said to Simon Peter, "Simon son of John, do you love me more than these?" He said to him, "Yes, Lord; you know that I love you." Jesus said to him, "Feed my lambs." A second time he said to him, "Simon son of John, do you love me?" He said to him, "Yes, Lord; you know that I love you." Jesus said to him, "Tend my sheep." He said to him the third time, "Simon son of John, do you love me?" Peter felt hurt because he said to him the third time, "Do you love me?" And he said to him, "Lord, you know everything; you know that I love you." Jesus said to him, "Feed my sheep. Very truly, I tell you, when you were younger, you used to fasten your own belt and to go wherever you wished. But when you grow old, you will stretch out your hands, and someone else will fasten a belt around you and take you where you do not wish to go." (He said this to indicate the kind of death by which he would glorify God.) After this he said to him, "Follow me."

John 21:15–19, NRSV

My Jesus, I love Thee, I know Thou art mine;
For Thee all the pleasures of sin I resign;
My gracious Redeemer, my Saviour art Thou,
If ever I loved Thee, my Jesus, 'tis now.

William Ralph Featherstone, 1842–70

Strength in unity

Behold, how good and how pleasant it is for brethren to dwell together in unity! It is like the precious ointment upon the head, that ran down upon the beard, even Aaron's beard: that went down to the skirts of his garments; as the dew of Hermon, and as the dew that descended upon the mountains of Zion: for there the LORD commanded the blessing, even life for evermore.

Psalm 133:1–3, KJV

Two are better than one; because they have a good reward for their labour. For if they fall, the one will lift up his fellow: but woe to him that is alone when he falleth; for he hath not another to help him up. Again, if two lie together, then they have heat: but how can one be warm alone? And if one prevail against him, two shall withstand him; and a threefold cord is not quickly broken.

Ecclesiastes 4:9–12, KJV

How beautiful the sight
  Of brethren who agree
In friendship to unite,
  And bonds of charity!
'Tis like the precious ointment shed
O'er all his robes from Aaron's head.

James Montgomery, 1771–1854

Salvation at the cross

The soldiers also came up and mocked him. They offered him wine vinegar and said, "If you are the king of the Jews, save yourself."

There was a written notice above him, which read: THIS IS THE KING OF THE JEWS.

One of the criminals who hung there hurled insults at him: "Aren't you the Christ? Save yourself and us!"

But the other criminal rebuked him. "Don't you fear God," he said, "since you are under the same sentence? We are punished justly, for we are getting what our deeds deserve. But this man has done nothing wrong."

Then he said, "Jesus, remember me when you come into your kingdom."

Jesus answered him, "I tell you the truth, today you will be with me in paradise."

Luke 23:36–43

There is a fountain filled with blood
   Drawn from Immanuel's veins;
And sinners, plunged beneath that flood,
   Lose all their guilty stains.

The dying thief rejoiced to see
   That fountain in his day;
And there have I, though vile as he,
   Washed all my sins away.

William Cowper, 1731–1800

The Spirit of God

But Peter, standing up with the eleven, raised his voice and said to them, "Men of Judea and all who dwell in Jerusalem, let this be known to you, and heed my words. For these are not drunk, as you suppose, since it is only the third hour of the day. But this is what was spoken by the prophet Joel: 'And it shall come to pass in the last days, says God, That I will pour out of My Spirit on all flesh; your sons and your daughters shall prophesy, your young men shall see visions, your old men shall dream dreams. And on My menservants and on My maidservants I will pour out My Spirit in those days; and they shall prophesy. I will show wonders in heaven above and signs in the earth beneath: blood and fire and vapor of smoke. The sun shall be turned into darkness, and the moon into blood, before the coming of the great and awesome day of the LORD. And it shall come to pass That whoever calls on the name of the LORD shall be saved.'"

Acts 2:14–21, NKJV

O Spirit of the living God,
  In all Thy plenitude of grace,
Where'er the foot of man hath trod,
  Descend on our apostate race.

Give tongues of fire and hearts of love
  To preach the reconciling word;
Give power and unction from above,
  Whene'er the joyful sound is heard.

Baptize the nations; far and nigh
  The triumphs of the cross record;
The Name of Jesus glorify
  Till every kindred call Him Lord.

James Montgomery, 1771–1854

Pure Father of light

Now Moses was pasturing the flock of Jethro his father-in-law, the priest of Midian; and he led the flock to the west side of the wilderness and came to Horeb, the mountain of God. The angel of the LORD appeared to him in a blazing fire from the midst of a bush; and he looked, and behold, the bush was burning with fire, yet the bush was not consumed. So Moses said, "I must turn aside now and see this marvelous sight, why the bush is not burned up." When the LORD saw that he turned aside to look, God called to him from the midst of the bush and said, "Moses, Moses!" And he said, "Here I am." Then He said, "Do not come near here; remove your sandals from your feet, for the place on which you are standing is holy ground." He said also, "I am the God of your father, the God of Abraham, the God of Isaac, and the God of Jacob." Then Moses hid his face, for he was afraid to look at God.

Exodus 3:1–6, NASB

Great Father of glory, pure Father of light,
Thine angels adore Thee, all veiling their sight;
All laud we would render; O help us to see
'Tis only the splendour of light hideth Thee.

Walter Chalmers Smith, 1824–1908

The sacred name

Then the LORD said, "I have observed the misery of my people who are in Egypt; I have heard their cry on account of their taskmasters. Indeed, I know their sufferings, and I have come down to deliver them from the Egyptians, and to bring them up out of that land to a good and broad land, a land flowing with milk and honey, to the country of the Canaanites, the Hittites, the Amorites, the Perizzites, the Hivites, and the Jebusites. The cry of the Israelites has now come to me; I have also seen how the Egyptians oppress them. So come, I will send you to Pharaoh to bring my people, the Israelites, out of Egypt." But Moses said to God, "Who am I that I should go to Pharaoh, and bring the Israelites out of Egypt?" He said, "I will be with you; and this shall be the sign for you that it is I who sent you: when you have brought the people out of Egypt, you shall worship God on this mountain."

But Moses said to God, "If I come to the Israelites and say to them, 'The God of your ancestors has sent me to you,' and they ask me, 'What is his name?' what shall I say to them?" God said to Moses, "I AM WHO I AM." He said further, "Thus you shall say to the Israelites, 'I AM has sent me to you.'" God also said to Moses, "Thus you shall say to the Israelites, 'The LORD, the God of your ancestors, the God of Abraham, the God of Isaac, and the God of Jacob, has sent me to you': This is my name forever, and this my title for all generations."

Exodus 3:7–15, NRSV

The God of Abraham praise,
  Who reigns enthroned above,
Ancient of everlasting days,
  And God of love.
Jehovah! Great I AM!
  By earth and heaven confessed;
I bow and bless the sacred Name
  For ever blessed.

Thomas Olivers, 1725–99

Be still

Come, behold the works of the LORD, what desolations he hath made in the earth. He maketh wars to cease unto the end of the earth; he breaketh the bow, and cutteth the spear in sunder; he burneth the chariot in the fire. Be still, and know that I am God: I will be exalted among the heathen, I will be exalted in the earth. The LORD of hosts is with us; the God of Jacob is our refuge.

Psalm 46:8–11, KJV

My heart is fixed, O God, my heart is fixed: I will sing and give praise. Awake up, my glory; awake, psaltery and harp: I myself will awake early. I will praise thee, O Lord, among the people: I will sing unto thee among the nations. For thy mercy is great unto the heavens, and thy truth unto the clouds. Be thou exalted, O God, above the heavens: let thy glory be above all the earth.

Psalm 57:7–11, KJV

Be still, my soul: the Lord is on thy side;
  Bear patiently the cross of grief or pain;
Leave to thy God to order and provide;
  In every change He faithful will remain.
Be still, my soul: thy best, thy heavenly Friend
Through thorny ways leads to a joyful end.

Katharina von Schlegel, b. 1697
translated by Jane Laurie Borthwick, 1813–97

Do not love the world

Do not love the world or the things in the world. If anyone loves the world, the love of the Father is not in him. For all that is in the world—the lust of the flesh, the lust of the eyes, and the pride of life—is not of the Father but is of the world. And the world is passing away, and the lust of it; but he who does the will of God abides forever.

Little children, it is the last hour; and as you have heard that the Antichrist is coming, even now many antichrists have come, by which we know that it is the last hour. They went out from us, but they were not of us; for if they had been of us, they would have continued with us; but they went out that they might be made manifest, that none of them were of us. But you have an anointing from the Holy One, and you know all things. I have not written to you because you do not know the truth, but because you know it, and that no lie is of the truth. Who is a liar but he who denies that Jesus is the Christ? He is antichrist who denies the Father and the Son. Whoever denies the Son does not have the Father either; he who acknowledges the Son has the Father also.

1 John 2:15–23, NKJV

> Let earth no more my heart divide,
> With Christ may I be crucified,
> To Thee with my whole soul aspire;
> Dead to the world and all its toys,
> Its idle pomp, and fading joys,
> Be Thou alone my one desire!

Charles Wesley, 1707–88

Because he first loved us

We love because he first loved us. If anyone says, "I love God," yet hates his brother, he is a liar. For anyone who does not love his brother, whom he has seen, cannot love God, whom he has not seen. And he has given us this command: Whoever loves God must also love his brother.

Everyone who believes that Jesus is the Christ is born of God, and everyone who loves the father loves his child as well. This is how we know that we love the children of God: by loving God and carrying out his commands. This is love for God: to obey his commands. And his commands are not burdensome, for everyone born of God overcomes the world. This is the victory that has overcome the world, even our faith. Who is it that overcomes the world? Only he who believes that Jesus is the Son of God.

1 John 4:19–5:5

I love thee because Thou hast first loved me,
And purchased my pardon on Calvary's tree;
I love Thee for wearing the thorns on Thy brow,
If ever I loved Thee, my Jesus, 'tis now.

William Ralph Featherstone, 1842–70

JULY 4

Praying to the Lord

This is the One who came by water and blood, Jesus Christ; not with the water only, but with the water and with the blood. It is the Spirit who testifies, because the Spirit is the truth. For there are three that testify: the Spirit and the water and the blood; and the three are in agreement. If we receive the testimony of men, the testimony of God is greater; for the testimony of God is this, that He has testified concerning His Son. The one who believes in the Son of God has the testimony in himself; the one who does not believe God has made Him a liar, because he has not believed in the testimony that God has given concerning His Son. And the testimony is this, that God has given us eternal life, and this life is in His Son. He who has the Son has the life; he who does not have the Son of God does not have the life.

These things I have written to you who believe in the name of the Son of God, so that you may know that you have eternal life. This is the confidence which we have before Him, that, if we ask anything according to His will, He hears us. And if we know that He hears us in whatever we ask, we know that we have the requests which we have asked from Him.

1 John 5:6–15, NASB

What a Friend we have in Jesus,
  All our sins and griefs to bear!
What a privilege to carry
  Everything to God in prayer!
O what peace we often forfeit,
  O what needless pain we bear,
All because we do not carry
  Everything to God in prayer!

Joseph Medlicott Scriven, 1819–86

New life in Christ

When the men had come to him, they said, "John the Baptist has sent us to you to ask, 'Are you the one who is to come, or are we to wait for another?'" Jesus had just then cured many people of diseases, plagues, and evil spirits, and had given sight to many who were blind. And he answered them, "Go and tell John what you have seen and heard: the blind receive their sight, the lame walk, the lepers are cleansed, the deaf hear, the dead are raised, the poor have good news brought to them. And blessed is anyone who takes no offense at me."

Luke 7:20–23, NRSV

But even though we were dead in our sins God, who is rich in mercy, because of the great love he had for us, gave us life together with Christ—it is, remember, by grace that you am saved.

Ephesians 2:4–5, PHILLIPS

O for a thousand tongues to sing
  My great Redeemer's praise,
The glories of my God and King,
  The triumphs of His grace!

Jesus! the Name that charms our fears,
  That bids our sorrows cease;
'Tis music in the sinner's ears,
  'Tis life, and health, and peace.

He speaks, and, listening to His voice,
  New life the dead receive,
The mournful, broken hearts rejoice,
  The humble poor believe.

Charles Wesley, 1707–88

A perfect sacrifice

If his offering is a burnt sacrifice of the herd, let him offer a male without blemish; he shall offer it of his own free will at the door of the tabernacle of meeting before the LORD. Then he shall put his hand on the head of the burnt offering, and it will be accepted on his behalf to make atonement for him. He shall kill the bull before the LORD; and the priests, Aaron's sons, shall bring the blood and sprinkle the blood all around on the altar that is by the door of the tabernacle of meeting. And he shall skin the burnt offering and cut it into its pieces. The sons of Aaron the priest shall put fire on the altar, and lay the wood in order on the fire. Then the priests, Aaron's sons, shall lay the parts, the head, and the fat in order on the wood that is on the fire upon the altar; but he shall wash its entrails and its legs with water. And the priest shall burn all on the altar as a burnt sacrifice, an offering made by fire, a sweet aroma to the LORD.

Leviticus 1:3–9, NKJV

And every priest stands ministering daily and offering repeatedly the same sacrifices, which can never take away sins. But this Man, after He had offered one sacrifice for sins forever, sat down at the right hand of God.

Hebrews 10:11–12, NKJV

Not all the blood of beasts,
  On Jewish altars slain,
Could give the guilty conscience peace
  Or wash away the stain.

But Christ, the heavenly Lamb,
  Takes all our sin away;
A sacrifice of nobler name,
  And richer blood than they.

Isaac Watts, 1674–1748

191

"I was blind but now I see"

So a second time they called the man who had been blind, and said to him, "Give glory to God; we know that this man is a sinner." He then answered, "Whether He is a sinner, I do not know; one thing I do know, that though I was blind, now I see." So they said to him, "What did He do to you? How did He open your eyes?" He answered them, "I told you already and you did not listen; why do you want to hear it again? You do not want to become His disciples too, do you?" They reviled him and said, "You are His disciple, but we are disciples of Moses. We know that God has spoken to Moses, but as for this man, we do not know where He is from." The man answered and said to them, "Well, here is an amazing thing, that you do not know where He is from, and yet He opened my eyes. We know that God does not hear sinners; but if anyone is God-fearing and does His will, He hears him. Since the beginning of time it has never been heard that anyone opened the eyes of a person born blind. If this man were not from God, He could do nothing." They answered him, "You were born entirely in sins, and are you teaching us?" So they put him out.

John 9:24–34, NASB

Lord, I was blind! I could not see
    In Thy marred visage any grace;
But now the beauty of Thy face
    In radiant vision dawns on me.

Lord, Thou hast made the blind to see;
    The deaf to hear, the dumb to speak,
The dead to live; and lo, I break
    The chains of my captivity!

William Tidd Matson, 1833–99

Overflowing praise

Great is the LORD, and greatly to be praised; and his greatness is unsearchable. One generation shall praise thy works to another, and shall declare thy mighty acts. I will speak of the glorious honour of thy majesty, and of thy wondrous works. And men shall speak of the might of thy terrible acts: and I will declare thy greatness. They shall abundantly utter the memory of thy great goodness, and shall sing of thy righteousness. The LORD is gracious, and full of compassion; slow to anger, and of great mercy. The LORD is good to all: and his tender mercies are over all his works. All thy works shall praise thee, O LORD; and thy saints shall bless thee. They shall speak of the glory of thy kingdom, and talk of thy power; to make known to the sons of men his mighty acts, and the glorious majesty of his kingdom. Thy kingdom is an everlasting kingdom, and thy dominion endureth throughout all generations.

Psalm 145:3–13, KJV

Holy, holy, holy, Lord God Almighty!
    All Thy works shall praise Thy Name, in earth and sky and sea;
Holy, holy, holy! merciful and mighty,
    God in Three Persons, blessed Trinity!

Reginald Heber, 1783–1826

Jesus brings the good news

Then Jesus, filled with the power of the Spirit, returned to Galilee, and a report about him spread through all the surrounding country. He began to teach in their synagogues and was praised by everyone.

When he came to Nazareth, where he had been brought up, he went to the synagogue on the sabbath day, as was his custom. He stood up to read, and the scroll of the prophet Isaiah was given to him. He unrolled the scroll and found the place where it was written: "The Spirit of the Lord is upon me, because he has anointed me to bring good news to the poor. He has sent me to proclaim release to the captives and recovery of sight to the blind, to let the oppressed go free, to proclaim the year of the Lord's favor." And he rolled up the scroll, gave it back to the attendant, and sat down. The eyes of all in the synagogue were fixed on him. Then he began to say to them, "Today this scripture has been fulfilled in your hearing." All spoke well of him and were amazed at the gracious words that came from his mouth. They said, "Is not this Joseph's son?"

Luke 4:14–22, NRSV

Hark, the glad sound! the Saviour comes,
  The Saviour promised long;
Let every heart prepare a throne,
  And every voice a song.

He comes the prisoners to release,
  In Satan's bondage held;
The gates of brass before Him burst,
  The iron fetters yield.

He comes the broken heart to bind,
  The bleeding soul to cure,
And with the treasures of His grace
  To enrich the humble poor.

Philip Doddridge, 1702–51

JULY 10

Responding to God's love

To the angel of the church in Laodicea write:

The Amen, the faithful and true Witness, the Beginning of the creation of God, says this:

"I know your deeds, that you are neither cold nor hot; I wish that you were cold or hot. So because you are lukewarm, and neither hot nor cold, I will spit you out of My mouth. Because you say, 'I am rich, and have become wealthy, and have need of nothing,' and you do not know that you are wretched and miserable and poor and blind and naked, I advise you to buy from Me gold refined by fire so that you may become rich, and white garments so that you may clothe yourself, and that the shame of your nakedness will not be revealed; and eye salve to anoint your eyes so that you may see. Those whom I love, I reprove and discipline; therefore be zealous and repent. Behold, I stand at the door and knock; if anyone hears My voice and opens the door, I will come in to him and will dine with him, and he with Me. He who overcomes, I will grant to him to sit down with Me on My throne, as I also overcame and sat down with My Father on His throne. He who has an ear, let him hear what the Spirit says to the churches."

Revelation 3:14–22, NASB

Jesus is seeking the wanderers yet;
  Why do they roam?
Love only waits to forgive and forget;
  Home! weary wanderer, home!
Wonderful love
Dwells in the heart of the Father above.

Robert Walmsley, 1831–1905

Saving others

But you, beloved, remember the words which were spoken before by the apostles of our Lord Jesus Christ: how they told you that there would be mockers in the last time who would walk according to their own ungodly lusts. These are sensual persons, who cause divisions, not having the Spirit.

But you, beloved, building yourselves up on your most holy faith, praying in the Holy Spirit, keep yourselves in the love of God, looking for the mercy of our Lord Jesus Christ unto eternal life. And on some have compassion, making a distinction; but others save with fear, pulling them out of the fire, hating even the garment defiled by the flesh.

Jude 17–23, NKJV

I want an even strong desire,
  I want a calmly fervent zeal
To save poor souls out of the fire
  To snatch them from the verge of hell,
And turn them to a pardoning God,
And quench the brands in Jesu's blood.

Enlarge, inflame, and fill my heart
  With boundless charity divine!
So shall I all my strength exert,
  And love them with a zeal like Thine;
And lead them to Thy open side,
The sheep for whom their Shepherd died.

Charles Wesley, 1707–88

God is faithful

In this confidence let us hold on to the hope that we profess without the slightest hesitation—for he is utterly dependable—and let us think of one another and how we can encourage each other to love and do good deeds. And let us not hold aloof from our church meetings, as some do. Let us do all we can to help one another's faith, and this the more earnestly as we see the final day drawing.

Hebrews 10:23–25, PHILLIPS

Write this to the angel of the Church in Smyrna:
These words are spoken by the first and the last, who died and came to life again. I know of your tribulation and of your poverty—though in fact you are rich! I know how you are slandered by those who call themselves Jews, but in fact are no Jews but a synagogue of Satan. Have no fear of what you will suffer. I tell you now that the devil is going to cast some of your number into prison where your faith will be tested and your distress win last for ten days. Be faithful in the face of death and I will give you the crown of life.

Revelation 2:8–10, PHILLIPS

How good is the God we adore,
  Our faithful, unchangeable Friend!
His love is as great as His power,
  And knows neither measure nor end!

'Tis Jesus, the First and the Last,
  Whose Spirit shall guide us safe home;
We'll praise Him for all that is past,
  And trust Him for all that's to come.

Joseph Hart, 1712–68

Wholehearted loyalty

But my servant Caleb . . . had another spirit with him, and hath followed me fully.

Numbers 14:24, KJV

Then the children of Judah came unto Joshua in Gilgal: and Caleb the son of Jephunneh the Kenezite said unto him, Thou knowest the thing that the LORD said unto Moses the man of God concerning me and thee in Kadesh-barnea. Forty years old was I when Moses the servant of the LORD sent me from Kadesh-barnea to espy out the land; and I brought him word again as it was in mine heart. Nevertheless my brethren that went up with me made the heart of the people melt: but I wholly followed the LORD my God. And Moses sware on that day, saying, Surely the land whereon thy feet have trodden shall be thine inheritance, and thy children's for ever, because thou hast wholly followed the LORD my God. And now, behold, the LORD hath kept me alive, as he said, these forty and five years, even since the LORD spake this word unto Moses, while the children of Israel wandered in the wilderness: and now, lo, I am this day fourscore and five years old. As yet I am as strong this day as I was in the day that Moses sent me: as my strength was then, even so is my strength now, for war, both to go out, and to come in.

Joshua 14:6–11, KJV

True-hearted, wholehearted, faithful and loyal,
    King of our lives, by Thy grace we will be:
Under Thy standard, exalted and royal,
    Strong in Thy strength, we will battle for Thee.

Peal out the watchword, and silence it never,
    Song of our spirits rejoicing and free:
"True-hearted, whole-hearted, now and for ever,
    King of our lives, by Thy grace we will be!"

Frances Ridley Havergal, 1836–79

Our security in God

But Zion said, "The LORD has forsaken me, the Lord has forgotten me. Can a mother forget the baby at her breast and have no compassion on the child she has borne? Though she may forget, I will not forget you! See, I have engraved you on the palms of my hands; your walls are ever before me."

Isaiah 49:14–16

Are not two sparrows sold for a penny? Yet not one of them will fall to the ground apart from your Father. And even the hairs of your head are all counted. So do not be afraid; you are of more value than many sparrows.

Matthew 10:29–31, NRSV

My name from the palms of His hands
    Eternity will not erase;
Impressed on His heart it remains,
    In marks of indelible grace;

Yes, I to the end shall endure,
    As sure as the earnest is given;
More happy, but not more secure,
    The glorified spirits in heaven.

Augustus Montague Toplady, 1740–78

The Lord, our hope

For thou art my hope, O Lord GOD: thou art my trust from my youth. By thee have I been holden up from the womb: thou art he that took me out of my mother's bowels: my praise shall be continually of thee. I am as a wonder unto many; but thou art my strong refuge. Let my mouth be filled with thy praise and with thy honour all the day. Cast me not off in the time of old age; forsake me not when my strength faileth.

Psalm 71:5–9, KJV

For a thousand years in thy sight are but as yesterday when it is past, and as a watch in the night. Thou carriest them away as with a flood; they are as a sleep: in the morning they are like grass which groweth up. In the morning it flourisheth, and groweth up; in the evening it is cut down, and withereth. For we are consumed by thine anger, and by thy wrath are we troubled. Thou hast set our iniquities before thee, our secret sins in the light of thy countenance. For all our days are passed away in thy wrath: we spend our years as a tale that is told. The days of our years are threescore years and ten; and if by reason of strength they be fourscore years, yet is their strength labour and sorrow; for it is soon cut off, and we fly away. Who knoweth the power of thine anger? even according to thy fear, so is thy wrath. So teach us to number our days, that we may apply our hearts unto wisdom.

Psalm 90:4–12, KJV

A thousand ages in Thy sight
  Are like an evening gone,
Short as the watch that ends the night
  Before the rising sun.

Our God, our help in ages past,
  Our hope for years to come,
Be thou our guard while troubles last,
  And our eternal home.

Isaac Watts, 1674–1748

Strong in Christ

You therefore, my son, be strong in the grace that is in Christ Jesus. And the things that you have heard from me among many witnesses, commit these to faithful men who will be able to teach others also. You therefore must endure hardship as a good soldier of Jesus Christ. No one engaged in warfare entangles himself with the affairs of this life, that he may please him who enlisted him as a soldier. And also if anyone competes in athletics, he is not crowned unless he competes according to the rules. The hardworking farmer must be first to partake of the crops. Consider what I say, and may the Lord give you understanding in all things.

2 Timothy 2:1–7, NKJV

Stand up stand up for Jesus!
  Stand in His strength alone:
The arm of flesh will fail you;
  Ye dare not trust your own.
Put on the gospel armour,
  Each piece put on with prayer;
Where duty calls, or danger,
  Be never wanting there.

Stand up, stand up for Jesus!
  The strife will not be long;
This day the noise of battle,
  The next the victor's song.
To him that overcometh
  A crown of life shall be;
He with the King of glory
  Shall reign eternally.

George Duffield, 1818–88

A lifetime of praise

Praise ye the LORD. Praise the LORD, O my soul. While I live will I praise the LORD: I will sing praises unto my God while I have any being. Put not your trust in princes, nor in the son of man, in whom there is no help. His breath goeth forth, he returneth to his earth; in that very day his thoughts perish. Happy is he that hath the God of Jacob for his help, whose hope is in the LORD his God: which made heaven, and earth, the sea, and all that therein is: which keepeth truth for ever: which executeth judgment for the oppressed: which giveth food to the hungry. The LORD looseth the prisoners: the LORD openeth the eyes of the blind: the LORD raiseth them that are bowed down: the LORD loveth the righteous: the LORD preserveth the strangers; he relieveth the fatherless and widow: but the way of the wicked he turneth upside down. The LORD shall reign for ever, even thy God, O Zion, unto all generations. Praise ye the LORD.

Psalm 146:1–10, KJV

I'll praise my Maker while I've breath,
And when my voice is lost in death,
Praise shall employ my nobler powers;
  My days of praise shall ne'er be past;
  While life, and thought, and being last,
Or immortality endures.

The Lord gives eyesight to the blind;
The Lord supports the fainting mind;
He sends the labouring conscience peace;
  He helps the stranger in distress,
  The widow and the fatherless,
And grants the prisoner sweet release.

Isaac Watts, 1674–1748

A purpose in suffering

O bless our God, ye people, and make the voice of his praise to be heard: which holdeth our soul in life, and suffereth not our feet to be moved. For thou, O God, hast proved us: thou hast tried us, as silver is tried.

Psalm 66:8–10, KJV

For my name's sake will I defer mine anger, and for my praise will I refrain for thee, that I cut thee not off. Behold, I have refined thee, but not with silver; I have chosen thee in the furnace of affliction. For mine own sake, even for mine own sake, will I do it: for how should my name be polluted? and I will not give my glory unto another.

Isaiah 48:9–11, KJV

Beloved, think it not strange concerning the fiery trial which is to try you, as though some strange thing happened unto you: But rejoice, inasmuch as ye are partakers of Christ's sufferings; that, when his glory shall be revealed, ye may be glad also with exceeding joy.

1 Peter 4:12–13, KJV

When through fiery trials thy pathway shall lie,
His grace all-sufficient shall be thy supply;
The flame shall not hurt thee, His only design
Thy dross to consume and thy gold to refine.

"K" in Rippon's *Selection,* 1787

JULY 19

Listening to God

The boy Samuel ministered before the LORD under Eli. In those days the word of the LORD was rare; there were not many visions.

One night Eli, whose eyes were becoming so weak that he could barely see, was lying down in his usual place. The lamp of God had not yet gone out, and Samuel was lying down in the temple of the LORD, where the ark of God was. Then the LORD called Samuel.

Samuel answered, "Here I am." And he ran to Eli and said, "Here I am; you called me."

But Eli said, "I did not call; go back and lie down." So he went and lay down.

Again the LORD called, "Samuel!" And Samuel got up and went to Eli and said, "Here I am; you called me."

"My son," Elli said, "I did not call; go back and lie down."

Now Samuel did not yet know the LORD: The word of the LORD had not yet been revealed to him.

The LORD called Samuel a third time, and Samuel got up and went to Eli and said, "Here I am; you called me."

Then Eli realized that the LORD was calling the boy. So Eli told Samuel, "Go and lie down, and if he calls you, say, 'Speak, LORD, for your servant is listening.' So Samuel went and lay down in his place.

The LORD came and stood there, calling as at the other times, "Samuel! Samuel!"

Then Samuel said, "Speak, for your servant is listening."

1 Samuel 3:1–10

Master, speak! Thy servant heareth,
  Waiting for Thy gracious word,
Longing for Thy voice that cheereth,
  Master, let it now be heard.
I am listening, Lord, for Thee;
What hast Thou to say to me?

Frances Ridley Havergal, 1836–79

The Lord is King!

Ascribe to the LORD, O families of the peoples, ascribe to the LORD glory and strength. Ascribe to the LORD the glory due his name; bring an offering, and come before him. Worship the LORD in holy splendor; tremble before him, all the earth. The world is firmly established; it shall never be moved. Let the heavens be glad, and let the earth rejoice, and let them say among the nations, "The LORD is king!"

1 Chronicles 16:28–31, NRSV

The LORD reigneth, he is clothed with majesty; the LORD is clothed with strength, wherewith he hath girded himself: the world also is stablished, that it cannot be moved. Thy throne is established of old: thou art from everlasting. The floods have lifted up, O LORD, the floods have lifted up their voice; the floods lift up their waves. The LORD on high is mightier than the noise of many waters, yea, than the mighty waves of the sea. Thy testimonies are very sure: holiness becometh thine house, O LORD, for ever.

Psalm 93:1–5, KJV

The Lord is King; lift up thy voice,
O earth, and all ye heavens rejoice!
From world to world the joy shall ring:
"The Lord Omnipotent is King!"

The Lord is King! child of the dust,
The Judge of all the earth is just:
Holy and true are all His ways;
Let every creature speak His praise.

Josiah Conder, 1789–1855

The King of glory

The earth is the LORD's, and the fulness thereof; the world, and they that dwell therein. For he hath founded it upon the seas, and established it upon the floods. Who shall ascend into the hill of the LORD? or who shall stand in his holy place? He that hath clean hands, and a pure heart; who hath not lifted up his soul unto vanity, nor sworn deceitfully. He shall receive the blessing from the LORD, and righteousness from the God of his salvation. This is the generation of them that seek him, that seek thy face, O Jacob. Selah. Lift up your heads, O ye gates; and be ye lift up, ye everlasting doors; and the King of glory shall come in. Who is this King of glory? The LORD strong and mighty, the LORD mighty in battle. Lift up your heads, O ye gates; even lift them up, ye everlasting doors; and the King of glory shall come in. Who is this King of glory? The LORD of hosts, he is the King of glory. Selah.

Psalm 24:1–10, KJV

King of glory! Soul of bliss!
  Hallelujah!
Everlasting life is this,
Thee to know, Thy power to prove,
Thus to sing, and thus to love.

Charles Wesley, 1707–88

Mary's song of praise

And Mary said: "My soul magnifies the Lord, and my spirit has rejoiced in God my Savior. For He has regarded the lowly state of His maidservant; for behold, henceforth all generations will call me blessed. For He who is mighty has done great things for me, and holy is His name. And His mercy is on those who fear Him from generation to generation. He has shown strength with His arm; He has scattered the proud in the imagination of their hearts. He has put down the mighty from their thrones, and exalted the lowly. He has filled the hungry with good things, and the rich He has sent away empty. He has helped His servant Israel, in remembrance of His mercy, as He spoke to our fathers, to Abraham and to his seed forever."

Luke 1:46–55, NKJV

Tell out, my soul, the greatness of the Lord,
  Unnumbered blessings give my spirit voice;
Tender to me the promise of His Word;
  In God my Saviour shall my heart rejoice.

Tell out, my soul, the greatness of His Name!
  Make known His might, the deeds His arm has done;
His mercy sure, from age to age the same;
  His Holy Name, the Lord, the Mighty One.

Tell out, my soul, the greatness of His might!
  Powers and dominions lay their glory by.
Proud hearts and stubborn wills are put to flight,
  The hungry fed, the humble lifted high.

Tell out, my soul, the glories of His Word!
  Firm is His promise, and His mercy sure.
Tell out, my soul, the greatness of the Lord
  To children's children and for evermore!

Timothy Dudley-Smith, b. 1926

In the strength of God

Then David said to the Philistine, "You come to me with a sword, a spear, and a javelin, but I come to you in the name of the LORD of hosts, the God of the armies of Israel, whom you have taunted. This day the LORD will deliver you up into my hands, and I will strike you down and remove your head from you. And I will give the dead bodies of the army of the Philistines this day to the birds of the sky and the wild beasts of the earth, that all the earth may know that there is a God in Israel, and that all this assembly may know that the LORD does not deliver by sword or by spear; for the battle is the LORD's and He will give you into our hands."

Then it happened when the Philistine rose and came and drew near to meet David, that David ran quickly toward the battle line to meet the Philistine. And David put his hand into his bag and took from it a stone and slung it, and struck the Philistine on his forehead. And the stone sank into his forehead, so that he fell on his face to the ground.

Thus David prevailed over the Philistine with a sling and a stone, and he struck the Philistine and killed him; but there was no sword in David's hand.

1 Samuel 17:45–50, NASB

"We rest on Thee," our Shield and our Defender!
  We go not forth alone against the foe;
Strong in Thy strength, safe in Thy keeping tender,
  "We rest on Thee, and in Thy Name we go."

Edith Adeline Gilling Cherry, 1872–97

The eternal God is our refuge

Then Moses and the sons of Israel sang this song to the LORD, and said, "I will sing to the LORD, for He is highly exalted; the horse and its rider He has hurled into the sea. The LORD is my strength and song, and He has become my salvation; this is my God, and I will praise Him; My father's God, and I will extol Him. The LORD is a warrior; the LORD is His name."

Exodus 15:1–3, NASB

There is no one like the God of Jeshurun, who rides the heavens to help you, and in His excellency on the clouds. The eternal God is your refuge, and underneath are the everlasting arms; He will thrust out the enemy from before you, and will say, "Destroy!" Then Israel shall dwell in safety, the fountain of Jacob alone, in a land of grain and new wine; His heavens shall also drop dew. Happy are you, O Israel! Who is like you, a people saved by the LORD, the shield of your help and the sword of your majesty! Your enemies shall submit to you, and you shall tread down their high places.

Deuteronomy 33:26–29, NKJV

We come unto our fathers' God;
  Their Rock is our salvation;
The eternal arms, their dear abode,
  We make our habitation;
We bring Thee, Lord, the praise they brought,
We seek Thee as Thy saints have sought
  In every generation.

Thomas Hornblower Gill, 1819–1906

Led by the Spirit

For those who live according to the flesh set their minds on the things of the flesh, but those who live according to the Spirit set their minds on the things of the Spirit. To set the mind on the flesh is death, but to set the mind on the Spirit is life and peace. For this reason the mind that is set on the flesh is hostile to God; it does not submit to God's law—indeed it cannot, and those who are in the flesh cannot please God.

But you are not in the flesh; you are in the Spirit, since the Spirit of God dwells in you. Anyone who does not have the Spirit of Christ does not belong to him. But if Christ is in you, though the body is dead because of sin, the Spirit is life because of righteousness. If the Spirit of him who raised Jesus from the dead dwells in you, he who raised Christ from the dead will give life to your mortal bodies also through his Spirit that dwells in you.

So then, brothers and sisters, we are debtors, not to the flesh, to live according to the flesh—for if you live according to the flesh, you will die; but if by the Spirit you put to death the deeds of the body, you will live. For all who are led by the Spirit of God are children of God.

Romans 8:5–14, NRSV

By Thine unerring Spirit led,
　We shall not in the desert stray;
We shall not full direction need,
　Nor miss our providential way;
As far from danger as from fear,
While love, almighty love, is near.

Charles Wesley, 1707–88

A life of faith

Is anyone among you suffering? Then he must pray. Is anyone cheerful? He is to sing praises. Is anyone among you sick? Then he must call for the elders of the church and they are to pray over him, anointing him with oil in the name of the Lord; and the prayer offered in faith will restore the one who is sick, and the Lord will raise him up, and if he has committed sins, they will be forgiven him. Therefore, confess your sins to one another, and pray for one another so that you may be healed. The effective prayer of a righteous man can accomplish much. Elijah was a man with a nature like ours, and he prayed earnestly that it would not rain, and it did not rain on the earth for three years and six months. Then he prayed again, and the sky poured rain and the earth produced its fruit.

My brethren, if any among you strays from the truth and one turns him back, let him know that he who turns a sinner from the error of his way will save his soul from death and will cover a multitude of sins.

James 5:13–20, NASB

While I am a pilgrim here,
Let Thy love my spirit cheer;
As my guide, my Guard, my Friend,
Lead me to my journey's end.

Show me what I have to do;
Every hour my strength renew;
Let me live a life of faith;
Let me die Thy people's death.

John Newton, 1725–1807

"You are very great"

Bless the LORD, O my soul. O LORD my God, thou art very great; thou art clothed with honour and majesty. Who coverest thyself with light as with a garment: who stretchest out the heavens like a curtain: who layeth the beams of his chambers in the waters: who maketh the clouds his chariot: who walketh upon the wings of the wind: who maketh his angels spirits; his ministers a flaming fire: who laid the foundations of the earth, that it should not be removed for ever. Thou coveredst it with the deep as with a garment: the waters stood above the mountains. At thy rebuke they fled; at the voice of thy thunder they hasted away. They go up by the mountains; they go down by the valleys unto the place which thou hast founded for them. Thou hast set a bound that they may not pass over; that they turn not again to cover the earth.

Psalm 104:1–9, KJV

Which in his times he shall shew, who is the blessed and only Potentate, the King of kings, and Lord of lords; who only hath immortality, dwelling in the light which no man can approach unto; whom no man hath seen, nor can see: to whom be honour and power everlasting. Amen.

1 Timothy 6:15–16, KJV

Immortal, invisible, God only wise,
In light inaccessible hid from our eyes,
Most blessed, most glorious, the Ancient of Days,
Almighty, victorious, thy great Name we praise.

Walter Chalmers Smith, 1824–1908

The Lord, my strength

I will love thee, O LORD, my strength. The LORD is my rock, and my fortress, and my deliverer; my God, my strength, in whom I will trust; my buckler, and the horn of my salvation, and my high tower. I will call upon the LORD, who is worthy to be praised: so shall I be saved from mine enemies. The sorrows of death compassed me, and the floods of ungodly men made me afraid. The sorrows of hell compassed me about: the snares of death prevented me. In my distress I called upon the LORD, and cried unto my God: he heard my voice out of his temple, and my cry came before him, even into his ears. Then the earth shook and trembled; the foundations also of the hills moved and were shaken, because he was wroth.

Psalm 18:1–7, KJV

Be Thou my vision, O Lord of my heart;
Nought be all else to me, save that Thou art;
Thou my best thought, by day or by night,
Waking or sleeping, Thy presence my light.

Be thou my battle-shield, sword for the fight;
Be thou my armour, be Thou my might;
Thou my soul's shelter, Thou my high tower;
Raise thou me heavenward, O Power of my power.

Irish, c. 8th century
translated by Mary Elizabeth Byrne, 1880–1931
versified by Eleanor Henrietta Hull, 1860–1935

To live is Christ

What then? Only that in every way, whether in pretense or in truth, Christ is preached; and in this I rejoice, yes, and will rejoice.

For I know that this will turn out for my deliverance through your prayer and the supply of the Spirit of Jesus Christ, according to my earnest expectation and hope that in nothing I shall be ashamed, but with all boldness, as always, so now also Christ will be magnified in my body, whether by life or by death. For to me, to live is Christ, and to die is gain. But if I live on in the flesh, this will mean fruit from my labor; yet what I shall choose I cannot tell. For I am hard-pressed between the two, having a desire to depart and be with Christ, which is far better. Nevertheless to remain in the flesh is more needful for you. And being confident of this, I know that I shall remain and continue with you all for your progress and joy of faith, that your rejoicing for me may be more abundant in Jesus Christ by my coming to you again.

Only let your conduct be worthy of the gospel of Christ, so that whether I come and see you or am absent, I may hear of your affairs, that you stand fast in one spirit, with one mind striving together for the faith of the gospel, and not in any way terrified by your adversaries, which is to them a proof of perdition, but to you of salvation, and that from God.

Philippians 1:18–28, NKJV

When peace, like a river, attendeth my way,
   When sorrows, like sea-billows, roll,
Whatever my lot, Thou hast taught me to say,
   It is well, it is well with my soul.

For me be it Christ, be it Christ hence to live!
   If Jordan above me shall roll,
No pang shall be mine, for in death as in life
   Thou wilt whisper Thy peace to my soul.

Horatio Gates Spafford, 1828–88

Christ's word in our hearts

Therefore, as the elect of God, holy and beloved, put on tender mercies, kindness, humility, meekness, longsuffering; bearing with one another, and forgiving one another, if anyone has a complaint against another; even as Christ forgave you, so you also must do. But above all these things put on love, which is the bond of perfection. And let the peace of God rule in your hearts, to which also you were called in one body; and be thankful. Let the word of Christ dwell in you richly in all wisdom, teaching and admonishing one another in psalms and hymns and spiritual songs, singing with grace in your hearts to the Lord. And whatever you do in word or deed, do all in the name of the Lord Jesus, giving thanks to God the Father through Him.

Colossians 3:12–17, NKJV

May the Word of God dwell richly
  In my heart from hour to hour.
So that all may see I triumph
  Only through His power.

Katie Barclay Wilkinson, 1859–1928

The call of wisdom

Does not wisdom call out? Does not understanding raise her voice? On the heights along the way, where the paths meet, she takes her stand; beside the gates leading into the city, at the entrances, she cries aloud: "To you, O men, I call out; I raise my voice to all mankind. You who are simple, gain prudence; you who are foolish, gain understanding. Listen, for I have worthy things to say; I open my lips to speak what is right. My mouth speaks what is true, for my lips detest wickedness. All the words of my mouth are just; none of them is crooked or perverse. To the discerning all of them are right; they are faultless to those who have knowledge. Choose my instruction instead of silver, knowledge rather than choice gold, for wisdom is more precious than rubies, and nothing you desire can compare with her."

Proverbs 8:1–11

Wisdom divine! who tells the price
Of wisdom's costly merchandise?
Wisdom to silver we prefer,
And gold is dross compared to her.

Charles Wesley, 1707–88

Jesus' entry into Jerusalem

When they were approaching Jerusalem and had come to Bethphage and Bethany near the Mount of Olives, he sent off two of his disciples with these instructions,

"Go into the village just ahead of you and as soon as you enter it you will find a tethered colt on which no one has yet ridden. Untie it, and bring it here. If anybody asks you, 'Why are you doing this?' just say, 'His master needs him, and will send him back immediately.'"

So they went off and found the colt tethered by a doorway outside in the open street, and they untied it. Some of the bystanders did say, "What are you doing, untying this colt?" but they made the reply Jesus told them to make, and the man raised no objection. So they brought the colt to Jesus, threw their coats on its back, and he took his seat upon it.

Many of the people spread out their coats in his path as he rode along, and others put down rushes which they had cut from the fields. The whole crowd, both those who were in front and those who were behind Jesus, shouted,

"God save him!—God bless the one who comes in the name of the Lord! God bless the coming kingdom of our father David! God save him from on high!"

Jesus entered Jerusalem and went into the Temple and looked round on all that was going on. And then, since it was already late in the day, he went out to Bethany with the twelve.

Mark 11:1–11, PHILLIPS

All glory, laud, and honour
    To Thee, Redeemer, King,
To whom the lips of children
    Made sweet hosannas ring!
Thou art the King of Israel,
    Thou David's royal Son,
Who in the Lord's Name comest,
    The King and blessed One.

Theodulph of Orleans, c. 750–821
translated by John Mason Neale, 1818–66

AUGUST 2

The peace of Christ

Jesus answered and said to him, "If anyone loves Me, he will keep My word; and My Father will love him, and We will come to him and make Our abode with him. He who does not love Me does not keep My words; and the word which you hear is not Mine, but the Father's who sent Me.

"These things I have spoken to you while abiding with you. But the Helper, the Holy Spirit, whom the Father will send in My name, He will teach you all things, and bring to your remembrance all that I said to you. Peace I leave with you; My peace I give to you; not as the world gives do I give to you. Do not let your heart be troubled, nor let it be fearful. You heard that I said to you, 'I go away, and I will come to you.' If you loved Me, you would have rejoiced because I go to the Father, for the Father is greater than I. Now I have told you before it happens, so that when it happens, you may believe. I will not speak much more with you, for the ruler of the world is coming, and he has nothing in Me; but so that the world may know that I love the Father, I do exactly as the Father commanded Me. Get up, let us go from here."

John 14:23–31, NASB

His for ever, only His;
  Who the Lord and me shall part?
Ah, with what a rest of bliss
  Christ can fill the loving heart!
Heaven and earth may fade and flee,
  First-born light in gloom decline,
But while God and I shall be,
  I am His and He is mine.

George Wade Robinson, 1828–77

218

The power of Jesus' name

Now as the lame man who was healed held on to Peter and John, all the people ran together to them in the porch which is called Solomon's, greatly amazed. So when Peter saw it, he responded to the people: "Men of Israel, why do you marvel at this? Or why look so intently at us, as though by our own power or godliness we had made this man walk? The God of Abraham, Isaac, and Jacob, the God of our fathers, glorified His Servant Jesus, whom you delivered up and denied in the presence of Pilate, when he was determined to let Him go. But you denied the Holy One and the Just, and asked for a murderer to be granted to you, and killed the Prince of life, whom God raised from the dead, of which we are witnesses. And His name, through faith in His name, has made this man strong, whom you see and know. Yes, the faith which comes through Him has given him this perfect soundness in the presence of you all."

Acts 3:11–16, NKJV

All hail the power of Jesus' Name!
  Let angels prostrate fall;
Bring forth the royal diadem
  To crown Him Lord of all.

O that with yonder sacred throng
  We at His feet may fall,
Join in the everlasting song,
  And crown Him Lord of all!

Edward Perronet, 1726–92
and
John Rippon, 1751–1836

God's perfect way

With the loyal you show yourself loyal; with the blameless you show yourself blameless; with the pure you show yourself pure, and with the crooked you show yourself perverse. You deliver a humble people, but your eyes are upon the haughty to bring them down. Indeed, you are my lamp, O LORD, the LORD lightens my darkness. By you I can crush a troop, and by my God I can leap over a wall. This God—his way is perfect; the promise of the LORD proves true; he is a shield for all who take refuge in him.

For who is God, but the LORD? And who is a rock, except our God? The God who has girded me with strength has opened wide my path. He made my feet like the feet of deer, and set me secure on the heights. He trains my hands for war, so that my arms can bend a bow of bronze. You have given me the shield of your salvation, and your help has made me great. You have made me stride freely, and my feet do not slip.

2 Samuel 22:26–37, NRSV

Thou God of truth and love,
  We seek Thy perfect way,
Ready Thy choice to approve,
  Thy providence to obey:
Enter into Thy wise design,
And sweetly lose our will in Thine.

Charles Wesley, 1707–88

Asking for wisdom

At Gibeon the LORD appeared to Solomon during the night in a dream, and God said, "Ask for whatever you want me to give you."

Solomon answered, "You have shown great kindness to your servant, my father David, because he was faithful to you and righteous and upright in heart. You have continued this great kindness to him and have given him a son to sit on his throne this very day.

"Now, O LORD my God, you have made your servant king in place of my father David. But I am only a little child and do not know how to carry out my duties. Your servant is here among the people you have chosen, a great people, too numerous to count or number. So give your servant a discerning heart to govern your people and to distinguish between right and wrong. For who is able to govern this great people of yours?"

The Lord was pleased that Solomon had asked for this. So God said to him, "Since you have asked for this and not for long life or wealth for yourself, nor have asked for the death of your enemies but for discernment in administering justice, I will do what you have asked. I will give you a wise and discerning heart, so that there will never have been anyone like you, nor will there ever be. Moreover, I will give you what you have not asked for—both riches and honor—so that in your lifetime you will have no equal among kings. And if you walk in my ways and obey my statutes and commands as David your father did, I will give you a long life." Then Solomon awoke—and he realized it had been a dream.

1 Kings 3:5–15

Be Thou my wisdom, Thou my true word;
I ever with Thee, Thou with me, Lord;
Thou my great Father, I Thy true son;
Thou in me dwelling, and I with Thee one.

Irish, c. 8th century
translated by Mary Elizabeth Byrne, 1880–1931
versified by Eleanor Henrietta Hull, 1860–1935

The quietness of God

And he came thither unto a cave, and lodged there; and, behold, the word of the LORD came to him, and he said unto him, What doest thou here, Elijah? And he said, I have been very jealous for the LORD God of hosts: for the children of Israel have forsaken thy covenant, thrown down thine altars, and slain thy prophets with the sword; and I, even I only, am left; and they seek my life, to take it away. And he said, Go forth, and stand upon the mount before the LORD. And, behold, the LORD passed by, and a great and strong wind rent the mountains, and brake in pieces the rocks before the LORD; but the LORD was not in the wind: and after the wind an earthquake; but the LORD was not in the earthquake: and after the earthquake a fire; but the LORD was not in the fire: and after the fire a still small voice. And it was so, when Elijah heard it, that he wrapped his face in his mantle, and went out, and stood in the entering in of the cave. And, behold, there came a voice unto him, and said, What doest thou here, Elijah? And he said, I have been very jealous for the LORD God of hosts: because the children of Israel have forsaken thy covenant, thrown down thine altars, and slain thy prophets with the sword; and I, even I only, am left; and they seek my life, to take it away. And the LORD said unto him, Go, return on thy way to the wilderness of Damascus: and when thou comest, anoint Hazael to be king over Syria.

1 Kings 19:9–15, KJV

Breathe through the heats of our desire
  Thy coolness and Thy balm;
Let sense be dumb—let flesh retire;
Speak through the earthquake, wind, and fire,
  O still small voice of calm!

John Greenleaf Whittier, 1807–92

My times are in your hand

But I trusted in thee, O LORD: I said, Thou art my God. My times are in thy hand: deliver me from the hand of mine enemies, and from them that persecute me. Make thy face to shine upon thy servant: save me for thy mercies' sake. Let me not be ashamed, O LORD; for I have called upon thee: let the wicked be ashamed, and let them be silent in the grave. Let the lying lips be put to silence; which speak grievous things proudly and contemptuously against the righteous. Oh how great is thy goodness, which thou hast laid up for them that fear thee; which thou hast wrought for them that trust in thee before the sons of men! Thou shalt hide them in the secret of thy presence from the pride of man: thou shalt keep them secretly in a pavilion from the strife of tongues. Blessed be the LORD: for he hath shewed me his marvellous kindness in a strong city. For I said in my haste, I am cut off from before thine eyes: nevertheless thou heardest the voice of my supplications when I cried unto thee. O love the LORD, all ye his saints: for the LORD preserveth the faithful, and plentifully rewardeth the proud doer. Be of good courage, and he shall strengthen your heart, all ye that hope in the LORD.

Psalm 31:14–24, KJV

My times are in Thy hand,
  Whatever they may be,
Pleasing or painful, dark or bright,
  As best may seem to Thee.

My times are in Thy hand:
  Why should I doubt or fear?
A Father's hand will never cause
  His child a needless tear.

William Freeman Lloyd, 1791–1853

The Ancient of Days

I watched till thrones were put in place, and the Ancient of Days was seated; His garment was white as snow, and the hair of His head was like pure wool. His throne was a fiery flame, its wheels a burning fire; a fiery stream issued and came forth from before Him. A thousand thousands ministered to Him; ten thousand times ten thousand stood before Him. The court was seated, and the books were opened. I watched then because of the sound of the pompous words which the horn was speaking; I watched till the beast was slain, and its body destroyed and given to the burning flame. As for the rest of the beasts, they had their dominion taken away, yet their lives were prolonged for a season and a time.

I was watching in the night visions, and behold, One like the Son of Man, coming with the clouds of heaven! He came to the Ancient of Days, and they brought Him near before Him. Then to Him was given dominion and glory and a kingdom, that all peoples, nations, and languages should serve Him. His dominion is an everlasting dominion, which shall not pass away, and His kingdom the one which shall not be destroyed.

Daniel 7:9–14, NKJV

O worship the King,
  All-glorious above,
O gratefully sing
  His power and His love:
Our Shield and Defender,
  The Ancient of Days,
Pavilioned in splendour
  And girded with praise.

Robert Grant, 1779–1838

Before the throne of God

Then one of the elders answered, saying to me, "Who are these arrayed in white robes, and where did they come from?" And I said to him, "Sir, you know." So he said to me, "These are the ones who come out of the great tribulation, and washed their robes and made them white in the blood of the Lamb. Therefore they are before the throne of God, and serve Him day and night in His temple. And He who sits on the throne will dwell among them. They shall neither hunger anymore nor thirst anymore; the sun shall not strike them, nor any heat; for the Lamb who is in the midst of the throne will shepherd them and lead them to living fountains of waters. And God will wipe away every tear from their eyes."

Revelation 7:13–17, NKJV

Glorious things of thee are spoken,
   Zion, city of our God!
He, whose word cannot be broken,
   Formed thee for His own abode.
On the Rock of Ages founded,
   What can shake thy sure repose?
With salvation's walls surrounded,
   Thou may'st smile at all thy foes.

Round each habitation hovering,
   See! the cloud and fire appear,
For a glory and a covering,
   Showing that the Lord is near:
Blest inhabitants of Zion,
   Washed in the Redeemer's blood—
Jesus, whom their souls rely on,
   Makes them kings and priests to God.

John Newton, 1725–1807

The unending reign

Then the seventh angel sounded; and there were loud voices in heaven, saying,

"The kingdom of the world has become the kingdom of our Lord and of His Christ; and He will reign forever and ever." And the twenty-four elders, who sit on their thrones before God, fell on their faces and worshiped God, saying,

"We give You thanks, O Lord God, the Almighty, who are and who were, because You have taken Your great power and have begun to reign. And the nations were enraged, and Your wrath came, and the time came for the dead to be judged, and the time to reward Your bond-servants the prophets and the saints and those who fear Your name, the small and the great, and to destroy those who destroy the earth."

And the temple of God which is in heaven was opened; and the ark of His covenant appeared in His temple, and there were flashes of lightning and sounds and peals of thunder and an earthquake and a great hailstorm.

Revelation 11:15–19, NASB

Praise Him, praise Him! Jesus, our blessed Redeemer;
  Sing, O earth, His wonderful love proclaim!
Hail Him, hail Him! highest archangels in glory,
  Strength and honour give to His holy Name.
Like a shepherd, Jesus will guard His children,
  In His arms He carries them all day long;
O ye saints that dwell in the mountains of Zion,
  Praise Him, praise Him! ever in joyful song.

Frances Jane Van Alstyne, 1820–1915

AUGUST 11

"They overcame him"

And there was war in heaven, Michael and his angels waging war with the dragon. The dragon and his angels waged war, and they were not strong enough, and there was no longer a place found for them in heaven. And the great dragon was thrown down, the serpent of old who is called the devil and Satan, who deceives the whole world; he was thrown down to the earth, and his angels were thrown down with him. Then I heard a loud voice in heaven, saying,

"Now the salvation, and the power, and the kingdom of our God and the authority of His Christ have come, for the accuser of our brethren has been thrown down, he who accuses them before our God day and night. And they overcame him because of the blood of the Lamb and because of the word of their testimony, and they did not love their life even when faced with death. For this reason, rejoice, O heavens and you who dwell in them. Woe to the earth and the sea, because the devil has come down to you, having great wrath, knowing that he has only a short time."

Revelation 12:7–12, NASB

Give me the wings of faith to rise
  Within the veil, and see
The saints above, how great their joys,
  How bright their glories be.

Once they were mourning here below,
  With sighing and with tears;
They wrestled hard, as we do now,
  With sins and doubts and fears.

I ask them whence their victory came;
  They, with united breath,
Ascribe their conquest to the Lamb,
  Their triumph to His death.

Isaac Watts, 1674–1748

AUGUST 12

Rest for the saints

And I saw another angel flying in midheaven, having an eternal gospel to preach to those who live on the earth, and to every nation and tribe and tongue and people; and he said with a loud voice, "Fear God, and give Him glory, because the hour of His judgment has come; worship Him who made the heaven and the earth and sea and springs of waters."

And another angel, a second one, followed, saying, "Fallen, fallen is Babylon the great, she who has made all the nations drink of the wine of the passion of her immorality."

Then another angel, a third one, followed them, saying with a loud voice, "If anyone worships the beast and his image, and receives a mark on his forehead or on his hand, he also will drink of the wine of the wrath of God, which is mixed in full strength in the cup of His anger; and he will be tormented with fire and brimstone in the presence of the holy angels and in the presence of the Lamb. And the smoke of their torment goes up forever and ever; they have no rest day and night, those who worship the beast and his image, and whoever receives the mark of his name." Here is the perseverance of the saints who keep the commandments of God and their faith in Jesus.

And I heard a voice from heaven, saying, "Write, 'Blessed are the dead who die in the Lord from now on!'" "Yes," says the Spirit, "so that they may rest from their labors, for their deeds follow with them."

Revelation 14:6–13, NASB

For all the saints who from their labours rest,
Who Thee by faith before the world confessed,
Thy name, O Jesu, be for ever blest.
  Alleluia!

Thou wast their Rock, their Fortress, and their Might;
Thou, Lord, their Captain in the well fought fight;
Thou in the darkness drear their one true Light.
  Alleluia!

O may Thy soldiers, faithful, true, and bold,
Fight as the saints who nobly fought of old,
And win, with them, the victor's crown of gold!
  Alleluia!

William Walsham How, 1823–97

True freedom

So Jesus said to the Jews who believed in him, "If you are faithful to what I have said, you are truly my disciples. And you will know the truth and the truth will set you free!"

"But we are descendants of Abraham," they replied, "and we have never in our lives been any man's slaves. How can you say to us, 'You will be set free'?"

Jesus returned, "Believe me when I tell you that every man who commits sin is a slave. For a slave is no permanent part of a household, but a son is. If the Son, then, sets you free, you are really free! I know that you are descended from Abraham, but some of you are looking for a way to kill me because you can't bear my words. I am telling you what I have seen in the presence of my Father, and you are doing what you have seen in the presence of your father."

"Our father is Abraham!" they retorted.

"If you were the children of Abraham, you would do the sort of things Abraham did. But in fact you are looking for a way to kill me, simply because I am a man who has told you the truth that I have heard from God. Abraham would never have done that. No, you are doing your father's work."

"We are not illegitimate!" they retorted. "We have one Father—God."

John 8:31–41, PHILLIPS

Long my imprisoned spirit lay
  Fast bound in sin and nature's night;
Thine eye diffused a quickening ray,
  I woke, the dungeon flamed with light;
My chains fell off, my heart was free,
I rose, went forth, and followed Thee.

Charles Wesley, 1707–88

Freedom in Christ

For freedom Christ has set us free. Stand firm, therefore, and do not submit again to a yoke of slavery.

Listen! I, Paul, am telling you that if you let yourselves be circumcised, Christ will be of no benefit to you. Once again I testify to every man who lets himself be circumcised that he is obliged to obey the entire law. You who want to be justified by the law have cut yourselves off from Christ; you have fallen away from grace. For through the Spirit, by faith, we eagerly wait for the hope of righteousness. For in Christ Jesus neither circumcision nor uncircumcision counts for anything; the only thing that counts is faith working through love.

You were running well; who prevented you from obeying the truth? Such persuasion does not come from the one who calls you. A little yeast leavens the whole batch of dough. I am confident about you in the Lord that you will not think otherwise. But whoever it is that is confusing you will pay the penalty. But my friends, why am I still being persecuted if I am still preaching circumcision? In that case the offense of the cross has been removed. I wish those who unsettle you would castrate themselves!

Galatians 5:1–12, NRSV

Give us holy freedom,
 Fill our hearts with love,
Draw us, holy Jesus,
 To the realms above.

George Rundle Prynne, 1818–1903

God, our friend

And Moses took the tabernacle, and pitched it without the camp, afar off from the camp, and called it the Tabernacle of the congregation. And it came to pass, that every one which sought the LORD went out unto the tabernacle of the congregation, which was without the camp. And it came to pass, when Moses went out unto the tabernacle, that all the people rose up, and stood every man at his tent door, and looked after Moses, until he was gone into the tabernacle. And it came to pass, as Moses entered into the tabernacle, the cloudy pillar descended, and stood at the door of the tabernacle, and the LORD talked with Moses. And all the people saw the cloudy pillar stand at the tabernacle door: and all the people rose up and worshipped, every man in his tent door. And the LORD spake unto Moses face to face, as a man speaketh unto his friend. And he turned again into the camp: but his servant Joshua, the son of Nun, a young man, departed not out of the tabernacle.

Exodus 33:7–11, KJV

A man that hath friends must shew himself friendly: and there is a friend that sticketh closer than a brother.

Proverbs 18:24, KJV

I've found a Friend, O such a Friend,
  So kind, and true, and tender!
So wise a Counsellor and Guide,
  So mighty a Defender!
From Him who loves me now so well
  What power my soul can sever?
Shall life or death, or earth or hell?
  No! I am His for ever.

James Grindlay Small, 1817–88

The final harvest

Another parable put he forth unto them, saying, The kingdom of heaven is likened unto a man which sowed good seed in his field: But while men slept, his enemy came and sowed tares among the wheat, and went his way. But when the blade was sprung up, and brought forth fruit, then appeared the tares also. So the servants of the householder came and said unto him, Sir, didst not thou sow good seed in thy field? from whence then hath it tares? He said unto them, An enemy hath done this. The servants said unto him, Wilt thou then that we go and gather them up? But he said, Nay; lest while ye gather up the tares, ye root up also the wheat with them. Let both grow together until the harvest: and in the time of harvest I will say to the reapers, Gather ye together first the tares, and bind them in bundles to burn them: but gather the wheat into my barn.

Matthew 13:24–30, KJV

All the world is God's own field,
Fruit unto His praise to yield;
Wheat and tares together sown,
Unto joy or sorrow grown;
First the blade, and then the ear,
Then the full corn shall appear:
Lord of harvest, grant that we
Wholesome grain and pure may be.

Even so, Lord, quickly come
To Thy final harvest-home:
Gather Thou Thy people in,
Free from sorrow, free from sin;
There, for ever purified,
In Thy presence to abide:
Come, with all Thine angels come,
Raise the glorious harvest-home.

Henry Alford, 1810–71

The light of God's word

Thy word is a lamp unto my feet, and a light unto my path. I have sworn, and I will perform it, that I will keep thy righteous judgments. I am afflicted very much: quicken me, O LORD, according unto thy word. Accept, I beseech thee, the freewill offerings of my mouth, O LORD, and teach me thy judgments. My soul is continually in my hand: yet do I not forget thy law. The wicked have laid a snare for me: yet I erred not from thy precepts. Thy testimonies have I taken as an heritage for ever: for they are the rejoicing of my heart. I have inclined mine heart to perform thy statutes alway, even unto the end.

Psalm 119:105–12, KJV

For as the rain cometh down, and the snow from heaven, and returneth not thither, but watereth the earth, and maketh it bring forth and bud, that it may give seed to the sower, and bread to the eater: So shall my word be that goeth forth out of my mouth: it shall not return unto me void, but it shall accomplish that which I please, and it shall prosper in the thing whereto I sent it.

Isaiah 55:10–11, KJV

O Word of God incarnate,
  O Wisdom from on high,
O Truth unchanged, unchanging,
  O Light of our dark sky,
We praise Thee for the radiance
  That from the hallowed page,
A lantern to our footsteps,
  Shines on from age to age.

William Walsham How, 1823–97

Melt my heart, O God

And he saith unto the man which had the withered hand, Stand forth. And he saith unto them, Is it lawful to do good on the sabbath days, or to do evil? to save life, or to kill? But they held their peace. And when he had looked round about on them with anger, being grieved for the hardness of their hearts, he saith unto the man, Stretch forth thine hand. And he stretched it out: and his hand was restored whole as the other. And the Pharisees went forth, and straightway took counsel with the Herodians against him, how they might destroy him.

Mark 3:3–6, KJV

Wherefore (as the Holy Ghost saith, To day if ye will hear his voice, harden not your hearts, as in the provocation, in the day of temptation in the wilderness: when your fathers tempted me, proved me, and saw my works forty years. Wherefore I was grieved with that generation, and said, They do alway err in their heart; and they have not known my ways. So I sware in my wrath, They shall not enter into my rest.)

Take heed, brethren, lest there be in any of you an evil heart of unbelief, in departing from the living God. But exhort one another daily, while it is called To day; lest any of you be hardened through the deceitfulness of sin.

Hebrews 3:7–13, KJV

The stone to flesh again convert,
  The veil of sin again remove;
Sprinkle thy blood upon my heart,
  And melt it by Thy dying love;
This rebel heart by love subdue,
And make it soft, and make it new.

Charles Wesley, 1707–88

"To whom shall we go?"

Therefore many of His disciples, when they heard this, said, "This is a hard saying; who can understand it?" When Jesus knew in Himself that His disciples complained about this, He said to them, "Does this offend you? What then if you should see the Son of Man ascend where He was before? It is the Spirit who gives life; the flesh profits nothing. The words that I speak to you are spirit, and they are life. But there are some of you who do not believe." For Jesus knew from the beginning who they were who did not believe, and who would betray Him. And He said, "Therefore I have said to you that no one can come to Me unless it has been granted to him by My Father." From that time many of His disciples went back and walked with Him no more. Then Jesus said to the twelve, "Do you also want to go away?" But Simon Peter answered Him, "Lord, to whom shall we go? You have the words of eternal life. Also we have come to believe and know that You are the Christ, the Son of the living God." Jesus answered them, "Did I not choose you, the twelve, and one of you is a devil?" He spoke of Judas Iscariot, the son of Simon, for it was he who would betray Him, being one of the twelve.

John 6:60–71, NKJV

I need thee every hour, most gracious Lord;
No tender voice like Thine can peace afford.

I need Thee, O I need Thee! every hour I need Thee;
O bless me now, my Saviour! I come to Thee.

Annie Sherwood Hawks, 1835–1918

The fellowship of the church

But to each one of us grace was given according to the measure of Christ's gift. Therefore He says: "When He ascended on high, He led captivity captive, and gave gifts to men." (Now this, "He ascended"— what does it mean but that He also first descended into the lower parts of the earth? He who descended is also the One who ascended far above all the heavens, that He might fill all things.) And He Himself gave some to be apostles, some prophets, some evangelists, and some pastors and teachers, for the equipping of the saints for the work of ministry, for the edifying of the body of Christ, till we all come to the unity of the faith and of the knowledge of the Son of God, to a perfect man, to the measure of the stature of the fullness of Christ; that we should no longer be children, tossed to and fro and carried about with every wind of doctrine, by the trickery of men, in the cunning craftiness of deceitful plotting, but, speaking the truth in love, may grow up in all things into Him who is the head—Christ—from whom the whole body, joined and knit together by what every joint supplies, according to the effective working by which every part does its share, causes growth of the body for the edifying of itself in love.

Ephesians 4:7–16, NKJV

Move and actuate and guide;
Divers gifts to each divide;
Placed according to Thy will,
Let us all our work fulfil;
Never from our office move;
Needful to each other prove;
Use the grace on each bestowed,
Tempered by the art of God.

Charles Wesley, 1707–88

AUGUST 21

Joy in Jerusalem

I was glad when they said unto me, Let us go into the house of the LORD. Our feet shall stand within thy gates, O Jerusalem. Jerusalem is builded as a city that is compact together: Whither the tribes go up, the tribes of the LORD, unto the testimony of Israel, to give thanks unto the name of the LORD. For there are set thrones of judgment, the thrones of the house of David. Pray for the peace of Jerusalem: they shall prosper that love thee. Peace be within thy walls, and prosperity within thy palaces. For my brethren and companions' sakes, I will now say, Peace be within thee. Because of the house of the LORD our God I will seek thy good.

Psalm 122:1–9, KJV

How pleased and blest was I
To hear the people cry,
  "Come, let us seek our God today!"
Yes, with a cheerful zeal
We haste to Zion's hill,
  And there our vows and honours pay.

My tongue repeats her vows,
Peace to this sacred house!
  For there my friends and kindred dwell;
And, since my glorious God
Makes thee His blest abode,
  My soul shall ever love thee well!

Isaac Watts, 1674–1748

The city of our God

Great is the LORD, and greatly to be praised in the city of our God, in the mountain of his holiness. Beautiful for situation, the joy of the whole earth, is mount Zion, on the sides of the north, the city of the great King. God is known in her palaces for a refuge. . . . As we have heard, so have we seen in the city of the LORD of hosts, in the city of our God: God will establish it for ever. Selah. We have thought of thy lovingkindness, O God, in the midst of thy temple. According to thy name, O God, so is thy praise unto the ends of the earth: thy right hand is full of righteousness. Let mount Zion rejoice, let the daughters of Judah be glad, because of thy judgments. Walk about Zion, and go round about her: tell the towers thereof. Mark ye well her bulwarks, consider her palaces; that ye may tell it to the generation following. For this God is our God for ever and ever: he will be our guide even unto death.

Psalm 48:1–3,8–14, KJV

The hill of Zion yields
  A thousand sacred sweets,
Before we reach the heavenly fields,
  Or walk the golden streets.

Then let our songs abound,
  And every tear be dry;
We're marching through Immanuel's ground
  To fairer worlds on high.

Isaac Watts, 1674–1748

The love of Jesus

The Revelation of Jesus Christ, which God gave Him to show to His bond-servants, the things which must soon take place; and He sent and communicated it by His angel to His bond-servant John, who testified to the word of God and to the testimony of Jesus Christ, even to all that he saw. Blessed is he who reads and those who hear the words of the prophecy, and heed the things which are written in it; for the time is near.

John to the seven churches that are in Asia: Grace to you and peace, from Him who is and who was and who is to come, and from the seven Spirits who are before His throne, and from Jesus Christ, the faithful witness, the firstborn of the dead, and the ruler of the kings of the earth. To Him who loves us and released us from our sins by His blood—and He has made us to be a kingdom, priests to His God and Father—to Him be the glory and the dominion forever and ever. Amen.

Revelation 1:1–6, NASB

Jesus loves me, this I know,
For the Bible tells me so;
Little ones to Him belong,
They are weak, but He is strong.

Yes, Jesus loves me,
Yes, Jesus loves me,
Yes, Jesus loves me,
The Bible tells me so.

Anna Bartlett Warner, 1827–1915

Fulfilling our calling

Blessed are you when people insult you, persecute you and falsely say all kinds of evil against you because of me. Rejoice and be glad, because great is your reward in heaven, for in the same way they persecuted the prophets who were before you.

You are the salt of the earth. But if the salt loses its saltiness, how can it be made salty again? It is no longer good for anything, except to be thrown out and trampled by men.

You are the light of the world. A city on a hill cannot be hidden. Neither do people light a lamp and put it under a bowl. Instead they put it on its stand, and it gives light to everyone in the house. In the same way, let your light shine before men, that they may see your good deeds and praise your Father in heaven.

Matthew 5:11–16

A charge to keep I have,
  A God to glorify,
A never-dying soul to save,
  And fit it for the sky:

To serve the present age,
  My calling to fulfil:
O may it all my powers engage
  To do my Master's will!

Charles Wesley, 1707–88

AUGUST 25

Christ, our cornerstone

Have done, then, with all evil and deceit, all pretence and jealousy and slander. You are babies, newborn in God's family, and you should be crying out for unadulterated spiritual milk to make you grow up to salvation! And so you will, if you have already tasted the goodness of the Lord.

You have come to the living Stone despised indeed by men but chosen and greatly honoured by God. So you yourselves, as living stones, must be built tip into a spiritual House of God, in which you become a holy priesthoods able to offer those sacrifices which are acceptable to God by Jesus Christ.

Behold, I lay in Zion a chief corner stone, elect, precious:

And he that believeth on him into shall not be put to shame. It is to you who believeth on him that he is "precious," but to those who disobey God, it is true that:

The stone which the builders rejected, The same was made the head of the corner. And he is, to them, A stone of stumbling and a rock of offence. Yes, they stumble at the Word of God for in their hearts they are unwilling to obey it—which makes stumbling a foregone conclusion.

1 Peter 2:1–8, PHILLIPS

Christ is our Corner-stone,
　On Him alone we build;
With His true saints alone
　The courts of heaven are filled;
On His great love
　Our hopes we place
　Of present grace
And joys above.

Latin, 6th or 7th century
translated by John Chandler, 1806–76

Seeing the King

He who walks righteously and speaks uprightly, he who despises the gain of oppressions, who gestures with his hands, refusing bribes, who stops his ears from hearing of bloodshed, and shuts his eyes from seeing evil: He will dwell on high; his place of defense will be the fortress of rocks; bread will be given him, his water will be sure.

Your eyes will see the King in His beauty; they will see the land that is very far off. Your heart will meditate on terror: "Where is the scribe? Where is he who weighs? Where is he who counts the towers?" You will not see a fierce people, a people of obscure speech, beyond perception, of a stammering tongue that you cannot understand.

Look upon Zion, the city of our appointed feasts; your eyes will see Jerusalem, a quiet home, a tabernacle that will not be taken down; not one of its stakes will ever be removed, nor will any of its cords be broken. But there the majestic LORD will be for us a place of broad rivers and streams.

Isaiah 33:15–21, NKJV

The King there, in His beauty,
   Without a veil is seen;
It were a well-spent journey,
   Though seven deaths lay between;
The Lamb with His fair army
   Doth on Mount Zion stand,
And glory, glory dwelleth
   In Immanuel's land.

The bride eyes not her garment,
   But her dear bridegroom's face;
I will not gaze at glory,
   But on my King of grace;
Not at the crown He giveth,
   But on His pierced hand:
The Lamb is all the glory
   Of Immanuel's land.

Anne Ross Cousin, 1824–1906

243

Delighting in the Lord

The LORD is the portion of mine inheritance and of my cup: thou maintainest my lot. The lines are fallen unto me in pleasant places; yea, I have a goodly heritage. I will bless the LORD, who hath given me counsel: my reins also instruct me in the night seasons. I have set the LORD always before me: because he is at my right hand, I shall not be moved. Therefore my heart is glad, and my glory rejoiceth: my flesh also shall rest in hope. For thou wilt not leave my soul in hell; neither wilt thou suffer thine Holy One to see corruption. Thou wilt shew me the path of life: in thy presence is fulness of joy; at thy right hand there are pleasures for evermore.

Psalm 16:5–11, KJV

Jesus, the very thought of Thee
　With sweetness fills my breast;
But sweeter far Thy face to see,
　And in Thy presence rest.

Jesus, our only joy be Thou,
　As Thou our prize wilt be;
Jesus, be Thou our glory now,
　And through eternity.

Bernard of Clairvaux, 1091–1153
translated by Edward Caswall, 1814–78

Finishing the course

In the presence of God and of Christ Jesus, who is to judge the living and the dead, and in view of his appearing and his kingdom, I solemnly urge you: proclaim the message; be persistent whether the time is favorable or unfavorable; convince, rebuke, and encourage, with the utmost patience in teaching. For the time is coming when people will not put up with sound doctrine, but having itching ears, they will accumulate for themselves teachers to suit their own desires, and will turn away from listening to the truth and wander away to myths. As for you, always be sober, endure suffering, do the work of an evangelist, carry out your ministry fully.

As for me, I am already being poured out as a libation, and the time of my departure has come. I have fought the good fight, I have finished the race, I have kept the faith. From now on there is reserved for me the crown of righteousness, which the Lord, the righteous judge, will give me on that day, and not only to me but also to all who have longed for his appearing.

2 Timothy 4:1–8, NRSV

Run the straight race through God's good grace,
Lift up thine eyes and seek His face;
Life with its path before thee lies,
Christ is the way, and Christ the prize.

Faint not nor fear, His arms are near;
He changeth not, and thou art dear;
Only believe, and thou shalt see
That Christ is all in all to thee.

John Samuel Bewley Monsell, 1811–75

AUGUST 29

The giver of all things

Blessed are You, O L ORD God of Israel our father, forever and ever.
Yours, O L ORD, is the greatness and the power and the glory and the
victory and the majesty, indeed everything that is in the heavens and
the earth; Yours is the dominion, O L ORD, and You exalt Yourself as
head over all. Both riches and honor come from You, and You rule
over all, and in Your hand is power and might; and it lies in Your
hand to make great and to strengthen everyone. Now therefore, our
God, we thank You, and praise Your glorious name.

But who am I and who are my people that we should be able to
offer as generously as this? For all things come from You, and from
Your hand we have given You. For we are sojourners before You, and
tenants, as all our fathers were; our days on the earth are like a
shadow, and there is no hope. O L ORD our God, all this abundance
that we have provided to build You a house for Your holy name, it is
from Your hand, and all is Yours.

1 Chronicles 29:10–16, NASB

O Lord of heaven, and earth, and sea,
To Thee all praise and glory be;
How shall we show our love to Thee,
  Who givest all?

To Thee from whom we all derive
Our life our gifts, our power to give!
O may we ever with Thee live,
  Who givest all!

Christopher Wordsworth, 1807–85

Loving the Savior

Let him kiss me with the kisses of his mouth! For your love is better than wine, your anointing oils are fragrant, your name is perfume poured out; therefore the maidens love you. Draw me after you, let us make haste. The king has brought me into his chambers. We will exult and rejoice in you; we will extol your love more than wine; rightly do they love you.

Song of Songs 1:2–4, NRSV

One of the Pharisees asked Jesus to eat with him, and he went into the Pharisee's house and took his place at the table. And a woman in the city, who was a sinner, having learned that he was eating in the Pharisee's house, brought an alabaster jar of ointment. She stood behind him at his feet, weeping, and began to bathe his feet with her tears and to dry them with her hair. Then she continued kissing his feet and anointing them with the ointment.

Luke 7:36–38, NRSV

There is a Name I love to hear;
  I love to sing its worth;
It sounds like music in mine ear,
  The sweetest Name on earth.

O how I love the Saviour's name,
  The sweetest name on earth.

Jesus, the Name I love so well,
  The Name I love to hear:
No saint on earth its worth can tell,
  No heart conceive how dear.

Frederick Whitfield, 1829–1904

The great Shepherd

You who bring good tidings to Zion, go up on a high mountain. You who bring good tidings to Jerusalem, lift up your voice with a shout, lift it up, do not be afraid; say to the towns of Judah, "Here is your God!" See, the Sovereign LORD comes with power, and his arm rules for him. See, his reward is with him, and his recompense accompanies him. He tends his flock like a shepherd: He gathers the lambs in his arms and carries them close to his heart; he gently leads those that have young.

Isaiah 40:9–11

For thus says the Lord GOD: "Indeed I Myself will search for My sheep and seek them out. As a shepherd seeks out his flock on the day he is among his scattered sheep, so will I seek out My sheep and deliver them from all the places where they were scattered on a cloudy and dark day. And I will bring them out from the peoples and gather them from the countries, and will bring them to their own land; I will feed them on the mountains of Israel, in the valleys and in all the inhabited places of the country. I will feed them in good pasture, and their fold shall be on the high mountains of Israel. There they shall lie down in a good fold and feed in rich pasture on the mountains of Israel. I will feed My flock, and I will make them lie down," says the Lord GOD. "I will seek what was lost and bring back what was driven away, bind up the broken and strengthen what was sick; but I will destroy the fat and the strong, and feed them in judgment."

Ezekiel 34:11–16, NKJV

Saviour, like a shepherd lead us,
  Much we need Thy tender care;
In Thy pleasant pastures feed us;
  For our use Thy folds prepare:
    Blessed Jesus!
  Thou hast bought us, Thine we are.

Anonymous

As white as snow

Hear the word of the LORD, ye rulers of Sodom; give ear unto the law of our God, ye people of Gomorrah. To what purpose is the multitude of your sacrifices unto me? saith the LORD: I am full of the burnt offerings of rams, and the fat of fed beasts; and I delight not in the blood of bullocks, or of lambs, or of he goats. When ye come to appear before me, who hath required this at your hand, to tread my courts? Bring no more vain oblations; incense is an abomination unto me; the new moons and sabbaths, the calling of assemblies, I cannot away with; it is iniquity, even the solemn meeting. Your new moons and your appointed feasts my soul hateth: they are a trouble unto me; I am weary to bear them. And when ye spread forth your hands, I will hide mine eyes from you: yea, when ye make many prayers, I will not hear: your hands are full of blood. Wash you, make you clean; put away the evil of your doings from before mine eyes; cease to do evil; learn to do well; seek judgment, relieve the oppressed, judge the fatherless, plead for the widow.

Come now, and let us reason together, saith the LORD: though your sins be as scarlet, they shall be as white as snow; though they be red like crimson, they shall be as wool.

Isaiah 1:10–18, KJV

What a wonderful redemption!
  Never can a mortal know
How my sin, tho' red like crimson,
  Can be whiter than the snow.

All that thrills my soul is Jesus;
  He is more than life to me;
And the fairest of ten thousand,
  In my blessed Lord I see.

Thoro Harris, 1874–1955

The Lord's servant

"Behold! My Servant whom I uphold, My Elect One in whom My soul delights! I have put My Spirit upon Him; He will bring forth justice to the Gentiles. He will not cry out, nor raise His voice, nor cause His voice to be heard in the street. A bruised reed He will not break, and smoking flax He will not quench; He will bring forth justice for truth. He will not fail nor be discouraged, till He has established justice in the earth; and the coastlands shall wait for His law."

Thus says God the LORD, who created the heavens and stretched them out, who spread forth the earth and that which comes from it, who gives breath to the people on it, and spirit to those who walk on it: "I, the LORD, have called You in righteousness, and will hold Your hand; I will keep You and give You as a covenant to the people, as a light to the Gentiles, to open blind eyes, to bring out prisoners from the prison, those who sit in darkness from the prison house."

Isaiah 42:1–7, NKJV

With joy we meditate the grace
    Of our High Priest above;
His heart is made of tenderness,
    And overflows with love.

He'll never quench the smoking flax,
    But raise it to a flame;
The bruised reed He never breaks,
    Nor scorns the meanest name.

Then let our humble faith address
    His mercy and His power:
We shall obtain delivering grace
    In the distressing hour.

Isaac Watts, 1674–1748

Clothed in God's righteousness

For I, the LORD, love justice; I hate robbery for burnt offering; I will direct their work in truth, and will make with them an everlasting covenant. Their descendants shall be known among the Gentiles, and their offspring among the people. All who see them shall acknowledge them, that they are the posterity whom the LORD has blessed.

I will greatly rejoice in the LORD, my soul shall be joyful in my God; for He has clothed me with the garments of salvation, He has covered me with the robe of righteousness, as a bridegroom decks himself with ornaments, and as a bride adorns herself with her jewels. For as the earth brings forth its bud, as the garden causes the things that are sown in it to spring forth, so the Lord GOD will cause righteousness and praise to spring forth before all the nations.

Isaiah 61:8–11, NKJV

A debtor to mercy alone,
  Of covenant mercy I sing;
Nor fear, with Thy righteousness on,
  My person and offering to bring;
The terrors of law and of God
  With me can have nothing to do;
My Saviour's obedience and blood
  Hide all my transgressions from view.

Augustus Montague Toplady, 1740–78

Resting in God

Therefore, since a promise remains of entering His rest, let us fear lest any of you seem to have come short of it. For indeed the gospel was preached to us as well as to them; but the word which they heard did not profit them, not being mixed with faith in those who heard it. For we who have believed do enter that rest, as He has said: "So I swore in My wrath, 'They shall not enter My rest,'" although the works were finished from the foundation of the world. For He has spoken in a certain place of the seventh day in this way: "And God rested on the seventh day from all His works"; and again in this place: "They shall not enter My rest."

Hebrews 4:1–5, NKJV

O give Thine own sweet rest to me,
  That I may speak with soothing power
A word in season, as from thee,
  To weary ones in needful hour.

Frances Ridley Havergal, 1836–79

Commitment from the heart

Because, whatever you do, eating or drinking or anything else, everything should be done to bring glory to God.

Do nothing that might make man stumble, whether they are Jews or Greeks or members of the church of God. I myself try to be agreeable to all men without considering my own advantage but that of the majority, that if possible they may be saved.

Copy me, my brothers, as I copy Christ himself.

1 Corinthians 10:31–11:1, PHILLIPS

We are near the end of all things now, and you should therefore be calm, self-controlled men of prayer. Above everything else be sure that you have real deep love for each other, remembering how love can cover a multitude of sins. Be hospitable to each lo other without secretly, wishing you hadn't got to be! Serve one another with the particular gifts God has given each of you, as faithful dispensers of the wonderfully varied grace of God. If any of you is a preacher then he should preach his message as from God. And in whatever way a man serves the Church he should do it recognizing the fact that God gives him his ability, so that God may be glorified in everything through Jesus Christ. To him belong glory and power for ever, amen!

1 Peter 4:7–11, PHILLIPS

Fill every part of me with praise;
　Let all my being speak
Of thee and of Thy love, O Lord,
　Poor though I be and weak.

So shall no part of day or night
　From sacredness be free;
But all my life, in every step,
　Be fellowship with Thee.

Horatius Bonar, 1808–89

Loved with everlasting love

"At that time," declares the LORD, "I will be the God of all the families of Israel, and they shall be My people."

Thus says the LORD, "The people who survived the sword found grace in the wilderness—Israel, when it went to find its rest." The LORD appeared to him from afar, saying, "I have loved you with an everlasting love; therefore I have drawn you with lovingkindness. Again I will build you and you will be rebuilt, O virgin of Israel! Again you will take up your tambourines, and go forth to the dances of the merrymakers. Again you will plant vineyards on the hills of Samaria; the planters will plant and will enjoy them. For there will be a day when watchmen on the hills of Ephraim call out, 'Arise, and let us go up to Zion, to the LORD our God.'"

Jeremiah 31:1–6, NASB

Loved with everlasting love,
  Led by grace that love to know,
Spirit, breathing from above,
  Thou hast taught me it is so.
O this full and perfect peace!
  O this transport all divine!
In a love which cannot cease,
  I am His and He is mine.

George Wade Robinson, 1838–77

Coming to life

He said to me, "Mortal, can these bones live?" I answered, "O Lord GOD, you know." Then he said to me, "Prophesy to these bones, and say to them: O dry bones, hear the word of the LORD. Thus says the Lord GOD to these bones: I will cause breath to enter you, and you shall live. I will lay sinews on you, and will cause flesh to come upon you, and cover you with skin, and put breath in you, and you shall live; and you shall know that I am the LORD."

So I prophesied as I had been commanded; and as I prophesied, suddenly there was a noise, a rattling, and the bones came together, bone to its bone. I looked, and there were sinews on them, and flesh had come upon them, and skin had covered them; but there was no breath in them. Then he said to me, "Prophesy to the breath, prophesy, mortal, and say to the breath: Thus says the Lord GOD: Come from the four winds, O breath, and breathe upon these slain, that they may live." I prophesied as he commanded me, and the breath came into them, and they lived, and stood on their feet, a vast multitude.

Ezekiel 37:3–10, NRSV

But God, who is rich in mercy, out of the great love with which he loved us even when we were dead through our trespasses, made us alive together with Christ—by grace you have been saved.

Ephesians 2:4–5, NRSV

Lord, I was dead! I could not stir
  My lifeless soul to come to Thee;
But now, since Thou hast quickened me,
  I rise from sin's dark sepulchre.

William Tidd Matson, 1833–99

Into Christ's fold

Then Jesus said, "Believe me when I tell you that anyone who does not enter the sheepfold through the door, but climbs in by some other way, is a thief and a rogue. It is the shepherd of the flock who goes in by the door. It is to him the doorkeeper opens the door and it is his voice that the sheep recognise. He calls his own sheep by name and leads them out of the fold, and when he has brought all his own flock outside, he goes in front of them himself, and the sheep follow him because they know his voice. They will never follow a stranger— indeed, they will run away from him, for they do not recognise strange voices."

Jesus gave them this illustration but they did not grasp the point of what he was saying to them. So Jesus said to them once more, "I do assure you that I myself am the door for the sheep. All who have gone before me are like thieves and rogues, but the sheep did not listen to them. I am the door. If a man goes in through me, he will be safe and sound; he can come in and out and find his food. The thief comes only to steal, to kill and to destroy, but I have come to bring them life in its fullness."

John 10:1–10, PHILLIPS

Out of the fear and dread of the tomb,
  Jesus, I come; Jesus, I come;
Into the joy and light of Thy home,
  Jesus, I come to Thee.
Out of the depths of ruin untold,
Into the peace of Thy sheltering fold,
Ever Thy glorious face to behold,
  Jesus, I come to Thee.

William True Sleeper, 1840–1920

Returning to God

"Come, let us return to the LORD. For He has torn us, but He will heal us; He has wounded us, but He will bandage us. He will revive us after two days; He will raise us up on the third day, that we may live before Him. So let us know, let us press on to know the LORD. His going forth is as certain as the dawn; and He will come to us like the rain, like the spring rain watering the earth."

What shall I do with you, O Ephraim? What shall I do with you, O Judah? For your loyalty is like a morning cloud and like the dew which goes away early.

Hosea 6:1–4, NASB

Come, let us to the Lord our God
  With contrite hearts return:
Our God is gracious, nor will leave
  The desolate to mourn.

Long hath the night of sorrow reigned;
  The dawn shall bring us light;
God shall appear, and we shall rise
  With gladness in His sight.

Our hearts, if God we seek to know,
  Shall know Him and rejoice;
His coming like the morn shall be,
  Like morning songs His voice.

Scottish Paraphrases, 1781

Preparing to meet God

Therefore thus I will do to you, O Israel; because I will do this to you, prepare to meet your God, O Israel!

For lo, the one who forms the mountains, creates the wind, reveals his thoughts to mortals, makes the morning darkness, and treads on the heights of the earth—the LORD, the God of hosts, is his name!

Hear this word that I take up over you in lamentation, O house of Israel:

Fallen, no more to rise, is maiden Israel; forsaken on her land, with no one to raise her up.

For thus says the Lord GOD: The city that marched out a thousand shall have a hundred left, and that which marched out a hundred shall have ten left.

For thus says the LORD to the house of Israel: Seek me and live; but do not seek Bethel, and do not enter into Gilgal or cross over to Beer-sheba; for Gilgal shall surely go into exile, and Bethel shall come to nothing.

Seek the LORD and live, or he will break out against the house of Joseph like fire, and it will devour Bethel, with no one to quench it.

Amos 4:12–5:6, NRSV

Prepare me, gracious God,
  To stand before Thy face!
Thy Spirit must the work perform,
  For it is all of grace.

In Christ's obedience clothe,
  And wash me in His blood:
So shall I lift my head with joy
  Among the sons of God.

Robert Elliott, 1763

The triumph of God's kingdom

Now it shall come to pass in the latter days that the mountain of the LORD's house shall be established on the top of the mountains, and shall be exalted above the hills; and peoples shall flow to it. Many nations shall come and say, "Come, and let us go up to the mountain of the LORD, to the house of the God of Jacob; He will teach us His ways, and we shall walk in His paths." For out of Zion the law shall go forth, and the word of the LORD from Jerusalem. He shall judge between many peoples, and rebuke strong nations afar off; they shall beat their swords into plowshares, and their spears into pruning hooks; nation shall not lift up sword against nation, neither shall they learn war anymore.

But everyone shall sit under his vine and under his fig tree, and no one shall make them afraid; for the mouth of the LORD of hosts has spoken. For all people walk each in the name of his god, but we will walk in the name of the LORD our God forever and ever.

Micah 4:1–5, NKJV

Jesus, immortal King, go on;
The glorious day will soon be won;
Thine enemies prepare to flee,
And leave the conquered world to Thee.

Then shall contending nations rest,
For love shall reign in every breast;
Weapons, for war designed, shall cease,
Or then be implements of peace.

Thomas Kelly, 1769–1855

The way to life

Art thou not from everlasting, O LORD my God, mine Holy One? we shall not die. O LORD, thou hast ordained them for judgment; and, O mighty God, thou hast established them for correction. Thou art of purer eyes than to behold evil, and canst not look on iniquity: wherefore lookest thou upon them that deal treacherously, and holdest thy tongue when the wicked devoureth the man that is more righteous than he?

Habakkuk 1:12–13, KJV

Wherewith shall I come before the LORD, and bow myself before the high God? shall I come before him with burnt offerings, with calves of a year old? Will the LORD be pleased with thousands of rams, or with ten thousands of rivers of oil? shall I give my firstborn for my transgression, the fruit of my body for the sin of my soul? He hath shewed thee, O man, what is good; and what doth the LORD require of thee, but to do justly, and to love mercy, and to walk humbly with thy God?

Micah 6:6–8, KJV

Wherewith, O God, Shall I draw near,
  And bow myself before Thy face?
How in Thy purer eyes appear?
  What shall I bring to gain Thy grace?

Jesus, the Lamb of God, hath bled;
  He bore our sins upon the tree;
Beneath our curse He bowed His head;
  'Tis finished! He hath died for me!

Who'er to Thee themselves approve
  Must take the path Thy Word hath showed,
Justice pursue, and mercy love,
  And humbly walk by faith with God.

Charles Wesley, 1707–88

When all is dark

Who is among you that feareth the LORD, that obeyeth the voice of his servant, that walketh in darkness, and hath no light? let him trust in the name of the LORD, and stay upon his God. Behold, all ye that kindle a fire, that compass yourselves about with sparks: walk in the light of your fire, and in the sparks that ye have kindled. This shall ye have of mine hand; ye shall lie down in sorrow.

Hearken to me, ye that follow after righteousness, ye that seek the LORD: look unto the rock whence ye are hewn, and to the hole of the pit whence ye are digged. Look unto Abraham your father, and unto Sarah that bare you: for I called him alone, and blessed him, and increased him. For the LORD shall comfort Zion: he will comfort all her waste places; and he will make her wilderness like Eden, and her desert like the garden of the LORD; joy and gladness shall be found therein, thanksgiving, and the voice of melody.

Isaiah 50:10–51:3, KJV

Lead, kindly Light, amid the encircling gloom
  Lead Thou me on!
The night is dark, and I am far from home;
  Lead Thou me on!
Keep Thou my feet, I do not ask to see
The distant scene; one step enough for me.

John Henry Newman, 1801–90

Heirs of God, co-heirs with Christ

Think what that means. If we are his children then we are God's heirs, and all that Christ inherits will belong to all of us as well! Yes, if we share in his sufferings we shall certainly share in his glory.

In my opinion whatever we may have to go through now is less than nothing compared with the magnificent future God has in store for us. The whole creation is on tiptoe to see the wonderful sight of the sons of God coming into their own. The world of creation cannot as yet see reality, not because it chooses to be blind, but because in God's purpose it has been so limited—yet it has been given hope. And the hope is that in the end the whole of created life will be rescued from the tyranny of change and decay, and have its share in that magnificent liberty which can only belong to the children of God!

Romans 8:17–21, PHILLIPS

What from Christ that soul shall sever,
　Bound by everlasting bands?
Once in Him, in Him for ever,
　Thus the eternal cov'nant stands:
　　None shall pluck thee
　From the Strength of Israel's hands.

Heirs of God, joint-heirs with Jesus,
　Long ere time its race begun;
To His Name eternal praises;
　O what wonders He hath done!
　　One with Jesus,
　By eternal union one.

John Kent, 1766–1843

The work of the Holy Spirit

We know that the whole creation has been groaning as in the pains of childbirth right up to the present time. Not only so, but we ourselves, who have the firstfruits of the Spirit, groan inwardly as we wait eagerly for our adoption as sons, the redemption of our bodies. For in this hope we were saved. But hope that is seen is no hope at all. Who hopes for what he already has? But if we hope for what we do not yet have, we wait for it patiently.

In the same way, the Spirit helps us in our weakness. We do not know what we ought to pray for, but the Spirit himself intercedes for us with groans that words cannot express.

Romans 8:22–26

His Holy Spirit dwelleth
  Within my willing heart,
Tames it, when it rebelleth,
  And soothes the keenest smart;
And when my soul is lying
  Weak, trembling and oppressed,
He pleads with groans and sighing
  That cannot be expressed.

To mine His Spirit speaketh
  Sweet words of soothing power,
How God, for him that seeketh
  For rest, hath rest in store:
There God Himself prepareth
  My heritage and lot,
And though my body weareth,
  My heaven shall fail me not.

Paul Gerhardt, 1607–76
translated by Richard Massie, 1800–1887

More than conquerors

What then are we to say about these things? If God is for us, who is against us? He who did not withhold his own Son, but gave him up for all of us, will he not with him also give us everything else? Who will bring any charge against God's elect? It is God who justifies. Who is to condemn? It is Christ Jesus, who died, yes, who was raised, who is at the right hand of God, who indeed intercedes for us. Who will separate us from the love of Christ? Will hardship, or distress, or persecution, or famine, or nakedness, or peril, or sword? As it is written, "For your sake we are being killed all day long; we are accounted as sheep to be slaughtered." No, in all these things we are more than conquerors through him who loved us. For I am convinced that neither death, nor life, nor angels, nor rulers, nor things present, nor things to come, nor powers, nor height, nor depth, nor anything else in all creation, will be able to separate us from the love of God in Christ Jesus our Lord.

Romans 8:31–39, NRSV

No more we doubt Thee, glorious Prince of life;
Life is nought without Thee: aid us in our strife,
Make us more than conquerors, through Thy deathless love;
Bring us safe through Jordan to Thy home above.

Thine be the glory, risen, conquering Son,
Endless is the victory Thou o'er death hast won!

Edmond Louis Budry, 1854–1932
translated by Richard Birch Hoyle, 1875–1939

Do not worry

And why are you worried about clothing? Observe how the lilies of the field grow; they do not toil nor do they spin, yet I say to you that not even Solomon in all his glory clothed himself like one of these. But if God so clothes the grass of the field, which is alive today and tomorrow is thrown into the furnace, will He not much more clothe you? You of little faith! Do not worry then, saying, "What will we eat?" or "What will we drink?" or "What will we wear for clothing?" For the Gentiles eagerly seek all these things; for your heavenly Father knows that you need all these things. But seek first His kingdom and His righteousness, and all these things will be added to you.

So do not worry about tomorrow; for tomorrow will care for itself. Each day has enough trouble of its own.

Matthew 6:28–34, NASB

Seek ye his first God's peace and blessing—
Ye have all if this possessing;
Come, your need and sin confessing:
  Seek Him first.

Seek this first, His promise trying—
It is sure, all need supplying;
Heavenly things—on Him relying—
  Seek ye first.

Georgianna Mary Taylor, 1848–1915

Built on rock

"Therefore whoever hears these sayings of Mine, and does them, I will liken him to a wise man who built his house on the rock: and the rain descended, the floods came, and the winds blew and beat on that house; and it did not fall, for it was founded on the rock. But everyone who hears these sayings of Mine, and does not do them, will be like a foolish man who built his house on the sand: and the rain descended, the floods came, and the winds blew and beat on that house; and it fell. And great was its fall." And so it was, when Jesus had ended these sayings, that the people were astonished at His teaching, for He taught them as one having authority, and not as the scribes.

Matthew 7:24–29, NKJV

When darkness seems to veil His face,
I rest on His unchanging grace;
In every high and stormy gale
My anchor holds within the veil.

On Christ, the solid Rock, I stand;
All other ground is sinking sand.

His oath, His covenant, and blood
Support me in the 'whelming flood:
When all around my soul gives way,
He then is all my hope and stay.

Edward Mote, 1797–1874,
and others

The gentle Father

Like as a father pitieth his children, so the LORD pitieth them that fear him. For he knoweth our frame; he remembereth that we are dust. As for man, his days are as grass: as a flower of the field, so he flourisheth. For the wind passeth over it, and it is gone; and the place thereof shall know it no more. But the mercy of the LORD is from everlasting to everlasting upon them that fear him, and his righteousness unto children's children; to such as keep his covenant, and to those that remember his commandments to do them. The LORD hath prepared his throne in the heavens; and his kingdom ruleth over all.

Psalm 103:13–19, KJV

Father-like, He tends and spares us,
   Well our feeble frame He knows;
In His hands He gently bears us,
   Rescues us from all our foes:
      Praise Him! Praise Him!
   Widely as His mercy flows.

Frail as summer's flower we flourish;
   Blows the wind, and it is gone;
But while mortals rise and perish
   God endures unchanging on.
      Praise Him! Praise Him!
   Praise the high eternal One.

Henry Francis Lyte, 1793–1847

Calming the storm

On the evening of that day, he said to them,
"Let us cross over to the other side of the lake."
So they sent the crowd home and took him with them in the small boat in which he had been sitting, accompanied by other small craft. Then came a violent squall of wind which drove the waves aboard the boat until it was almost swamped. Jesus was in the stern asleep on the cushion. They awoke him with the words,
"Master, don't you care that we're drowning?"
And he woke up, rebuked the wind, and said to the waves,
"Hush now! Be still!"
The wind dropped and there was a dead calm.
"Why are you so frightened? Do you not trust me even yet?" he asked them.
But sheer awe swept over them, and they kept saying to each other,
"Who ever can he be?—even the wind and the waves do what he tells them!"

Mark 4:35–41, PHILLIPS

Praise to the Lord, Who, when tempests their warfare are waging,
Who, when the elements madly around Thee are raging,
  Biddeth them cease,
  Turneth their fury to peace,
Whirlwinds and waters assuaging.

Joachim Neander, 1650–80
translated by Catherine Winkworth, 1829–78,
and others

The Friend of sinners

"For I say to you, among those born of women there is not a greater prophet than John the Baptist; but he who is least in the kingdom of God is greater than he." And when all the people heard Him, even the tax collectors justified God, having been baptized with the baptism of John. But the Pharisees and lawyers rejected the will of God for themselves, not having been baptized by him. And the Lord said, "To what then shall I liken the men of this generation, and what are they like? They are like children sitting in the marketplace and calling to one another, saying: 'We played the flute for you, and you did not dance; we mourned to you, and you did not weep.' For John the Baptist came neither eating bread nor drinking wine, and you say, 'He has a demon.' The Son of Man has come eating and drinking, and you say, 'Look, a glutton and a winebibber, a friend of tax collectors and sinners!' But wisdom is justified by all her children."

Luke 7:28–35, NKJV

One there is above all others,
   Well deserves the name of Friend;
His is love beyond a brother's,
   Costly, free, and knows no end:
They who once His kindness prove,
Find it everlasting love.

When He lived on earth abased
   "Friend of sinners" was His Name;
Now above all glory raised,
   He rejoices in the same;
Still He calls them brethren, friends,
And to all their wants attends.

John Newton, 1725–1807

Bearing fruit for God

"A sower went out to sow his seed. And as he sowed, some fell by the wayside; and it was trampled down, and the birds of the air devoured it. Some fell on rock; and as soon as it sprang up, it withered away because it lacked moisture. And some fell among thorns, and the thorns sprang up with it and choked it. But others fell on good ground, sprang up, and yielded a crop a hundredfold." When He had said these things He cried, "He who has ears to hear, let him hear!" . . .

"Now the parable is this: The seed is the word of God. Those by the wayside are the ones who hear; then the devil comes and takes away the word out of their hearts, lest they should believe and be saved. But the ones on the rock are those who, when they hear, receive the word with joy; and these have no root, who believe for a while and in time of temptation fall away. Now the ones that fell among thorns are those who, when they have heard, go out and are choked with cares, riches, and pleasures of life, and bring no fruit to maturity. But the ones that fell on the good ground are those who, having heard the word with a noble and good heart, keep it and bear fruit with patience."

Luke 8:5–8,11–15, NKJV

Let not the foe of Christ and man
   This holy seed remove,
But give it root in every heart
   To bring forth fruits of love.

Let not the world's deceitful cares
   The rising plant destroy,
But let it yield a hundredfold
   The fruits of peace and joy.

John Cawood, 1775–1852

Our King of glory

Then [Jesus] said to them all, "If any want to become my followers, let them deny themselves and take up their cross daily and follow me. For those who want to save their life will lose it, and those who lose their life for my sake will save it. What does it profit them if they gain the whole world, but lose or forfeit themselves? Those who are ashamed of me and of my words, of them the Son of Man will be ashamed when he comes in his glory and the glory of the Father and of the holy angels."

Luke 9:23–26, NRSV

Therefore God exalted him to the highest place and gave him the name that is above every name, that at the name of Jesus every knee should bow, in heaven and on earth and under the earth, and every tongue confess that Jesus Christ is Lord, to the glory of God the Father.

Philippians 2:9–11

At the Name of Jesus
 Every knee shall bow,
Every tongue confess Him
 King of glory now.
'Tis the Father's pleasure
 We should call Him Lord,
Who from the beginning
 Was the mighty Word.

Brothers, this Lord Jesus
 Shall return again
With His Father's glory,
 With His angel train;
For all wreaths of empire
 Meet upon His brow,
And our hearts confess Him
 King of glory now.

Caroline Maria Noel, 1817–77

271

The harvest field

Jesus now traveled through all the towns and villages, teaching in their synagogues, proclaiming the gospel of the kingdom, and healing all kinds of illness and disability. As he looked at the vast crowds he was deeply moved with pity for them, for they were as bewildered and miserable as a flock of sheep with no shepherd.

"The harvest is great enough," he remarked to his disciples, "but the reapers are few. So you must pray to the Lord of the harvest to send men out to bring it in."

Matthew 9:35–38, PHILLIPS

Revive us, Lord! Is zeal abating
  While harvest fields are vast and white?
Revive us, Lord, the world is waiting,
  Equip Thy church to spread the light.

Elizabeth A. P. Head, 1850–1936

Let earth receive the King

O sing unto the Lord a new song; for he hath done marvellous things: his right hand, and his holy arm, hath gotten him the victory. The Lord hath made known his salvation: his righteousness hath he openly shewed in the sight of the heathen. He hath remembered his mercy and his truth toward the house of Israel: all the ends of the earth have seen the salvation of our God. Make a joyful noise unto the Lord, all the earth: make a loud noise, and rejoice, and sing praise. Sing unto the Lord with the harp; with the harp, and the voice of a psalm. With trumpets and sound of cornets make a joyful noise before the Lord, the King. Let the sea roar, and the fulness thereof; the world, and they that dwell therein. Let the floods clap their hands: let the hills be joyful together before the Lord; for he cometh to judge the earth: with righteousness shall he judge the world, and the people with equity.

Psalm 98:1–9, KJV

Joy to the world! the Lord is come!
  Let earth receive her King;
Let every heart prepare Him room,
  And heaven and nature sing.

Joy to the earth! the Saviour reigns!
  Let men their songs employ;
While fields and floods, rocks, hills and plains,
  Repeat the sounding joy.

He rules the world with truth and grace,
  And makes the nations prove
The glories of His righteousness,
  The wonders of His love.

Isaac Watts, 1674–1748

Our Lord God Almighty reigns!

And the twenty-four elders and the four living creatures fell down and worshiped God who sat on the throne, saying, "Amen! Alleluia!" Then a voice came from the throne, saying, "Praise our God, all you His servants and those who fear Him, both small and great!" And I heard, as it were, the voice of a great multitude, as the sound of many waters and as the sound of mighty thunderings, saying, "Alleluia! For the Lord God Omnipotent reigns! Let us be glad and rejoice and give Him glory, for the marriage of the Lamb has come, and His wife has made herself ready." And to her it was granted to be arrayed in fine linen, clean and bright, for the fine linen is the righteous acts of the saints. Then he said to me, "Write: 'Blessed are those who are called to the marriage supper of the Lamb!'" And he said to me, "These are the true sayings of God." And I fell at his feet to worship him. But he said to me, "See that you do not do that! I am your fellow servant, and of your brethren who have the testimony of Jesus. Worship God! For the testimony of Jesus is the spirit of prophecy."

Revelation 19:4–10, NKJV

He reigns! ye saints, exalt your strains:
Your God is King, your Father reigns;
And He is at the Father's side,
The Man of love, the Crucified.

One Lord, one empire, all secures:
He reigns—and life and death are yours;
Through earth and heaven one song shall ring,
"The Lord Omnipotent is King!"

Josiah Conder, 1789–1855

Looking at Christ

And I will pour out on the house of David and the inhabitants of Jeru-salem a spirit of grace and supplication. They will look on me, the one they have pierced, and they will mourn for him as one mourns for an only child, and grieve bitterly for him as one grieves for a first-born son.

Zechariah 12:10

Instead, one of the soldiers pierced his side with a spear, and at once blood and water came out. (He who saw this has testified so that you also may believe. His testimony is true, and he knows that he tells the truth.) These things occurred so that the scripture might be fulfilled, "None of his bones shall be broken." And again another passage of scripture says, "They will look on the one whom they have pierced."

John 19:34–37, NRSV

Since then it is by faith that we are justified, let us grasp the fact that we have peace with God through our Lord Jesus Christ.

Romans 5:1, PHILLIPS

I hear the words of love,
  I gaze upon the blood,
I see the mighty sacrifice,
  And I have peace with God.

'Tis everlasting peace,
  Sure as Jehovah's Name;
'Tis stable as His steadfast throne,
  For evermore the same.

Horatius Bonar, 1808–89

Loving God

Hear, O Israel: The LORD our God, the LORD is one! You shall love the LORD your God with all your heart, with all your soul, and with all your strength.

And these words which I command you today shall be in your heart. You shall teach them diligently to your children, and shall talk of them when you sit in your house, when you walk by the way, when you lie down, and when you rise up. You shall bind them as a sign on your hand, and they shall be as frontlets between your eyes. You shall write them on the doorposts of your house and on your gates.

Deuteronomy 6:4–9, NKJV

"Teacher, which is the great commandment in the law?" Jesus said to him, "'You shall love the LORD your God with all your heart, with all your soul, and with all your mind.' This is the first and great commandment. And the second is like it: 'You shall love your neighbor as yourself.' On these two commandments hang all the Law and the Prophets."

Matthew 22:36–40, NKJV

Thee will I love, my strength, my tower,
  Thee will I love, my joy, my crown,
Thee will I love with all my power,
  In all Thy works and Thee alone;
Thee will I love, till the pure fire
Fill my whole soul with chaste desire.

Johann Scheffler, 1624–77
translated by John Wesley, 1703–91

Watching for the Lord's coming

Be dressed in readiness, and keep your lamps lit. Be like men who are waiting for their master when he returns from the wedding feast, so that they may immediately open the door to him when he comes and knocks. Blessed are those slaves whom the master will find on the alert when he comes; truly I say to you, that he will gird himself to serve, and have them recline at the table, and will come up and wait on them. Whether he comes in the second watch, or even in the third, and finds them so, blessed are those slaves.

But be sure of this, that if the head of the house had known at what hour the thief was coming, he would not have allowed his house to be broken into. You too, be ready; for the Son of Man is coming at an hour that you do not expect.

Luke 12:35–40, NASB

Let all your lamps be bright,
   And trim the golden flame;
Gird up your loins as in His sight,
   For holy is His Name.

Watch! 'tis your Lord's command,
   And while we speak He's near;
Mark the first signal of His hand,
   And ready all appear.

Christ shall the banquet spread
   With His own royal hand,
And raise that faithful servant's head
   Amid the angelic band.

Philip Doddridge, 1702–51

"Increase our faith!"

He said to His disciples, "It is inevitable that stumbling blocks come, but woe to him through whom they come! It would be better for him if a millstone were hung around his neck and he were thrown into the sea, than that he would cause one of these little ones to stumble. Be on your guard! If your brother sins, rebuke him; and if he repents, forgive him. And if he sins against you seven times a day, and returns to you seven times, saying, 'I repent,' forgive him."

The apostles said to the Lord, "Increase our faith!" And the Lord said, "If you had faith like a mustard seed, you would say to this mulberry tree, 'Be uprooted and be planted in the sea'; and it would obey you."

Luke 17:1–6, NASB

O for a faith that will not shrink,
  Though pressed by many a foe;
That will not tremble on the brink
  Of poverty or woe;
Lord, give me such a faith as this,
  And then, whate'er may come,
I taste e'en now the hallowed bliss
  Of an eternal home.

William Hiley Bathurst, 1796–1877

OCTOBER 1

Growing in Christ

Therefore I also, after I heard of your faith in the Lord Jesus and your love for all the saints, do not cease to give thanks for you, making mention of you in my prayers: that the God of our Lord Jesus Christ, the Father of glory, may give to you the spirit of wisdom and revelation in the knowledge of Him, the eyes of your understanding being enlightened; that you may know what is the hope of His calling, what are the riches of the glory of His inheritance in the saints, and what is the exceeding greatness of His power toward us who believe, according to the working of His mighty power which He worked in Christ when He raised Him from the dead and seated Him at His right hand in the heavenly places, far above all principality and power and might and dominion, and every name that is named, not only in this age but also in that which is to come. And He put all things under His feet, and gave Him to be head over all things to the church, which is His body, the fullness of Him who fills all in all.

Ephesians 1:15–23, NKJV

Lo! Thy presence now is filling
　All Thy church in every place;
Fill my heart too, make me willing
　In this season of Thy grace;
Come, Thou King of glory, come,
Deign to make my heart Thy home,
There abide and rule alone,
As upon Thy heavenly throne!

Gerhard Tersteegen, 1697–1769
translated by Catherine Winkworth, 1827–78

The presence of God

And Moses said unto the LORD, See, thou sayest unto me, Bring up this people: and thou hast not let me know whom thou wilt send with me. Yet thou hast said, I know thee by name, and thou hast also found grace in my sight. Now therefore, I pray thee, if I have found grace in thy sight, shew me now thy way, that I may know thee, that I may find grace in thy sight: and consider that this nation is thy people. And he said, My presence shall go with thee, and I will give thee rest. And he said unto him, If thy presence go not with me, carry us not up hence. For wherein shall it be known here that I and thy people have found grace in thy sight? is it not in that thou goest with us? so shall we be separated, I and thy people, from all the people that are upon the face of the earth. And the LORD said unto Moses, I will do this thing also that thou hast spoken: for thou hast found grace in my sight, and I know thee by name.

Exodus 33:12–17, KJV

Lord, it is not life to live
  If Thy presence Thou deny;
Lord, if Thou Thy presence give,
  'Tis no longer death to die:
Source and giver of repose,
Singly from Thy smile it flows;
Peace and happiness are Thine;
Mine they are, if Thou art mine.

Augustus Montague Toplady, 1740–78

"Show me your glory"

And he said, I beseech thee, shew me thy glory. And he said, I will make all my goodness pass before thee, and I will proclaim the name of the LORD before thee; and will be gracious to whom I will be gracious, and will shew mercy on whom I will shew mercy. And he said, Thou canst not see my face: for there shall no man see me, and live. And the LORD said, Behold, there is a place by me, and thou shalt stand upon a rock: And it shall come to pass, while my glory passeth by, that I will put thee in a clift of the rock, and will cover thee with my hand while I pass by: And I will take away mine hand, and thou shalt see my back parts: but my face shall not be seen.

Exodus 33:18–23, KJV

Show me Thy face!—one transient gleam
  Of loveliness divine,
And I shall never think or dream
  Of other love save Thine;
All lesser light will darken quite,
  All lower glories wane;
The beautiful of earth will scarce
  Seem beautiful again.

Show me Thy face!—my faith and love
  Shall henceforth fixed be,
And nothing here have power to move
  My soul's serenity;
My life shall seem a trance, a dream,
  And all I feel and see,
Illusive, visionary—Thou
  The one reality!

Anonymous

OCTOBER 4

Trusting God for pardon

Then he gave this illustration to certain people who were confident of their own goodness and looked down on others:

"Two men went up to the Temple to pray, one was a Pharisee, the other was a tax-collector. The Pharisee stood and prayed like this with himself, 'O God, I do thank thee that I am not like the rest of mankind, greedy, dishonest, impure, or even like that tax-collector over there. I fast twice every week; I give away a tenth-part of all my income.' But the tax-collector stood in a distant corner, scarcely daring to look up to Heaven, and with a gesture of despair, said, 'God, have mercy on a sinner like me.' I assure you that he was the man who went home justified in God's sight, rather than the other one. For everyone who sets himself up as somebody will become a nobody, and the man who makes himself nobody will become somebody."

Luke 18:9–14, PHILLIPS

I am trusting Thee for pardon,
  At Thy feet I bow;
For Thy grace and tender mercy,
  Trusting now.

I am trusting Thee for cleansing
  In the crimson flood;
Trusting Thee to make me holy
  By Thy blood.

Frances Ridley Havergal, 1836–79

OCTOBER 5

Doing good to all

My friends, if anyone is detected in a transgression, you who have received the Spirit should restore such a one in a spirit of gentleness. Take care that you yourselves are not tempted. Bear one another's burdens, and in this way you will fulfill the law of Christ. For if those who are nothing think they are something, they deceive themselves. All must test their own work; then that work, rather than their neighbor's work, will become a cause for pride. For all must carry their own loads.

Those who are taught the word must share in all good things with their teacher.

Do not be deceived; God is not mocked, for you reap whatever you sow. If you sow to your own flesh, you will reap corruption from the flesh; but if you sow to the Spirit, you will reap eternal life from the Spirit. So let us not grow weary in doing what is right, for we will reap at harvest time, if we do not give up. So then, whenever we have an opportunity, let us work for the good of all, and especially for those of the family of faith.

Galatians 6:1–10, NRSV

Lord, speak to me, that I may speak
  In living echoes of Thy tone;
As Thou hast sought, so let me seek
  Thy erring children lost and lone.

O lead me, Lord, that I may lead
  The wandering and the wavering feet,
O feed me, Lord, that I may feed
  Thy hungering ones with manna sweet,

O strengthen me, that, while I stand
  Firm on the rock, and strong in Thee,
I may stretch out a loving hand
  To wrestlers with the troubled sea.

Frances Ridley Havergal, 1836–79

His love endures for ever

Give thanks to the LORD, for he is good.

His love endures forever.

Give thanks to the God of gods.

His love endures forever.

Give thanks to the Lord of lords:

His love endures forever.

to him who alone does great wonders,

His love endures forever.

who by his understanding made the heavens,

His love endures forever.

who spread out the earth upon the waters,

His love endures forever.

who made the great lights—

His love endures forever.

the sun to govern the day,

His love endures forever.

the moon and stars to govern the night;

His love endures forever.

to him who struck down the firstborn of Egypt

His love endures forever.

and brought Israel out from among them

His love endures forever.

with a mighty hand and outstretched arm;

His love endures forever.

Psalm 136:1–12

Give to our God immortal praise;
Mercy and truth are all His ways;
Wonders of grace to God belong,
Repeat His mercies in your song.

Give to the Lord of lords renown,
The King of kings with glory crown:
His mercies ever shall endure,
When lords and kings are known no more.

He built the earth, He spread the sky,
And fixed the starry lights on high:
Wonders of grace to God belong,
Repeat His mercies in your song.

Isaac Watts, 1674–1748

OCTOBER 7

God's great love

Now the LORD descended in the cloud and stood with him there, and proclaimed the name of the LORD. And the LORD passed before him and proclaimed, "The LORD, the LORD God, merciful and gracious, long-suffering, and abounding in goodness and truth, keeping mercy for thousands, forgiving iniquity and transgression and sin, by no means clearing the guilty, visiting the iniquity of the fathers upon the children and the children's children to the third and the fourth generation." So Moses made haste and bowed his head toward the earth, and worshiped. Then he said, "If now I have found grace in Your sight, O Lord, let my Lord, I pray, go among us, even though we are a stiff-necked people; and pardon our iniquity and our sin, and take us as Your inheritance."

And He said: "Behold, I make a covenant. Before all your people I will do marvels such as have not been done in all the earth, nor in any nation; and all the people among whom you are shall see the work of the LORD. For it is an awesome thing that I will do with you. Observe what I command you this day. Behold, I am driving out from before you the Amorite and the Canaanite and the Hittite and the Perizzite and the Hivite and the Jebusite."

Exodus 34:5–11, NKJV

There's a wideness in God's mercy,
  Like the wideness of the sea;
There's a kindness in His justice,
  Which is more than liberty.

For the love of God is broader
  Than the measures of man's mind;
And the heart of the Eternal
  Is most wonderfully kind.

Frederick William Faber, 1814–63

"My glory all the cross"

Behold, a king shall reign in righteousness, and princes shall rule in judgment. And a man shall be as an hiding place from the wind, and a covert from the tempest; as rivers of water in a dry place, as the shadow of a great rock in a weary land.

Isaiah 32:1–2, KJV

For Christ sent me not to baptize, but to preach the gospel: not with wisdom of words, lest the cross of Christ should be made of none effect. For the preaching of the cross is to them that perish foolishness; but unto us which are saved it is the power of God. For it is written, I will destroy the wisdom of the wise, and will bring to nothing the understanding of the prudent.

1 Corinthians 1:17–19, KJV

Upon that cross of Jesus
  Mine eye at times can see
The very dying form of One
  Who suffered there for me;
And from my smitten heart, with tears,
  Two wonders I confess—
The wonders of His glorious love,
  And my own worthlessness.

I take, O cross, thy shadow,
  For my abiding place;
I ask no other sunshine than
  The sunshine of His face;
Content to let the world go by,
  To know no gain nor loss—
My sinful self my only shame,
  My glory all the cross.

Elizabeth Cecilia Clephane, 1830–69

Working with all our heart

Wives, be subject to your husbands, as is fitting in the Lord. Husbands, love your wives and do not be embittered against them. Children, be obedient to your parents in all things, for this is well-pleasing to the Lord. Fathers, do not exasperate your children, so that they will not lose heart.

Slaves, in all things obey those who are your masters on earth, not with external service, as those who merely please men, but with sincerity of heart, fearing the Lord. Whatever you do, do your work heartily, as for the Lord rather than for men, knowing that from the Lord you will receive the reward of the inheritance. It is the Lord Christ whom you serve. For he who does wrong will receive the consequences of the wrong which he has done, and that without partiality.

Masters, grant to your slaves justice and fairness, knowing that you too have a Master in heaven.

Colossians 3:18–4:1, NASB

Teach me, my God and King,
  In all things Thee to see,
And what I do in anything
  To do it as for Thee.

George Herbert, 1593–1633

The pure in heart

Blessed are the pure in heart: for they shall see God.

Matthew 5:8, KJV

As for me, I will behold thy face in righteousness: I shall be satisfied, when I awake, with thy likeness.

Psalm 17:15, KJV

Truly God is good to Israel, even to such as are of a clean heart.

Psalm 73:1, KJV

Follow peace with all men, and holiness, without which no man shall see the Lord.

Hebrews 12:14, KJV

Blest are the pure in heart,
  For they shall see their God;
The secret of the Lord is theirs;
  Their soul is Christ's abode.

Still to the lowly soul
  He doth Himself impart,
And for His dwelling and His throne
  Chooseth the pure in heart.

Lord, we Thy presence seek:
  May ours this blessing be;
Give us a pure and lowly heart,—
  A temple meet for Thee.

John Keble, 1792–1866,
and
William John Hall, 1793–1861

Christ in us

John answered, "No one can receive anything except what has been given from heaven. You yourselves are my witnesses that I said, 'I am not the Messiah, but I have been sent ahead of him.' He who has the bride is the bridegroom. The friend of the bridegroom, who stands and hears him, rejoices greatly at the bridegroom's voice. For this reason my joy has been fulfilled. He must increase, but I must decrease." The one who comes from above is above all; the one who is of the earth belongs to the earth and speaks about earthly things.

The one who comes from heaven is above all. He testifies to what he has seen and heard, yet no one accepts his testimony. Whoever has accepted his testimony has certified this, that God is true. He whom God has sent speaks the words of God, for he gives the Spirit without measure. The Father loves the Son and has placed all things in his hands. Whoever believes in the Son has eternal life; whoever disobeys the Son will not see life, but must endure God's wrath.

John 3:27–36, NRSV

My dear children, for whom I am again in the pains of childbirth until Christ is formed in you.

Galatians 4:19

Each day let Thy supporting might
  My weakness still embrace;
My darkness vanish in Thy light,
  Thy life my death efface.

Make this poor self grow less and less,
  Be Thou my life and aim;
O make me daily, through Thy grace,
  More meet to bear. Thy Name!

Johann Caspar Lavater, 1741–1801
translated by Elizabeth Lee Smith, 1817–98

OCTOBER 12

Trusting in God

The LORD is my light and my salvation; whom shall I fear? the LORD is the strength of my life; of whom shall I be afraid? When the wicked, even mine enemies and my foes, came upon me to eat up my flesh, they stumbled and fell. Though an host should encamp against me, my heart shall not fear: though war should rise against me, in this will I be confident. One thing have I desired of the LORD, that will I seek after; that I may dwell in the house of the LORD all the days of my life, to behold the beauty of the LORD, and to inquire in his temple. . . . Hide not thy face far from me; put not thy servant away in anger: thou hast been my help; leave me not, neither forsake me, O God of my salvation. When my father and my mother forsake me, then the LORD will take me up. Teach me thy way, O LORD, and lead me in a plain path, because of mine enemies. Deliver me not over unto the will of mine enemies: for false witnesses are risen up against me, and such as breathe out cruelty. I had fainted, unless I had believed to see the goodness of the LORD in the land of the living. Wait on the LORD: be of good courage, and he shall strengthen thine heart: wait, I say, on the LORD.

Psalm 27:1–4, 9–14, KJV

God is my strong salvation;
  What foe have I to fear?
In darkness and temptation
  My light, my help is near.

Though hosts encamp around me,
  Firm to the fight I stand;
What terror can confound me,
  With God at my right hand?

James Montgomery, 1771–1854

Real worship

O come, let us sing unto the LORD: let us make a joyful noise to the rock of our salvation. Let us come before his presence with thanksgiving, and make a joyful noise unto him with psalms. For the LORD is a great God, and a great King above all gods. In his hand are the deep places of the earth: the strength of the hills is his also. The sea is his, and he made it: and his hands formed the dry land. O come, let us worship and bow down: let us kneel before the LORD our maker. For he is our God; and we are the people of his pasture, and the sheep of his hand. To day if ye will hear his voice, harden not your heart, as in the provocation, and as in the day of temptation in the wilderness.

Psalm 95:1–8, KJV

My God, how wonderful Thou art!
   Thy majesty how bright!
How beautiful Thy mercy-seat,
   In depths of burning light!

How wonderful, how beautiful,
   The sight of Thee must be,
Thine endless wisdom, boundless power,
   And aweful purity!

Frederick William Faber, 1814–63

The Lord has done great things

When the LORD turned again the captivity of Zion, we were like them that dream. Then was our mouth filled with laughter, and our tongue with singing: then said they among the heathen, The LORD hath done great things for them. The LORD hath done great things for us; whereof we are glad. Turn again our captivity, O LORD, as the streams in the south. They that sow in tears shall reap in joy. He that goeth forth and weepeth, bearing precious seed, shall doubtless come again with rejoicing, bringing his sheaves with him.

Psalm 126:1–6, KJV

Now thank we all our God,
  With hearts, and hands, and voices;
Who wondrous things hath done,
  In whom His world rejoices;
Who, from our mothers' arms,
  Hath blessed us on our way
With countless gifts of love,
And still is ours today.

Martin Rinkart, 1586–1649
translated by Catherine Winkworth, 1827–78

What God has prepared for his own

And I, brethren, when I came to you, did not come with excellence of speech or of wisdom declaring to you the testimony of God. For I determined not to know anything among you except Jesus Christ and Him crucified. I was with you in weakness, in fear, and in much trembling. And my speech and my preaching were not with persuasive words of human wisdom, but in demonstration of the Spirit and of power, that your faith should not be in the wisdom of men but in the power of God.

However, we speak wisdom among those who are mature, yet not the wisdom of this age, nor of the rulers of this age, who are coming to nothing. But we speak the wisdom of God in a mystery, the hidden wisdom which God ordained before the ages for our glory, which none of the rulers of this age knew; for had they known, they would not have crucified the Lord of glory. But as it is written: "Eye has not seen, nor ear heard, nor have entered into the heart of man the things which God has prepared for those who love Him." But God has revealed them to us through His Spirit. For the Spirit searches all things, yes, the deep things of God.

1 Corinthians 2:1–10, NKJV

Glories upon glories
  Has our God prepared,
By the souls that love Him
  One day to be shared;
Eye has not beheld them,
  Ear has never heard,
Nor of these has uttered
  Thought or speech a word.
Forward, marching forward,
  Clad in armour bright,
Till the veil be lifted,
  Till our faith be sight.

Henry Alford, 1810–71

Wisdom from the Spirit

But God has revealed them to us through His Spirit. For the Spirit searches all things, yes, the deep things of God. For what man knows the things of a man except the spirit of the man which is in him? Even so no one knows the things of God except the Spirit of God. Now we have received, not the spirit of the world, but the Spirit who is from God, that we might know the things that have been freely given to us by God. These things we also speak, not in words which man's wisdom teaches but which the Holy Spirit teaches, comparing spiritual things with spiritual. But the natural man does not receive the things of the Spirit of God, for they are foolishness to him; nor can he know them, because they are spiritually discerned. But he who is spiritual judges all things, yet he himself is rightly judged by no one. For "who has known the mind of the LORD that he may instruct Him?" But we have the mind of Christ.

1 Corinthians 2:10–16, NKJV

Send us the Spirit of Thy Son,
To make the depths of Godhead known,
To make us share the life divine;
  Send Him the sprinkled blood to apply,
  Send Him our souls to sanctify,
And show and seal us ever Thine.

So shall we pray, and never cease,
So shall we thankfully confess
Thy wisdom, truth, and power, and love;
  With joy unspeakable adore,
  And bless and praise Thee evermore,
And serve Thee as Thy hosts above.

Charles Wesley, 1707–88

The paradise to come

The spirit of the LORD shall rest on him, the spirit of wisdom and understanding, the spirit of counsel and might, the spirit of knowledge and the fear of the LORD. His delight shall be in the fear of the LORD.

He shall not judge by what his eyes see, or decide by what his ears hear; but with righteousness he shall judge the poor, and decide with equity for the meek of the earth; he shall strike the earth with the rod of his mouth, and with the breath of his lips he shall kill the wicked. Righteousness shall be the belt around his waist, and faithfulness the belt around his loins.

The wolf shall live with the lamb, the leopard shall lie down with the kid, the calf and the lion and the fatling together, and a little child shall lead them. The cow and the bear shall graze, their young shall lie down together; and the lion shall eat straw like the ox. The nursing child shall play over the hole of the asp, and the weaned child shall put its hand on the adder's den. They will not hurt or destroy on all my holy mountain; for the earth will be full of the knowledge of the LORD as the waters cover the sea.

Isaiah 11:2–9, NRSV

God is working His purpose out as year succeeds to year.
God is working His purpose out, and the time is drawing near;
Nearer and nearer draws the time, the time that shall surely be,
When the earth shall be filled with the glory of God as the waters
    cover the sea.

Arthur Campell Ainger, 1841–1919

"Teach me your way"

Shew me thy ways, O LORD; teach me thy paths. Lead me in thy truth, and teach me: for thou art the God of my salvation; on thee do I wait all the day. Remember, O LORD, thy tender mercies and thy loving-kindnesses; for they have been ever of old. Remember not the sins of my youth, nor my transgressions: according to thy mercy remember thou me for thy goodness' sake, O LORD. Good and upright is the LORD: therefore will he teach sinners in the way. The meek will he guide in judgment: and the meek will he teach his way. All the paths of the LORD are mercy and truth unto such as keep his covenant and his testimonies. For thy name's sake, O LORD, pardon mine iniquity; for it is great. What man is he that feareth the LORD? him shall he teach in the way that he shall choose. His soul shall dwell at ease; and his seed shall inherit the earth. The secret of the LORD is with them that fear him; and he will shew them his covenant.

Psalm 25:4–14, KJV

Long as my life shall last,
  Teach me Thy way;
Where'er my lot be cast,
  Teach me Thy way;
Until the race is run,
Until the journey's done,
Until the crown is won,
  Teach me Thy way.

Benjamin Mansell Ramsey, 1849–1923

God's great mercy

Oh, the depth of the riches both of the wisdom and knowledge of God! How unsearchable are His judgments and His ways past finding out! "For who has known the mind of the LORD? Or who has become His counselor? Or who has first given to Him and it shall be repaid to him?" For of Him and through Him and to Him are all things, to whom be glory forever. Amen.

I beseech you therefore, brethren, by the mercies of God, that you present your bodies a living sacrifice, holy, acceptable to God, which is your reasonable service. And do not be conformed to this world, but be transformed by the renewing of your mind, that you may prove what is that good and acceptable and perfect will of God.

Romans 11:33–12:2, NKJV

> When all Thy mercies, O my God,
>   My rising soul surveys,
> Transported with the view, I'm lost
>   In wonder, love, and praise.
>
> Through every period of my life
>   Thy goodness I'll pursue,
> And after death in distant worlds
>   The glorious theme renew.
>
> Through all eternity to Thee
>   A joyful song I'll raise;
> But O! eternity's too short
>   To utter all Thy praise!

Joseph Addison, 1672–1719

Growing in grace

All over the world this gospel is bearing fruit and growing, just as it has been doing among you since the day you heard it and understood God's grace in all its truth. You learned it from Epaphras, our dear fellow servant, who is a faithful minister of Christ on our behalf, and who also told us of your love in the Spirit.

For this reason, since the day we heard about you, we have not stopped praying for you and asking God to fill you with the knowledge of his will through all spiritual wisdom and understanding. And we pray this in order that you may live a life worthy of the Lord and may please him in every way: bearing fruit in every good work, growing in the knowledge of God, being strengthened with all power according to his glorious might so that you may have great endurance and patience, and joyfully giving thanks to the Father, who has qualified you to share in the inheritance of the saints in the kingdom of light. For he has rescued us from the dominion of darkness and brought us into the kingdom of the Son he loves, in whom we have redemption, the forgiveness of sins.

Colossians 1:6–14

It passeth praises, that dear love of Thine,
My Saviour, Jesus, yet this heart of mine
Would sing that love, so full, so rich, so free,
Which brings a rebel sinner, such as me,
  Nigh unto God.

O fill me, Jesus, Saviour, with Thy love!
Lead, lead me to the living fount above;
Thither may I, in simple faith, draw nigh,
And never to another fountain fly,
  But unto Thee.

Mary Shekleton, 1827–83

OCTOBER 21

The supremacy of Christ

He is the image of the invisible God, the firstborn of all creation. For by Him all things were created, both in the heavens and on earth, visible and invisible, whether thrones or dominions or rulers or authorities—all things have been created through Him and for Him. He is before all things, and in Him all things hold together. He is also head of the body, the church; and He is the beginning, the firstborn from the dead, so that He Himself will come to have first place in everything. For it was the Father's good pleasure for all the fullness to dwell in Him, and through Him to reconcile all things to Himself, having made peace through the blood of His cross; through Him, I say, whether things on earth or things in heaven.

Colossians 1:15–20, NASB

Thou art the Everlasting Word,
  The Father's only Son;
God manifestly seen and heard,
  And heaven's beloved One.

Worthy, O Lamb of God, art Thou,
That every knee to Thee should bow!

In Thee, most perfectly expressed,
  The Father's glories shine:
Of the full Deity possessed,
  Eternally divine:

True image of the Infinite,
  Whose essence is concealed;
Brightness of uncreated light;
  The heart of God revealed.

Josiah Conder, 1789–1855

Coming to Christ

Therefore, knowing the fear of the Lord, we persuade men, but we are made manifest to God; and I hope that we are made manifest also in your consciences. We are not again commending ourselves to you but are giving you an occasion to be proud of us, so that you will have an answer for those who take pride in appearance and not in heart. For if we are beside ourselves, it is for God; if we are of sound mind, it is for you. For the love of Christ controls us, having concluded this, that one died for all, therefore all died; and He died for all, so that they who live might no longer live for themselves, but for Him who died and rose again on their behalf.

Therefore from now on we recognize no one according to the flesh; even though we have known Christ according to the flesh, yet now we know Him in this way no longer. Therefore if anyone is in Christ, he is a new creature; the old things passed away; behold, new things have come.

2 Corinthians 5:11–17, NASB

Come, ye sinners, poor and wretched,
  Weak and wounded, sick and sore;
Jesus ready stands to save you,
  Full of pity joined with power;
    He is able,
He is willing; doubt no more!

Lo, the incarnate God, ascended,
  Pleads the merit of His blood;
Venture on Him, venture wholly,
  Let no other trust intrude;
    None but Jesus
Can do helpless sinners good.

Joseph Hart, 1712–68

Christ, the curse of the law

For as many as are of the works of the law are under the curse; for it is written, "Cursed is everyone who does not continue in all things which are written in the book of the law, to do them." But that no one is justified by the law in the sight of God is evident, for "the just shall live by faith." Yet the law is not of faith, but "the man who does them shall live by them." Christ has redeemed us from the curse of the law, having become a curse for us (for it is written, "Cursed is everyone who hangs on a tree"), that the blessing of Abraham might come upon the Gentiles in Christ Jesus, that we might receive the promise of the Spirit through faith.

Galatians 3:10–14, NKJV

Guilty, vile, and helpless, we;
Spotless Lamb of God was He:
Full atonement!—can it be?
  Hallelujah! what a Saviour!

Philipp Paul Bliss, 1838–76

Forever with the Lord

"If only you had been here, Lord," said Martha, "My brother would never have died. And I know that, even now, God will give you whatever you ask from him."

"Your brother will rise again," Jesus replied to her.

"I know," said Martha "that he will rise again in the resurrection on the last day."

"I myself am the resurrection and the life," Jesus told her. "The man who believes in me will live even though he dies, and anyone who is alive and believes in me will never die at all. Can you believe that?"

"Yes, Lord," replied Martha. "I do believe that you are Christ, the Son of God, the one who was to come into the world."

John 11:21–27, PHILLIPS

One word of command, one shout from the archangel, one blast from the trumpet of God and the Lord himself will come down from Heaven! Those who have died in Christ will be the first to rise, and then we who are still living will be swept up with them into the clouds to meet the Lord in the air. And after that we shall be with him for ever.

1 Thessalonians 4:16–17, PHILLIPS

So when my latest breath
  Shall rend the veil in twain,
By death I shall escape from death,
  And life eternal gain.
That resurrection-word,
  That shout of victory;
Once more, "For ever with the Lord!"
  Amen, so let it be!

James Montgomery, 1771–1854

The full measure of Christ's love

Now before the feast of the Passover, when Jesus knew that His hour had come that He should depart from this world to the Father, having loved His own who were in the world, He loved them to the end. And supper being ended, the devil having already put it into the heart of Judas Iscariot, Simon's son, to betray Him, Jesus, knowing that the Father had given all things into His hands, and that He had come from God and was going to God, rose from supper and laid aside His garments, took a towel and girded Himself. After that, He poured water into a basin and began to wash the disciples' feet, and to wipe them with the towel with which He was girded.

John 13:1–5, NKJV

He came from His blest throne,
　Salvation to bestow:
But men made strange, and none
　The longed-for Christ would know.
But O, my Friend!
　My Friend indeed,
　Who at my need
His life did spend!

　　　Samuel Crossman, 1624–83

A new commandment

So after he [Jesus] had washed their feet, and had taken his garments, and was set down again, he said unto them, Know ye what I have done to you? Ye call me Master and Lord: and ye say well; for so I am. If I then, your Lord and Master, have washed your feet; ye also ought to wash one another's feet. For I have given you an example, that ye should do as I have done to you. Verily, verily, I say unto you, The servant is not greater than his lord; neither he that is sent greater than he that sent him. If ye know these things, happy are ye if ye do them.

John 13:12–17, KJV

A new commandment I give unto you, That ye love one another; as I have loved you, that ye also love one another. By this shall all men know that ye are my disciples, if ye have love one to another.

John 13:34–35, KJV

Beloved, let us love:
  Love is of God;
In God alone hath love
  Its true abode.

Horatius Bonar, 1808–89

"You are not your own"

All things are lawful for me, but all things are not helpful. All things are lawful for me, but I will not be brought under the power of any. Foods for the stomach and the stomach for foods, but God will destroy both it and them. Now the body is not for sexual immorality but for the Lord, and the Lord for the body. And God both raised up the Lord and will also raise us up by His power. Do you not know that your bodies are members of Christ? Shall I then take the members of Christ and make them members of a harlot? Certainly not! Or do you not know that he who is joined to a harlot is one body with her? For "the two," He says, "shall become one flesh." But he who is joined to the Lord is one spirit with Him. Flee sexual immorality. Every sin that a man does is outside the body, but he who commits sexual immorality sins against his own body. Or do you not know that your body is the temple of the Holy Spirit who is in you, whom you have from God, and you are not your own? For you were bought at a price; therefore glorify God in your body and in your spirit, which are God's.

1 Corinthians 6:12–20, NKJV

All to Thee is yielded,
  I am not my own;
Blissful, glad surrender—
  I am Thine alone.

E. May Grimes, 1868–1927

To every believer the promise of God

Jesus answered and said to him, "Are you the teacher of Israel and do not understand these things? Truly, truly, I say to you, we speak of what we know and testify of what we have seen, and you do not accept our testimony. If I told you earthly things and you do not believe, how will you believe if I tell you heavenly things? No one has ascended into heaven, but He who descended from heaven: the Son of Man. As Moses lifted up the serpent in the wilderness, even so must the Son of Man be lifted up; so that whoever believes will in Him have eternal life.

"For God so loved the world, that He gave His only begotten Son, that whoever believes in Him shall not perish, but have eternal life. For God did not send the Son into the world to judge the world, but that the world might be saved through Him. He who believes in Him is not judged; he who does not believe has been judged already, because he has not believed in the name of the only begotten Son of God."

John 3:10–18, NASB

O perfect redemption, the purchase of blood!
To every believer the promise of God;
The vilest offender who truly believes,
That moment from Jesus a pardon receives.

Praise the Lord! praise the Lord! Let the earth hear His voice!
Praise the Lord! praise the Lord! Let the people rejoice!
O come to the Father through Jesus the Son:
And give Him the glory! great things He hath done!

Frances Jane Van Alstyne, 1820–1915

Jesus comforts his disciples

"Do not let your hearts be troubled. Believe in God, believe also in me. In my Father's house there are many dwelling places. If it were not so, would I have told you that I go to prepare a place for you? And if I go and prepare a place for you, I will come again and will take you to myself, so that where I am, there you may be also. And you know the way to the place where I am going." Thomas said to him, "Lord, we do not know where you are going. How can we know the way?" Jesus said to him, "I am the way, and the truth, and the life. No one comes to the Father except through me. If you know me, you will know my Father also. From now on you do know him and have seen him."

Philip said to him, "Lord, show us the Father, and we will be satis-fied." Jesus said to him, "Have I been with you all this time, Philip, and you still do not know me? Whoever has seen me has seen the Father. How can you say, 'Show us the Father'? Do you not believe that I am in the Father and the Father is in me? The words that I say to you I do not speak on my own; but the Father who dwells in me does his works."

John 14:1–10, NRSV

Thou art gone up before us, Lord,
　To make for us a place,
That we may be where now Thou art,
　And look upon God's face.

Lift up our hearts, lift up our minds;
　Let Thy dear grace be given,
That, while we wander here below,
　Our treasure be in heaven.

Cecil Frances Alexander, 1818–95

"Simply trusting thee, Lord Jesus"

I am the true vine, and my Father is the gardener. He cuts off every branch in me that bears no fruit, while every branch that does bear fruit he prunes so that it will be even more fruitful. You are already clean because of the word I have spoken to you. Remain in me, and I will remain in you. No branch can bear fruit by itself; it must remain in the vine. Neither can you bear fruit unless you remain in me.

I am the vine; you are the branches. If a man remains in me and I in him, he will bear much fruit; apart from me you can do nothing. If anyone does not remain in me, he is like a branch that is thrown away and withers; such branches are picked up, thrown into the fire and burned. If you remain in me and my words remain in you, ask whatever you wish, and it will be given you. This is to my Father's glory, that you bear much fruit, showing yourselves to be my disciples.

John 15:1–8

Jesus, I am resting, resting
  In the joy of what Thou art;
I am finding out the greatness
  Of Thy loving heart.
Thou hast bid me gaze upon Thee,
  And Thy beauty fills my soul,
For by Thy transforming power
  Thou hast made me whole.

Simply trusting Thee, Lord Jesus,
  I behold Thee as Thou art,
And Thy love, so pure, so changeless,
  Satisfies my heart;
Satisfies its deepest longings,
  Meets, supplies its every need,
Compasseth me round with blessings;
  Thine is love indeed!

Jean Sophia Pigott, 1845–82

The Shepherd of the sheep

By him therefore let us offer the sacrifice of praise to God continually, that is, the fruit of our lips giving thanks to his name. But to do good and to communicate forget not: for with such sacrifices God is well pleased. Obey them that have the rule over you, and submit yourselves: for they watch for your souls, as they that must give account, that they may do it with joy, and not with grief: for that is unprofitable for you. Pray for us: for we trust we have a good conscience, in all things willing to live honestly. But I beseech you the rather to do this, that I may be restored to you the sooner. Now the God of peace, that brought again from the dead our Lord Jesus, that great shepherd of the sheep, through the blood of the everlasting covenant, make you perfect in every good work to do his will, working in you that which is well-pleasing in his sight, through Jesus Christ; to whom be glory for ever and ever. Amen.

Hebrews 13:15–21, KJV

Now may He, who from the dead
  Brought the Shepherd of the sheep,
Jesus Christ, our King and Head,
  All our souls in safety keep.

May He teach us to fulfil
  What is pleasing in His sight,
Perfect us in all His will,
  And preserve us day and night.

To that dear Redeemer's praise,
  Who the covenant sealed with blood,
Let our hearts and voices raise
  Loud thanksgivings to our God.

John Newton, 1725–1807

Peace with God

Therefore, having been justified by faith, we have peace with God through our Lord Jesus Christ, through whom also we have access by faith into this grace in which we stand, and rejoice in hope of the glory of God. And not only that, but we also glory in tribulations, knowing that tribulation produces perseverance; and perseverance, character; and character, hope. Now hope does not disappoint, because the love of God has been poured out in our hearts by the Holy Spirit who was given to us.

Romans 5:1–5, NKJV

I hear the words of love,
  I gaze upon the blood,
I see the mighty sacrifice,
  And I have peace with God.

'Tis everlasting peace,
  Sure as Jehovah's Name;
'Tis stable as His steadfast throne,
  For evermore the same.

My love is oft-times low,
  My joy still ebbs and flows;
But peace with Him remains the same—
  No change Jehovah knows.

Horatius Bonar, 1808–89

The promise of the Spirit

Believe me that I am in the Father and the Father is in me; but if you do not, then believe me because of the works themselves. Very truly, I tell you, the one who believes in me will also do the works that I do and, in fact, will do greater works than these, because I am going to the Father. I will do whatever you ask in my name, so that the Father may be glorified in the Son. If in my name you ask me for anything, I will do it.

"If you love me, you will keep my commandments. And I will ask the Father, and he will give you another Advocate, to be with you forever. This is the Spirit of truth, whom the world cannot receive, because it neither sees him nor knows him. You know him, because he abides with you, and he will be in you.

"I will not leave you orphaned; I am coming to you. In a little while the world will no longer see me, but you will see me; because I live, you also will live. On that day you will know that I am in my Father, and you in me, and I in you. They who have my commandments and keep them are those who love me; and those who love me will be loved by my Father, and I will love them and reveal myself to them."

John 14:11–21, NRSV

And so the yearning strong,
With which the soul will long,
  Shall far outpass the power of human telling;
For none can guess its grace,
Till he become the place
  Wherein the Holy Spirit makes His dwelling.

Bianco da Siena, c. 1350–1434
translated by Richard Frederick Littledale, 1833–90

The way of faith

For we know that if the earthly tent which is our house is torn down, we have a building from God, a house not made with hands, eternal in the heavens. For indeed in this house we groan, longing to be clothed with our dwelling from heaven, inasmuch as we, having put it on, will not be found naked. For indeed while we are in this tent, we groan, being burdened, because we do not want to be unclothed but to be clothed, so that what is mortal will be swallowed up by life. Now He who prepared us for this very purpose is God, who gave to us the Spirit as a pledge.

Therefore, being always of good courage, and knowing that while we are at home in the body we are absent from the Lord—for we walk by faith, not by sight—we are of good courage, I say, and prefer rather to be absent from the body and to be at home with the Lord. Therefore we also have as our ambition, whether at home or absent, to be pleasing to Him. For we must all appear before the judgment seat of Christ, so that each one may be recompensed for his deeds in the body, according to what he has done, whether good or bad.

2 Corinthians 5:1–10, NASB

Teach me Thy way, O Lord,
  Teach me Thy way;
Thy gracious aid afford,
  Teach me Thy way;
Help me to walk aright,
More by faith, less by sight;
Lead me with heavenly light:
  Teach me Thy way.

Benjamin Mansell Ramsey, 1849–1923

God's precious word

The law of the LORD is perfect, converting the soul: the testimony of the LORD is sure, making wise the simple. The statutes of the LORD are right, rejoicing the heart: the commandment of the LORD is pure, enlightening the eyes. The fear of the LORD is clean, enduring for ever: the judgments of the LORD are true and righteous altogether. More to be desired are they than gold, yea, than much fine gold: sweeter also than honey and the honeycomb. Moreover by them is thy servant warned: and in keeping of them there is great reward. Who can understand his errors? cleanse thou me from secret faults. Keep back thy servant also from presumptuous sins; let them not have dominion over me: then shall I be upright, and I shall be innocent from the great transgression. Let the words of my mouth, and the meditation of my heart, be acceptable in thy sight, O LORD, my strength, and my redeemer.

Psalm 19:7–14, KJV

Who can tell the pleasure,
Who recount the treasure,
By Thy Word imparted,
To the simple-hearted?

Word of mercy, giving
Succour to the living;
Word of life, supplying
Comfort to the dying!

Henry Williams Baker, 1821–77

The great banquet

When one of those at the table with him heard this, he said to Jesus, "Blessed is the man who will eat at the feast in the kingdom of God."

Jesus replied: "A certain man was preparing a great banquet and invited many guests. At the time of the banquet he sent his servant to tell those who had been invited, 'Come, for everything is now ready.'

"But they all alike began to make excuses. The first said, 'I have just bought a field, and I must go and see it. Please excuse me.'

"Another said, 'I have just bought five yoke of oxen, and I'm on my way to try them out. Please excuse me.'

"Still another said, 'I just got married, so I can't come.'

"The servant came back and reported this to his master. Then the owner of the house became angry and ordered his servant, 'Go out quickly into the streets and alleys of the town and bring in the poor, the crippled, the blind and the lame.'

"'Sir,' the servant said, 'what you ordered has been done, but there is still room.'

"Then the master told his servant, 'Go out to the roads and country lanes and make them come in, so that my house will be full. I tell you, not one of those men who were invited will get a taste of my banquet.'"

Luke 14:15–24

Sent by my Lord, on you I call,
The invitation is to all:
Come, all the world; come, sinner, thou!
All things in Christ are ready now.

His love is mighty to compel;
His conquering love consent to feel,
Yield to His love's resistless power,
And fight against your God no more.

Charles Wesley, 1707–88

"Abba, Father"

For you are all sons of God through faith in Christ Jesus. For as many of you as were baptized into Christ have put on Christ. There is neither Jew nor Greek, there is neither slave nor free, there is neither male nor female; for you are all one in Christ Jesus. And if you are Christ's, then you are Abraham's seed, and heirs according to the promise.

Now I say that the heir, as long as he is a child, does not differ at all from a slave, though he is master of all, but is under guardians and stewards until the time appointed by the father. Even so we, when we were children, were in bondage under the elements of the world. But when the fullness of the time had come, God sent forth His Son, born of a woman, born under the law, to redeem those who were under the law, that we might receive the adoption as sons. And because you are sons, God has sent forth the Spirit of His Son into your hearts, crying out, "Abba, Father!" Therefore you are no longer a slave but a son, and if a son, then an heir of God through Christ.

Galatians 3:26–4:7, NKJV

If in our Father's love
  We share a filial part,
Send down Thy Spirit like a dove
  To rest upon each heart.

We would no longer lie
  Like slaves beneath Thy throne;
Our faith shall "Abba, Father" cry,
  And Thou the kindred own.

Isaac Watts, 1674–1748

Work out your salvation

Therefore, my beloved, as you have always obeyed, not as in my presence only, but now much more in my absence, work out your own salvation with fear and trembling; for it is God who works in you both to will and to do for His good pleasure. Do all things without complaining and disputing, that you may become blameless and harmless, children of God without fault in the midst of a crooked and perverse generation, among whom you shine as lights in the world, holding fast the word of life, so that I may rejoice in the day of Christ that I have not run in vain or labored in vain. Yes, and if I am being poured out as a drink offering on the sacrifice and service of your faith, I am glad and rejoice with you all. For the same reason you also be glad and rejoice with me.

Philippians 2:12–18, NKJV

Thou canst keep my feet from falling,
  Even my poor wayward feet—
Thou who dost present me faultless,
  In Thy righteousness complete;
Jesus, Lord, in knowing Thee,
O what strength and victory!

Make my life a bright outshining
  Of Thy life, that all may see
Thine own resurrection power
  Mightily put forth in me;
Ever let my heart become
Yet more consciously Thy home.

Jean Sophia Pigott, 1845–82

NOVEMBER 8

He will meet all our needs

Nor do I mean that I have been in actual need, for I have learned to be content, whatever the circumstances may be. I know now how to live when things are difficult and I know how to live when things are prosperous. In general and in particular I have learned the secret of eating well or going hungry—of facing either plenty or poverty. I am ready for anything through the strength of the One who lives within me. Nevertheless I am very grateful for the way in which you were willing to share my troubles. You Philippians will remember that in the early days of the gospel when I left Macedonia, you were the only church who shared with me the fellowship of giving and receiving. Even in Thessalonica you sent me help when I was in need, not once but twice. . . .

My God will supply all that you need from his glorious resources in Christ Jesus. And may glory be to our God and our Father for ever and ever, amen!

Philippians 4:11–16,19–20, PHILLIPS

My every need He richly will supply,
Nor will His mercy ever let me die;
In Him there dwells a treasure all divine,
And matchless grace has made that treasure mine.

William Gadsby, 1773–1844

NOVEMBER 9

Submitting to God

Where do wars and fights come from among you? Do they not come from your desires for pleasure that war in your members? You lust and do not have. You murder and covet and cannot obtain. You fight and war. Yet you do not have because you do not ask. You ask and do not receive, because you ask amiss, that you may spend it on your pleasures. Adulterers and adulteresses! Do you not know that friendship with the world is enmity with God? Whoever therefore wants to be a friend of the world makes himself an enemy of God. Or do you think that the Scripture says in vain, "The Spirit who dwells in us yearns jealously"? But He gives more grace. Therefore He says: "God resists the proud, But gives grace to the humble."

Therefore submit to God. Resist the devil and he will flee from you. Draw near to God and He will draw near to you. Cleanse your hands, you sinners; and purify your hearts, you double-minded. Lament and mourn and weep! Let your laughter be turned to mourning and your joy to gloom. Humble yourselves in the sight of the Lord, and He will lift you up.

James 4:1–10, NKJV

Here from the world we turn,
  Jesus to seek;
Here may His loving voice
  Tenderly speak.
Jesus, our dearest Friend,
While at Thy feet we bend,
O let Thy smile descend!
  'Tis Thee we seek.

Frances Jane Van Alstyne, 1820–1915

The mediator, the man Christ Jesus

First of all, then, I urge that entreaties and prayers, petitions and thanksgivings, be made on behalf of all men, for kings and all who are in authority, so that we may lead a tranquil and quiet life in all godliness and dignity. This is good and acceptable in the sight of God our Savior, who desires all men to be saved and to come to the knowledge of the truth. For there is one God, and one mediator also between God and men, the man Christ Jesus, who gave Himself as a ransom for all, the testimony given at the proper time. For this I was appointed a preacher and an apostle (I am telling the truth, I am not lying) as a teacher of the Gentiles in faith and truth.

1 Timothy 2:1–7, NASB

For ever God, for ever Man,
  My Jesus shall endure;
And fixed on Him, my hope remains
  Eternally secure.

Edward Caswall, 1814–78

NOVEMBER 11

You are my hiding place

For this shall every one that is godly pray unto thee in a time when thou mayest be found: surely in the floods of great waters they shall not come nigh unto him. Thou art my hiding place; thou shalt preserve me from trouble; thou shalt compass me about with songs of deliverance. Selah. I will instruct thee and teach thee in the way which thou shalt go: I will guide thee with mine eye. Be ye not as the horse, or as the mule, which have no understanding: whose mouth must be held in with bit and bridle, lest they come near unto thee. Many sorrows shall be to the wicked: but he that trusteth in the LORD, mercy shall compass him about. Be glad in the LORD, and rejoice, ye righteous: and shout for joy, all ye that are upright in heart.

Psalm 32:6–11, KJV

O safe to the Rock that is higher than I
My soul in its conflicts and sorrows would fly;
So sinful, so weary, Thine, Thine would I be;
Thou blest Rock of Ages, I'm hiding in Thee!

Hiding in Thee! hiding in Thee!
Thou blest Rock of Ages, I'm hiding in Thee!

William Orcutt Cushing, 1823–1903

Our gracious, powerful God

Praise waiteth for thee, O God, in Sion: and unto thee shall the vow be performed. O thou that hearest prayer, unto thee shall all flesh come. Iniquities prevail against me: as for our transgressions, thou shalt purge them away. Blessed is the man whom thou choosest, and causest to approach unto thee, that he may dwell in thy courts: we shall be satisfied with the goodness of thy house, even of thy holy temple. By terrible things in righteousness wilt thou answer us, O God of our salvation; who art the confidence of all the ends of the earth, and of them that are afar off upon the sea: Which by his strength setteth fast the mountains; being girded with power: Which stilleth the noise of the seas, the noise of their waves, and the tumult of the people. They also that dwell in the uttermost parts are afraid at thy tokens: thou makest the outgoings of the morning and evening to rejoice.

Psalm 65:1–8, KJV

Praise, Lord, for Thee in Zion waits;
Prayer shall besiege Thy temple gates;
All flesh shall to Thy throne repair,
And find, through Christ, salvation there.

How blest Thy saints! how safely led!
How surely kept! how richly fed!
Saviour of all in earth and sea,
How happy they who rest in Thee!

Henry Francis Lyte, 1793–1847

"Whom have I in heaven but you?"

Nevertheless I am continually with thee: thou hast holden me by my right hand. Thou shalt guide me with thy counsel, and afterward receive me to glory. Whom have I in heaven but thee? and there is none upon earth that I desire beside thee. My flesh and my heart faileth: but God is the strength of my heart, and my portion for ever. For, lo, they that are far from thee shall perish: thou hast destroyed all them that go a whoring from thee. But it is good for me to draw near to God: I have put my trust in the Lord GOD, that I may declare all thy works.

Psalm 73:23–28, KJV

Whom have I on earth below?
Thee, and only Thee, I know;
Whom have I in heaven but Thee?
Thou art all in all to me.

All my treasure is above,
All my riches is Thy love:
Who the worth of love can tell?
Infinite, unsearchable.

Charles Wesley, 1707–88

Looking at Jesus

Therefore we also, since we are surrounded by so great a cloud of witnesses, let us lay aside every weight, and the sin which so easily ensnares us, and let us run with endurance the race that is set before us, looking unto Jesus, the author and finisher of our faith, who for the joy that was set before Him endured the cross, despising the shame, and has sat down at the right hand of the throne of God. For consider Him who endured such hostility from sinners against Himself, lest you become weary and discouraged in your souls. You have not yet resisted to bloodshed, striving against sin. And you have forgotten the exhortation which speaks to you as to sons: "My son, do not despise the chastening of the LORD, nor be discouraged when you are rebuked by Him; for whom the LORD loves He chastens, and scourges every son whom He receives."

Hebrews 12:1–6, NKJV

Onward! Christian soldiers,
  Marching as to war,
Looking unto Jesus,
  Who is gone before:
Christ, the royal Master,
  Leads against the foe;
Forward into battle,
  See, His banners go!

Onward! Christian soldiers,
  Marching as to war,
Looking unto Jesus,
  Who is gone before.

Sabine Baring-Gould, 1834–1924

The choir of creation

Praise ye the LORD. Praise ye the LORD from the heavens: praise him in the heights. Praise ye him, all his angels: praise ye him, all his hosts. Praise ye him, sun and moon: praise him, all ye stars of light. Praise him, ye heavens of heavens, and ye waters that be above the heavens. Let them praise the name of the LORD: for he commanded, and they were created. He hath also stablished them for ever and ever: he hath made a decree which shall not pass. Praise the LORD from the earth, ye dragons, and all deeps: fire, and hail; snow, and vapour; stormy wind fulfilling his word: mountains, and all hills; fruit-ful trees, and all cedars: beasts, and all cattle; creeping things, and flying fowl: kings of the earth, and all people; princes, and all judges of the earth: both young men, and maidens; old men, and children.

Psalm 148:1–12, KJV

For the beauty of the earth,
  For the beauty of the skies,
For the love which from our birth
  Over and around us lies:

Gracious God, to Thee we raise
This our sacrifice of praise.

For each perfect gift of Thine
  To our race so freely given,
Graces human and divine,
  Flowers of earth and buds of heaven.

Folliott Stanford Pierpoint, 1835–1917

Crowned with glory and honor

For God did not put the future world of men under the control of angels, and it is this world that we are now talking about.

But someone has truly said:

What is man, that thou art mindful of him?

Or the son of man, that thou visitest him?

Thou madest him a little lower than the angels;

Thou crownedst him with glory and honour,

And didst set him over the works of thy hands;

Thou didst put all things in subjection under his feet.

Notice that the writer puts "all things" under the sovereignty of man: he left nothing outside his control. But we do not yet see "all things" under his control.

What we see is Jesus, after being made temporarily inferior to the angels and so subject to death, in order that he should, by God's grace, taste death for every man, now crowned with glory and honour. It was right and proper that in bringing many sons to glory, God (from whom and by whom everything exists) should make the leader of their salvation perfect through his sufferings. For the one who makes men holy and the men who are made holy share a common humanity. So that he is not ashamed to call them his brothers.

Hebrews 2:5–11, PHILLIPS

Crown Him the Lord of years,
  The Potentate of time,
Creator of the rolling spheres,
  Ineffably sublime!
All hail. Redeemer, hail!
  For Thou hast died for me:
Thy praise shall never, never fail
  Throughout eternity.

Matthew Bridges, 1800–1894
and
Godfrey Thring, 1823–1903

The shedding of Christ's blood

Christ is consequently the administrator of an entirely new agreement having the power, by virtue of his death, to redeem transgressions committed under the first agreement: to enable those who obey God's call to enjoy the promises of the eternal inheritance. For, as in the case of a will, the agreement is only valid after death. While the testator lives, a will has no legal power. And indeed we find that even the first agreement of God's will was not put into force without the shedding of blood. For when Moses had told the people every command of the Law he took calves' and goats' blood with water and scarlet wool, and sprinkled both the book and all the people with a sprig of hyssop, saying: "This is the blood of the agreement God makes with you." Moses also sprinkled with blood the tent itself and all the sacred vessels. And you will find that in the Law almost all cleansing is made by means of blood—it implies again and again: "No shedding of blood, no remission of sin."

Hebrews 9:15–22, PHILLIPS

Christ is my peace; He died for me,
  For me He gave His blood;
And, as my wondrous sacrifice,
  Offered Himself to God.

John Mason, c. 1646–94

God's good gifts

Blessed is the man who endures temptation; for when he has been approved, he will receive the crown of life which the Lord has promised to those who love Him. Let no one say when he is tempted, "I am tempted by God"; for God cannot be tempted by evil, nor does He Himself tempt anyone. But each one is tempted when he is drawn away by his own desires and enticed. Then, when desire has conceived, it gives birth to sin; and sin, when it is full-grown, brings forth death. Do not be deceived, my beloved brethren. Every good gift and every perfect gift is from above, and comes down from the Father of lights, with whom there is no variation or shadow of turning. Of His own will He brought us forth by the word of truth, that we might be a kind of firstfruits of His creatures.

James 1:12–18, NKJV

All good gifts around us
  Are sent from heaven above,
Then thank the Lord, O thank the Lord,
  For all His love.

Matthias Claudius, 1740–1815
translated by Jane Montgomery Campbell, 1817–78

What he says, we will do

So then, my beloved brethren, let every man be swift to hear, slow to speak, slow to wrath; for the wrath of man does not produce the righteousness of God.

Therefore lay aside all filthiness and overflow of wickedness, and receive with meekness the implanted word, which is able to save your souls. But be doers of the word, and not hearers only, deceiving yourselves. For if anyone is a hearer of the word and not a doer, he is like a man observing his natural face in a mirror; for he observes himself, goes away, and immediately forgets what kind of man he was. But he who looks into the perfect law of liberty and continues in it, and is not a forgetful hearer but a doer of the work, this one will be blessed in what he does.

James 1:19–25, NKJV

Then in fellowship sweet
We will sit at His feet,
  Or we'll walk by His side in the way;
What He says we will do,
Where He sends we will go—
  Never fear, only trust and obey!

Trust and obey!
For there's no other way
 To be happy in Jesus
But to trust and obey.

John Henry Sammis, 1846–1919

Taming the tongue

Even so the tongue is a little member and boasts great things. See how great a forest a little fire kindles! And the tongue is a fire, a world of iniquity. The tongue is so set among our members that it defiles the whole body, and sets on fire the course of nature; and it is set on fire by hell. For every kind of beast and bird, of reptile and creature of the sea, is tamed and has been tamed by mankind. But no man can tame the tongue. It is an unruly evil, full of deadly poison. With it we bless our God and Father, and with it we curse men, who have been made in the similitude of God. Out of the same mouth proceed blessing and cursing. My brethren, these things ought not to be so.

James 3:5–10, NKJV

Take my voice, and let me sing
Always, only for my King;
Take my lips, and let them be
Filled with messages from Thee.

Frances Ridley Havergal, 1836–79

Dead to sin

What shall we say, then? Shall we go on sinning so that grace may increase? By no means! We died to sin; how can we live in it any longer? Or don't you know that all of us who were baptized into Christ Jesus were baptized into his death? We were therefore buried with him through baptism into death in order that, just as Christ was raised from the dead through the glory of the Father, we too may live a new life.

If we have been united with him like this in his death, we will certainly also be united with him in his resurrection. For we know that our old self was crucified with him so that the body of sin might be done away with, that we should no longer be slaves to sin—because anyone who has died has been freed from sin.

Now if we died with Christ, we believe that we will also live with him. For we know that since Christ was raised from the dead, he cannot die again; death no longer has mastery over him. The death he died, he died to sin once for all; but the life he lives, he lives to God.

In the same way, count yourselves dead to sin but alive to God in Christ Jesus.

Romans 6:1–11

As dead indeed to sin,
    From its dominion free,
Henceforth, as not our own, but Thine,
    We follow only Thee.

Baptised into Thy death,
    With Thee again we rise,
To newness of a life of faith,
    To new and endless joys.

Anonymous

The coming King

Give the king thy judgments, O God, and thy righteousness unto the king's son. He shall judge thy people with righteousness, and thy poor with judgment. The mountains shall bring peace to the people, and the little hills, by righteousness. He shall judge the poor of the people, he shall save the children of the needy, and shall break in pieces the oppressor. They shall fear thee as long as the sun and moon endure, throughout all generations. He shall come down like rain upon the mown grass: as showers that water the earth. In his days shall the righteous flourish; and abundance of peace so long as the moon endureth. He shall have dominion also from sea to sea, and from the river unto the ends of the earth.

Psalm 72:1–8, KJV

Hail to the Lord's Anointed,
　　Great David's greater Son!
Hail, in the time appointed,
　　His reign on earth begun!
He comes to break oppression,
　　To set the captive free,
To take away transgression,
　　And rule in equity.

He shall come down like showers
　　Upon the fruitful earth,
And love, joy, hope, like flowers,
　　Spring in His path to birth:
Before Him on the mountains
　　Shall peace, the herald, go;
And righteousness, in fountains,
　　From hill to valley flow.

James Montgomery, 1771–1854

"Stay with us"

As they came near the village to which they were going, he walked ahead as if he were going on. But they urged him strongly, saying, "Stay with us, because it is almost evening and the day is now nearly over." So he went in to stay with them. When he was at the table with them, he took bread, blessed and broke it, and gave it to them. Then their eyes were opened, and they recognized him; and he vanished from their sight. They said to each other, "Were not our hearts burning within us while he was talking to us on the road, while he was opening the scriptures to us?" That same hour they got up and returned to Jerusalem; and they found the eleven and their companions gathered together. They were saying, "The Lord has risen indeed, and he has appeared to Simon!" Then they told what had happened on the road, and how he had been made known to them in the breaking of the bread.

Luke 24:28–35, NRSV

Our restless spirits yearn for Thee
    Where'er our changeful lot is cast;
Glad, when Thy gracious smile we see;
    Blest, when our faith can hold Thee fast.

O Jesus, ever with us stay;
    Make all our moments calm and bright;
Chase the dark night of sin away;
    Shed o'er our souls Thy holy light.

Latin, c. 11th century
translated by Ray Palmer, 1808–87

The world for the gospel

Then [Jesus] said to them, "These are my words that I spoke to you while I was still with you—that everything written about me in the law of Moses, the prophets, and the psalms must be fulfilled." Then he opened their minds to understand the scriptures, and he said to them, "Thus it is written, that the Messiah is to suffer and to rise from the dead on the third day, and that repentance and forgiveness of sins is to be proclaimed in his name to all nations, beginning from Jerusalem. You are witnesses of these things. And see, I am sending upon you what my Father promised; so stay here in the city until you have been clothed with power from on high."

Then he led them out as far as Bethany, and, lifting up his hands, he blessed them. While he was blessing them, he withdrew from them and was carried up into heaven. And they worshiped him, and returned to Jerusalem with great joy; and they were continually in the temple blessing God.

Luke 24:44–53, NRSV

"For my sake and the gospel's, go
  And tell redemption's story";
His heralds answer, "Be it so,
  And Thine, Lord, all the glory!"
They preach His birth, His life, His cross,
  The love of His atonement,
For whom they count the world but loss,
  His Easter, His enthronement.

Edward Henry Bickersteth, 1825–1906

God, our refuge

He that dwelleth in the secret place of the most High shall abide under the shadow of the Almighty. I will say of the LORD, He is my refuge and my fortress: my God; in him will I trust. Surely he shall deliver thee from the snare of the fowler, and from the noisome pestilence. He shall cover thee with his feathers, and under his wings shalt thou trust: his truth shall be thy shield and buckler. Thou shalt not be afraid for the terror by night; nor for the arrow that flieth by day; nor for the pestilence that walketh in darkness; nor for the destruction that wasteth at noonday. A thousand shall fall at thy side, and ten thousand at thy right hand; but it shall not come nigh thee. Only with thine eyes shalt thou behold and see the reward of the wicked.

Psalm 91:1–8, KJV

Inspirer and Hearer of prayer,
  Thou Shepherd and Guardian of Thine,
My all to Thy covenant care
  I sleeping and waking resign.
If Thou art my Shield and my Sun,
  The night is no darkness to me;
And fast as my moments roll on,
  They bring me but nearer to Thee.

Augustus Montague Toplady, 1740–78

Continuing in prayer

Then He spoke a parable to them, that men always ought to pray and not lose heart, saying: "There was in a certain city a judge who did not fear God nor regard man. Now there was a widow in that city; and she came to him, saying, 'Get justice for me from my adversary.' And he would not for a while; but afterward he said within himself, 'Though I do not fear God nor regard man, yet because this widow troubles me I will avenge her, lest by her continual coming she weary me.'" Then the Lord said, "Hear what the unjust judge said. And shall God not avenge His own elect who cry out day and night to Him, though He bears long with them? I tell you that He will avenge them speedily. Nevertheless, when the Son of Man comes, will He really find faith on the earth?"

Luke 18:1–8, NKJV

Prayer is the burden of a sigh,
  The falling of a tear;
The upward glancing of an eye,
  When none but God is near.

Prayer is the Christian's vital breath,
  The Christian's native air;
His watchword at the gates of death;
  He enters heaven with prayer.

James Montgomery, 1771–1854

Trusting in God

They wandered in the wilderness in a solitary way; they found no city to dwell in. Hungry and thirsty, their soul fainted in them. Then they cried unto the LORD in their trouble, and he delivered them out of their distresses. And he led them forth by the right way, that they might go to a city of habitation. Oh that men would praise the LORD for his goodness, and for his wonderful works to the children of men! For he satisfieth the longing soul, and filleth the hungry soul with goodness.

Psalm 107:4–9, KJV

In the fear of the LORD is strong confidence: and his children shall have a place of refuge. The fear of the LORD is a fountain of life, to depart from the snares of death.

Proverbs 14:26–27, KJV

Put thou thy trust in God,
  In duty's path go on;
Walk in His strength with faith and hope,
  So shall thy work be done.

Commit thy ways to Him,
  Thy works into His hands,
And rest on His unchanging word,
  Who heaven and earth commands.

Leave to His sovereign sway
  To choose and to command;
So shalt thou, wondering, own His way,
  How wise, how strong, His hand.

Paul Gerhardt, 1607–76
translated by John Wesley, 1703–91

A life's journey

Remember the word unto thy servant, upon which thou hast caused me to hope. This is my comfort in my affliction: for thy word hath quickened me. The proud have had me greatly in derision: yet have I not declined from thy law. I remembered thy judgments of old, O LORD; and have comforted myself. Horror hath taken hold upon me because of the wicked that forsake thy law. Thy statutes have been my songs in the house of my pilgrimage. I have remembered thy name, O LORD, in the night, and have kept thy law. This I had, because I kept thy precepts.

Psalm 119:49–56, KJV

Children of the heavenly King,
As ye journey, sweetly sing;
Sing your Saviour's worthy praise,
Glorious in His works and ways.

We are travelling home to God
In the way the fathers trod;
They are happy now, and we
Soon their happiness shall see.

Lord, obediently we go,
Gladly leaving all below:
Only Thou our Leader be,
And we still will follow Thee.

John Cennick, 1718–55

Jesus our Lord

"I am the Alpha and the Omega," says the Lord God, "who is and who was and who is to come, the Almighty."

I, John, your brother and fellow partaker in the tribulation and kingdom and perseverance which are in Jesus, was on the island called Patmos because of the word of God and the testimony of Jesus. I was in the Spirit on the Lord's day, and I heard behind me a loud voice like the sound of a trumpet, saying, "Write in a book what you see, and send it to the seven churches: to Ephesus and to Smyrna and to Pergamum and to Thyatira and to Sardis and to Philadelphia and to Laodicea."

Revelation 1:8–11, NASB

Love divine, all loves excelling,
  Joy of heaven, to earth come down,
Fix in us Thy humble dwelling,
  All Thy faithful mercies crown.
Jesus, Thou art all compassion,
  Pure, unbounded love Thou art;
Visit us with Thy salvation,
  Enter every trembling heart.

Breathe, O breathe Thy loving Spirit
  Into every troubled breast;
Let us all in Thee inherit,
  Let us find Thy promised rest.
Take away the love of sinning,
  Alpha and Omega be;
End of faith, as its beginning,
  Set our hearts at liberty.

Charles Wesley, 1707–88

He lives forever!

Then I turned to see whose voice it was that spoke to me, and on turning I saw seven golden lampstands, and in the midst of the lampstands I saw one like the Son of Man, clothed with a long robe and with a golden sash across his chest. His head and his hair were white as white wool, white as snow; his eyes were like a flame of fire, his feet were like burnished bronze, refined as in a furnace, and his voice was like the sound of many waters. In his right hand he held seven stars, and from his mouth came a sharp, two-edged sword, and his face was like the sun shining with full force.

When I saw him, I fell at his feet as though dead. But he placed his right hand on me, saying, "Do not be afraid; I am the first and the last, and the living one. I was dead, and see, I am alive forever and ever; and I have the keys of Death and of Hades."

Revelation 1:12–18, NRSV

Rejoice and be glad! the Redeemer hath come:
Go, look on His cradle, His cross, and His tomb.

Sound His praises, tell the story of Him who was slain;
Sound His praises, tell with gladness He liveth again.

Rejoice and be glad! for the Lamb that was slain
O'er death is triumphant, and liveth again.

Horatius Bonar, 1808–89

"My Lord and my God!"

Now Thomas, called the Twin, one of the twelve, was not with them when Jesus came. The other disciples therefore said to him, "We have seen the Lord." So he said to them, "Unless I see in His hands the print of the nails, and put my finger into the print of the nails, and put my hand into His side, I will not believe." And after eight days His disciples were again inside, and Thomas with them. Jesus came, the doors being shut, and stood in the midst, and said, "Peace to you!" Then He said to Thomas, "Reach your finger here, and look at My hands; and reach your hand here, and put it into My side. Do not be unbelieving, but believing." And Thomas answered and said to Him, "My Lord and my God!" Jesus said to him, "Thomas, because you have seen Me, you have believed. Blessed are those who have not seen and yet have believed."

John 20:24–29, NKJV

Lord, in this blest and hallowed hour
Reveal Thy presence and Thy power;
Show to my faith Thy hands and side,
My Lord and God, the Crucified!

Josiah Conder, 1789–1855

The city of our God

In that day this song will be sung in the land of Judah: We have a strong city; God makes salvation its walls and ramparts. Open the gates that the righteous nation may enter, the nation that keeps faith. You will keep in perfect peace him whose mind is steadfast, because he trusts in you. Trust in the LORD forever, for the LORD, the LORD, is the Rock eternal. . . .

The path of the righteous is level; O upright One, you make the way of the righteous smooth. Yes, LORD, walking in the way of your laws, we wait for you; your name and renown are the desire of our hearts. My soul yearns for you in the night; in the morning my spirit longs for you. When your judgments come upon the earth, the people of the world learn righteousness.

Isaiah 26:1–4,7–9

How glorious Zion's courts appear,
　The city of our God!
His throne He hath established here,
　Here fixed His loved abode.

Its walls, defended by His grace,
　No power shall e'er o'erthrow,
Salvation is its bulwark sure
　Against the assaulting foe.

Here shall ye taste unmingled joys,
　And dwell in perfect peace,
Ye, who have known Jehovah's Name,
　And trusted in His grace.

Scottish Paraphrases, 1781

"Turn to me and be saved"

"Look to Me, and be saved, all you ends of the earth! For I am God, and there is no other. I have sworn by Myself; the word has gone out of My mouth in righteousness, and shall not return, that to Me every knee shall bow, every tongue shall take an oath. He shall say, 'Surely in the LORD I have righteousness and strength. To Him men shall come, and all shall be ashamed who are incensed against Him. In the LORD all the descendants of Israel shall be justified, and shall glory.'"

Isaiah 45:22–25, NKJV

For by grace you have been saved through faith, and that not of yourselves; it is the gift of God, not of works, lest anyone should boast.

Ephesians 2:8–9, NKJV

Look unto Him, ye nations, own
  Your God, ye fallen race;
Look, and be saved through faith alone,
  Be justified by grace.

Charles Wesley, 1707–88

The good news of peace

How beautiful upon the mountains are the feet of him who brings good news, who proclaims peace, who brings glad tidings of good things, who proclaims salvation, who says to Zion, "Your God reigns!" Your watchmen shall lift up their voices, with their voices they shall sing together; for they shall see eye to eye when the Lord brings back Zion. Break forth into joy, sing together, you waste places of Jerusalem! For the Lord has comforted His people, He has redeemed Jerusalem. The Lord has made bare His holy arm in the eyes of all the nations; and all the ends of the earth shall see the salvation of our God.

Isaiah 52:7–10, NKJV

How beauteous are their feet
  Who stand on Zion's hill,
Who bring salvation on their tongues
  And words of peace reveal!

The Lord makes bare His arm
  Through all the earth abroad;
Let every nation now behold
  Their Saviour and their God.

Isaac Watts, 1674–1748

The triumph of grace

And one shall say, "Heap it up! Heap it up! Prepare the way, take the stumbling block out of the way of My people." For thus says the High and Lofty One Who inhabits eternity, whose name is Holy: "I dwell in the high and holy place, with him who has a contrite and humble spirit, to revive the spirit of the humble, and to revive the heart of the contrite ones. For I will not contend forever, nor will I always be angry; for the spirit would fail before Me, and the souls which I have made. For the iniquity of his covetousness I was angry and struck him; I hid and was angry, and he went on backsliding in the way of his heart. I have seen his ways, and will heal him; I will also lead him, and restore comforts to him and to his mourners. I create the fruit of the lips: Peace, peace to him who is far off and to him who is near," says the LORD, "and I will heal him."

Isaiah 57:14–19, NKJV

O how I fear Thee, living God,
  With deepest, tenderest fears,
And worship Thee with trembling hope
  And penitential tears!

Yet I may love Thee, too, O Lord,
  Almighty as Thou art;
For Thou hast stooped to ask of me
  The love of my poor heart.

Frederick William Faber, 1814–63

Coming to Christ

Come unto me, all ye that labour and are heavy laden, and I will give you rest. Take my yoke upon you, and learn of me; for I am meek and lowly in heart: and ye shall find rest unto your souls. For my yoke is easy, and my burden is light.

Matthew 11:28–30, KJV

For God so loved the world, that he gave his only begotten Son, that whosoever believeth in him should not perish, but have everlasting life.

John 3:16, KJV

Jesu, lover of my soul,
  Let me to Thy bosom fly,
While the nearer waters roll,
  While the tempest still is high:
Hide me, O my Saviour, hide,
  Till the storm of life be past;
Safe into the haven guide;
  O receive my soul at last!

Other refuge have I none;
  Hangs my helpless soul on Thee;
Leave, ah! leave me not alone,
  Still support and comfort me:
All my trust on Thee is stayed,
  All my help from Thee I bring;
Cover my defenceless head
  With the shadow of Thy wing.

Charles Wesley, 1707–88

Our sovereign protector

Because thou hast made the LORD, which is my refuge, even the most High, thy habitation; there shall no evil befall thee, neither shall any plague come nigh thy dwelling. For he shall give his angels charge over thee, to keep thee in all thy ways. They shall bear thee up in their hands, lest thou dash thy foot against a stone. Thou shalt tread upon the lion and adder: the young lion and the dragon shalt thou trample under feet. Because he hath set his love upon me, therefore will I deliver him: I will set him on high, because he hath known my name. He shall call upon me, and I will answer him: I will be with him in trouble; I will deliver him, and honour him. With long life will I satisfy him, and shew him my salvation.

Psalm 91:9–16, KJV

A sovereign Protector I have,
  Unseen, yet for ever at hand,
Unchangeably faithful to save,
  Almighty to rule and command.
He smiles, and my comforts abound;
  His grace as the dew shall descend;
And walls of salvation surround
  The soul He delights to defend.

Augustus Montague Toplady, 1740–78

Rejoice in the Lord!

Though the fig tree should not blossom and there be no fruit on the vines, though the yield of the olive should fail and the fields produce no food, though the flock should be cut off from the fold and there be no cattle in the stalls, yet I will exult in the LORD, I will rejoice in the God of my salvation. The Lord GOD is my strength, and He has made my feet like hinds' feet, and makes me walk on my high places. For the choir director, on my stringed instruments.

Habakkuk 3:17–19, NASB

Rejoice in the Lord always; again I will say, rejoice!

Philippians 4:4, NASB

Though vine nor fig-tree neither
  Their wonted fruit should bear,
Though all the field should wither,
  Nor flocks nor herds be there,
Yet God the same abiding,
  His praise shall tune my voice;
For while in Him confiding,
  I cannot but rejoice.

William Cowper, 1731–1800

Christ in us

I became its servant according to God's commission that was given to me for you, to make the word of God fully known, the mystery that has been hidden throughout the ages and generations but has now been revealed to his saints. To them God chose to make known how great among the Gentiles are the riches of the glory of this mystery, which is Christ in you, the hope of glory. It is he whom we proclaim, warning everyone and teaching everyone in all wisdom, so that we may present everyone mature in Christ. For this I toil and struggle with all the energy that he powerfully inspires within me.

For I want you to know how much I am struggling for you, and for those in Laodicea, and for all who have not seen me face to face. I want their hearts to be encouraged and united in love, so that they may have all the riches of assured understanding and have the knowledge of God's mystery, that is, Christ himself, in whom are hidden all the treasures of wisdom and knowledge. I am saying this so that no one may deceive you with plausible arguments. For though I am absent in body, yet I am with you in spirit, and I rejoice to see your morale and the firmness of your faith in Christ.

Colossians 1:25–2:5, NRSV

Jesus, Prince of Peace, be near us,
  Fix in all our hearts Thy home;
With Thy gracious presence cheer us,
  Let Thy sacred kingdom come.
Raise to heaven our expectation;
  Give our ransomed souls to prove
Glorious and complete salvation
  In the realms of bliss above.

Charles Wesley, 1707–88

Longing for home

How amiable are thy tabernacles, O LORD of hosts! My soul longeth, yea, even fainteth for the courts of the LORD: my heart and my flesh crieth out for the living God. Yea, the sparrow hath found an house, and the swallow a nest for herself, where she may lay her young, even thine altars, O LORD of hosts, my King, and my God. Blessed are they that dwell in thy house: they will be still praising thee. Selah. Blessed is the man whose strength is in thee; in whose heart are the ways of them. Who passing through the valley of Baca make it a well; the rain also filleth the pools. They go from strength to strength, every one of them in Zion appeareth before God.

Psalm 84:1–7, KJV

Pleasant are Thy courts above,
In the land of light and love;
Pleasant are Thy courts below,
In this land of sin and woe.
O! my spirit longs and faints
For the converse of Thy saints,
For the brightness of Thy face,
For Thy fulness, God of grace!

Happy souls! their praises flow
Even in this vale of woe;
Waters in the desert rise,
Manna feeds them from the skies.
On they go from strength to strength,
Till they reach Thy throne at length,
At Thy feet adoring fall,
Who hast led them safe through all.

Henry Francis Lyte, 1793–1847

The greatness of Christ

These things I write to you, though I hope to come to you shortly; but if I am delayed, I write so that you may know how you ought to conduct yourself in the house of God, which is the church of the living God, the pillar and ground of the truth. And without controversy great is the mystery of godliness: God was manifested in the flesh, justified in the Spirit, seen by angels, preached among the Gentiles, believed on in the world, received up in glory.

1 Timothy 3:14–16, NKJV

And the Word was made flesh, and dwelt among us.

John 1:14, KJV

Let earth and heaven combine,
  Angels and men agree,
To praise in songs divine,
  The incarnate Deity,
Our God contracted to a span,
Incomprehensibly made man.

Unsearchable the love
  That hath the Saviour brought;
The grace is far above
  Or man or angel's thought:
Suffice for us that God, we know,
Our God, is manifest below.

Charles Wesley, 1707–88

The majestic King

The Lord gave the word: great was the company of those that pub-
lished it. Kings of armies did flee apace: and she that tarried at home
divided the spoil. . . . The chariots of God are twenty thousand, even
thousands of angels: the Lord is among them, as in Sinai, in the holy
place. Thou hast ascended on high, thou hast led captivity captive:
thou hast received gifts for men; yea, for the rebellious also, that the
LORD God might dwell among them. Blessed be the Lord, who daily
loadeth us with benefits, even the God of our salvation. Selah. He
that is our God is the God of salvation; and unto GOD the Lord belong
the issues from death.

Psalm 68:11–12,17–20, KJV

Songs of praise the angels sang,
Heaven with hallelujahs rang,
When creation was begun,
When God spake and it was done.

Songs of praise awoke the morn,
When the Prince of Peace was born;
Songs of praise arose, when He
Captive led captivity.

Heaven and earth must pass away,
Songs of praise shall crown that day;
God will make new heavens, new earth,
Songs of praise shall hail their birth.

James Montgomery, 1771–1854

God helps us

I called upon the LORD in distress: the LORD answered me, and set me in a large place. The LORD is on my side; I will not fear: what can man do unto me? The LORD taketh my part with them that help me: therefore shall I see my desire upon them that hate me. It is better to trust in the LORD than to put confidence in man. It is better to trust in the LORD than to put confidence in princes.

Psalm 118:5–9, KJV

But my God shall supply all your need according to his riches in glory by Christ Jesus.

Philippians 4:19, KJV

Why should I fear the darkest hour,
Or tremble at the tempter's power?
Jesus vouchsafes to be my tower.

Though hot the fight, why quit the field?
Why must I either fly or yield,
Since Jesus is my mighty shield?

I know not what may soon betide,
Or how my wants shall be supplied;
But Jesus knows, and will provide.

John Newton, 1725–1807

Casting our cares on the Lord

Cast thy burden upon the LORD, and he shall sustain thee: he shall never suffer the righteous to be moved.

Psalm 55:22, KJV

Be anxious for nothing, but in everything by prayer and supplication, with thanksgiving, let your requests be made known to God; and the peace of God, which surpasses all understanding, will guard your hearts and minds through Christ Jesus.

Finally, brethren, whatever things are true, whatever things are noble, whatever things are just, whatever things are pure, whatever things are lovely, whatever things are of good report, if there is any virtue and if there is anything praiseworthy—meditate on these things. The things which you learned and received and heard and saw in me, these do, and the God of peace will be with you.

Philippians 4:6–9, NKJV

How gentle God's commands,
 How kind His precepts are!
Come, cast your burdens on the Lord,
 And trust His constant care.

While providence supports,
 Let saints securely dwell;
That hand which bears all Nature up
 Shall guide His children well.

Why should this anxious load
 Press down your weary mind?
Haste to your heavenly Father's throne,
 And sweet refreshment find.

Philip Doddridge, 1702–51

Christ above all

So he [God's Son] became as much superior to the angels as the name he has inherited is superior to theirs.

For to which of the angels did God ever say, "You are my Son; today I have become your Father"? Or again, "I will be his Father, and he will be my Son"? And again, when God brings his firstborn into the world, he says, "Let all God's angels worship him." In speaking of the angels he says, "He makes his angels winds, his servants flames of fire." But about the Son he says, "Your throne, O God, will last for ever and ever, and righteousness will be the scepter of your kingdom. You have loved righteousness and hated wickedness; therefore God, your God, has set you above your companions by anointing you with the oil of joy."

Hebrews 1:4–9

Name of Jesus! highest Name!
  Name that earth and heaven adore!
From the heart of God it came,
  Leads me to God's heart once more.

Only Jesus! fairest Name!
  Life, and rest, and peace, and bliss,
Jesus, evermore the same,
  He is mine, and I am His.

Gerhard Tersteegen, 1697–1769
translated by Emma Frances Bevan, 1827–1909

The final judgment

And then I saw a great white throne, and One seated upon it from whose presence both earth and sky fled and vanished.

Then; I saw the dead, great and small, standing before the throne; and the books were opened. And another book was opened, which is the book of life. And the dead were judged by what was written in the books concerning what they had done. The sea gave up its dead, and death and the grave gave up the dead which were in them. And men were judged, each according to what he had done.

Then death and the grave were themselves hurled into the lake of fire, which is the second death. If anyone's name was not found written in the book of life he was thrown into the lake of fire.

Revelation 20:11–15, PHILLIPS

Behold! on flying clouds He comes,
    And all earth's nations then shall see
The glorious face of Him from whom
    Both heaven and earth away shall flee.

The unbelieving world shall wail,
    While we rejoice to see the day;
Come, Lord, nor let Thy promise fail,
    Nor let Thy chariots long delay!

Isaac Watts, 1674–1748

DECEMBER 17

The new Jerusalem

Then I saw a new Heaven and a new earth, for the first Heaven and the first earth had disappeared and the sea was no more. I saw the holy city, the new Jerusalem, descending from God out of Heaven, prepared as a bride dressed in beauty for her husband. Then I heard a great voice from the throne crying,

"See! The home of God is with men, and he will live among them. They shall be his people, and God himself shall be with them, and will wipe away every tear from their eyes. Death shall he no more, and never again shall there be sorrow or crying or pain. For all those former things are past and gone."

Then he who is seated upon the throne said,

"See, I am making all things new!"

And he added,

"Write this down for my words are true and to be trusted."

Then he said to me,

"It is done! I am Alpha and Omega, the beginning and the end. I will give to the thirsty water without price from the fountain of life. The victorious shall inherit these things, and I will be God to him and he will be son to me."

Revelation 21:1–7, PHILLIPS

O Christ, He is the fountain,
  The deep, sweet well of love;
The streams on earth I've tasted,
  More deep I'll drink above;
There, to an ocean fulness,
  His mercy doth expand,
And glory, glory dwelleth
  In Immanuel's land.

Anne Ross Cousin, 1824–1906

The river of life

Then he showed me the river of the water of life, sparkling like crystal as it flowed from the throne of God and of the Lamb. In the middle of the street of the city and on either bank of the river grew the tree of life, bearing twelve fruits, a different kind for each month. The leaves of the tree were for the healing of the nations.

Nothing that has cursed mankind shall exist any longer; the throne of God and of the Lamb shall be within the city. His servants shall worship him; they shall see his face, and his name will be upon their foreheads. Night shall be no more; they have no more need for either lamplight or sunlight, for the Lord God will shed his light upon them and they shall reign as kings for timeless ages.

Revelation 22:1–5, PHILLIPS

There is a land of pure delight,
  Where saints immortal reign;
Infinite day excludes the night,
  And pleasures banish pain.

Isaac Watts, 1674–1748

The sign of Immanuel

Then the LORD spoke again to Ahaz, saying, "Ask a sign for yourself from the LORD your God; make it deep as Sheol or high as heaven." But Ahaz said, "I will not ask, nor will I test the LORD!" Then he said, "Listen now, O house of David! Is it too slight a thing for you to try the patience of men, that you will try the patience of my God as well? Therefore the Lord Himself will give you a sign: Behold, a virgin will be with child and bear a son, and she will call His name Immanuel. He will eat curds and honey at the time He knows enough to refuse evil and choose good. For before the boy will know enough to refuse evil and choose good, the land whose two kings you dread will be forsaken. The LORD will bring on you, on your people, and on your father's house such days as have never come since the day that Ephraim separated from Judah, the king of Assyria."

Isaiah 7:10–17, NASB

Christ by highest heaven adored,
Christ the Everlasting Lord,
Late in time behold Him come,
Offspring of a virgin's womb.
Veiled in flesh the Godhead see!
Hail the incarnate Deity!
Pleased as Man with man to dwell,
Jesus, our Immanuel.

Hark! the herald angels sing
Glory to the new-born King.

Charles Wesley, 1707–88

The wonderful counselor

The people who walk in darkness will see a great light; those who live in a dark land, the light will shine on them. You shall multiply the nation, You shall increase their gladness; they will be glad in Your presence as with the gladness of harvest, as men rejoice when they divide the spoil. For You shall break the yoke of their burden and the staff on their shoulders, the rod of their oppressor, as at the battle of Midian. For every boot of the booted warrior in the battle tumult, and cloak rolled in blood, will be for burning, fuel for the fire. For a child will be born to us, a son will be given to us; and the government will rest on His shoulders; and His name will be called Wonderful Counselor, Mighty God, Eternal Father, Prince of Peace. There will be no end to the increase of His government or of peace, on the throne of David and over his kingdom, to establish it and to uphold it with justice and righteousness from then on and forevermore. The zeal of the LORD of hosts will accomplish this.

Isaiah 9:2–7, NASB

Thou whose Name is called Jesus,
  Risen Lord of life and power,
O it is so sweet to trust Thee
  Every day and every hour!
Of Thy wondrous grace I sing,
Saviour, Counsellor and King.

Jean Sophia Pigott, 1845–82

The Ruler from Bethlehem

Now gather yourself in troops, O daughter of troops; he has laid siege against us; they will strike the judge of Israel with a rod on the cheek.

"But you, Bethlehem Ephrathah, though you are little among the thousands of Judah, yet out of you shall come forth to Me the One to be Ruler in Israel, whose goings forth are from of old, from everlasting."

Therefore He shall give them up, Until the time that she who is in labor has given birth; then the remnant of His brethren shall return to the children of Israel. And He shall stand and feed His flock in the strength of the LORD, in the majesty of the name of the LORD His God; and they shall abide, for now He shall be great to the ends of the earth; and this One shall be peace.

Micah 5:1–5, NKJV

Jesus was born in Bethlehem in Judea, during the time of King Herod.

Matthew 2:1

O holy Child of Bethlehem,
  Descend to us, we pray;
Cast out our sin, and enter in;
  Be born in us today.
We hear the Christmas angels
  The great glad tidings tell;
O come to us, abide with us,
  Our Lord Immanuel.

Phillips Brooks, 1835–93

Jesus' birth foretold

In the sixth month, God sent the angel Gabriel to Nazareth, a town in Galilee, to a virgin pledged to be married to a man named Joseph, a descendant of David. The virgin's name was Mary. The angel went to her and said, "Greetings, you who are highly favored! The Lord is with you."

Mary was greatly troubled at his words and wondered what kind of greeting this might be. But the angel said to her, "Do not be afraid, Mary, you have found favor with God. You will be with child and give birth to a son, and you are to give him the name Jesus. He will be great and will be called the Son of the Most High. The Lord God will give him the throne of his father David, and he will reign over the house of Jacob forever; his kingdom will never end."

"How will this be," Mary asked the angel, "since I am a virgin?"

The angel answered, "The Holy Spirit will come upon you, and the power of the Most High will overshadow you. So the holy one to be born will be called the Son of God. Even Elizabeth your relative is going to have a child in her old age, and she who was said to be barren is in her sixth month. For nothing is impossible with God."

"I am the Lord's servant," Mary answered. "May it be to me as you have said." Then the angel left her.

Luke 1:26–38

Silent night! holy night!
Son of God, love's pure light
Radiant beams from Thy holy face,
With the dawn of redeeming grace,
Jesus, Lord, at Thy birth.

Joseph Mohr, 1792–1848

Zechariah's prophecy

Zechariah was filled with the Holy Spirit and prophesied: "Praise be to the Lord, the God of Israel, because he has come and has redeemed his people. He has raised up a horn of salvation for us in the house of his servant David (as he said through his holy prophets of long ago), salvation from our enemies and from the hand of all who hate us—to show mercy to our fathers and to remember his holy covenant, the oath he swore to our father Abraham: to rescue us from the hand of our enemies, and to enable us to serve him without fear in holiness and righteousness before him all our days."

Luke 1:67–75

O come, O come, Immanuel,
And ransom captive Israel,
That mourns in lonely exile here
Until the Son of God appear.

Rejoice! rejoice! Immanuel
Shall come to thee, O Israel!

Latin, 12th century
translated by John Mason Neale, 1818–66

O come let us adore him!

In the beginning was the Word, and the Word was with God, and the Word was God. He was in the beginning with God. All things came into being through Him, and apart from Him nothing came into being that has come into being. In Him was life, and the life was the Light of men. The Light shines in the darkness, and the darkness did not comprehend it.

There came a man sent from God, whose name was John. He came as a witness, to testify about the Light, so that all might believe through him. He was not the Light, but he came to testify about the Light.

There was the true Light which, coming into the world, enlightens every man. . . .

And the Word became flesh, and dwelt among us, and we saw His glory, glory as of the only begotten from the Father, full of grace and truth.

John 1:1–9,14, NASB

O come, all ye faithful,
Joyful and triumphant,
O come ye, O come ye to Bethlehem;
Come and behold Him,
Born the King of angels:

O come, let us adore Him,
O come, let us adore Him,
O come, let us adore Him, Christ the Lord!

God of God,
Light of Light,
Lo, He abhors not the Virgin's womb;
Very God,
Begotten, not created.

Latin, 17th century
translated by Frederick Oakeley, 1802–80

The Savior is born

And it came to pass in those days, that there went out a decree from Caesar Augustus, that all the world should be taxed. (And this taxing was first made when Cyrenius was governor of Syria.) And all went to be taxed, every one into his own city. And Joseph also went up from Galilee, out of the city of Nazareth, into Judaea, unto the city of David, which is called Bethlehem; (because he was of the house and lineage of David:) to be taxed with Mary his espoused wife, being great with child. And so it was, that, while they were there, the days were accomplished that she should be delivered. And she brought forth her firstborn son, and wrapped him in swaddling clothes, and laid him in a manger; because there was no room for them in the inn.

Luke 2:1–7, KJV

Once in royal David's city
  Stood a lowly cattle-shed,
Where a mother laid her Baby
  In a manger for His bed.
Mary was that mother mild,
Jesus Christ her little Child.

He came down to earth from heaven
  Who is God and Lord of all,
And His shelter was a stable,
  And His cradle was a stall.
With the poor, and mean, and lowly
Lived on earth our Saviour holy.

Cecil Frances Alexander, 1818–95

DECEMBER 26

The shepherds and the angels

And there were in the same country shepherds abiding in the field, keeping watch over their flock by night. And, lo, the angel of the Lord came upon them, and the glory of the Lord shone round about them: and they were sore afraid. And the angel said unto them, Fear not: for, behold, I bring you good tidings of great joy, which shall be to all people. For unto you is born this day in the city of David a Saviour, which is Christ the Lord. And this shall be a sign unto you; Ye shall find the babe wrapped in swaddling clothes, lying in a manger. And suddenly there was with the angel a multitude of the heavenly host praising God, and saying, Glory to God in the highest, and on earth peace, good will toward men. And it came to pass, as the angels were gone away from them into heaven, the shepherds said one to another, Let us now go even unto Bethlehem, and see this thing which is come to pass, which the Lord hath made known unto us.

Luke 2:8–15, KJV

Then to the watchful shepherds it was told,
Who heard the angelic herald's voice, "Behold,
I bring good tidings of a Saviour's birth
To you and all the nations upon earth;
This day hath God fulfilled His promised word,
This day is born a Saviour, Christ the Lord."

He spake; and straightway the celestial choir
In hymns of joy unknown before conspire;
The praises of redeeming love they sang,
And heaven's whole orb with hallelujahs rang;
God's highest glory was their anthem still,
"Peace upon earth, and unto men goodwill."

John Byrom, 1692–1768

The Magi worship Jesus

In the time of King Herod, after Jesus was born in Bethlehem of Judea, wise men from the East came to Jerusalem, asking, "Where is the child who has been born king of the Jews? For we observed his star at its rising, and have come to pay him homage." . . .

Then Herod secretly called for the wise men and learned from them the exact time when the star had appeared. Then he sent them to Bethlehem, saying, "Go and search diligently for the child; and when you have found him, bring me word so that I may also go and pay him homage." When they had heard the king, they set out; and there, ahead of them, went the star that they had seen at its rising, until it stopped over the place where the child was. When they saw that the star had stopped, they were overwhelmed with joy. On entering the house, they saw the child with Mary his mother; and they knelt down and paid him homage. Then, opening their treasure chests, they offered him gifts of gold, frankincense, and myrrh. And having been warned in a dream not to return to Herod, they left for their own country by another road.

Matthew 2:1–2,7–12, NRSV

Then entered in those wise men three
Full reverently on bended knee,
And offered there, in His presence,
Their gold, and myrrh, and frankincense.

Nowell, Nowell, Nowell, Nowell,
Born is the King of Israel.

Then let us all with one accord
Sing praises to our heavenly Lord,
That hath made heaven and earth of nought,
And with His blood mankind hath bought.

Traditional, c. 17th century

Outcast yet Lord of all

Now after they had left, an angel of the Lord appeared to Joseph in a dream and said, "Get up, take the child and his mother, and flee to Egypt, and remain there until I tell you; for Herod is about to search for the child, to destroy him." Then Joseph got up, took the child and his mother by night, and went to Egypt, and remained there until the death of Herod. This was to fulfill what had been spoken by the Lord through the prophet, "Out of Egypt I have called my son."

When Herod saw that he had been tricked by the wise men, he was infuriated, and he sent and killed all the children in and around Bethlehem who were two years old or under, according to the time that he had learned from the wise men. Then was fulfilled what had been spoken through the prophet Jeremiah: "A voice was heard in Ramah, wailing and loud lamentation, Rachel weeping for her children; she refused to be consoled, because they are no more."

Matthew 2:13–18, NRSV

Child in the manger, infant of Mary;
   Outcast and stranger, Lord of all;
Child who inherits all our transgressions,
   All our demerits on him fall.

Once the most holy child of salvation
   Gently and lowly lived below;
Now as our glorious mighty Redeemer,
   See him victorious o'er each foe.

Prophets foretold him, infant of wonder;
   Angels behold him on his throne;
Worthy our Saviour of all their praises;
   Happy for ever are his own.

Mary Macdonald, 1789–1872
translated by Lachlan Macbean, 1853–1931

The long-expected Jesus

And behold, there was a man in Jerusalem whose name was Simeon, and this man was just and devout, waiting for the Consolation of Israel, and the Holy Spirit was upon him. And it had been revealed to him by the Holy Spirit that he would not see death before he had seen the Lord's Christ. So he came by the Spirit into the temple. And when the parents brought in the Child Jesus, to do for Him according to the custom of the law, he took Him up in his arms and blessed God and said: "Lord, now You are letting Your servant depart in peace, According to Your word; for my eyes have seen Your salvation which You have prepared before the face of all peoples, a light to bring revelation to the Gentiles, and the glory of Your people Israel."

Luke 2:25–32, NKJV

Come, Thou long-expected Jesus,
　Born to set Thy people free;
From our fears and sins release us,
　Let us find our rest in Thee.

Israel's strength and consolation,
　Hope of all the earth Thou art;
Dear desire of every nation,
　Joy of every longing heart.

Charles Wesley, 1707–88

Hallelujah!

Praise ye the LORD. Praise God in his sanctuary: praise him in the firmament of his power. Praise him for his mighty acts: praise him according to his excellent greatness. Praise him with the sound of the trumpet: praise him with the psaltery and harp. Praise him with the timbrel and dance: praise him with stringed instruments and organs. Praise him upon the loud cymbals: praise him upon the high sounding cymbals. Let every thing that hath breath praise the LORD. Praise ye the LORD.

Psalm 150:1–6, KJV

O praise ye the Lord!
  Praise Him in the height;
Rejoice in His Word,
  Ye angels of light;
Ye heavens, adore Him
  By whom ye were made,
And worship before Him,
  In brightness arrayed.

O praise ye the Lord!
  Thanksgiving and song
To Him be outpoured
  All ages along:
For love in creation,
  For heaven restored,
For grace of salvation
  O praise ye the Lord!

Henry Williams Baker, 1821–77

Come, Lord Jesus!

"I, Jesus, have sent my angel to give you this testimony for the churches. I am the Root and the Offspring of David, and the bright Morning Star."

The Spirit and the bride say, "Come!" And let him who hears say, "Come!" Whoever is thirsty, let him come; and whoever wishes, let him take the free gift of the water of life.

I warn everyone who hears the words of the prophecy of this book: If anyone adds anything to them, God will add to him the plagues described in this book. And if anyone takes words away from this book of prophecy, God will take away from him his share in the tree of life and in the holy city, which are described in this book.

He who testifies to these things says, "Yes, I am coming soon."

Amen. Come, Lord Jesus.

The grace of the Lord Jesus be with God's people. Amen.

Revelation 22:16–21

Yea, Amen! let all adore Thee,
  High on Thine eternal throne!
Saviour, take the power and glory;
  Claim the kingdom for Thine own:
    O come quickly!
  Hallelujah, come, Lord, come!

John Cennick, 1718–55,
and
Charles Wesley, 1707–88

ACKNOWLEDGMENTS

Frank Houghton, "Facing a Task," is quoted on page 50 courtesy of OMF International.

Katharine Agnes May Kelly, "Give Me a Sight," is quoted on page 62 courtesy of National Young Life Campaign.

Thomas O. Chisholm, "Great Is Thy Faithfulness," is quoted on page 63. Words: Thomas O. Chisholm. Music: William M. Runyan. © 1923, Ren. 1951 by Hope Publishing Co., Carol Stream, IL 60188. All rights reserved. Used by permission.

Timothy Dudley-Smith, "Tell Out, My Soul," is quoted on page 207. Words: Timothy Dudley-Smith. Words © 1962, Ren. 1990 by Hope Publishing Co., Carol Stream, IL 60188. All rights reserved. Used by permission.

Thoro Harris, "All That Thrills My Soul," is quoted on page 249. © 1931 Nazarene Publishing House (administered by the Copyright Company, Nashville, Tenn.). All rights reserved. International copyright secured. Used by permission.